ALGEBRA NATION - How It Works

Welcome to Algebra Nation! Our goal is to help you and all other students across Michigan master Algebra 1. Algebra is essential for success in future math and science courses, on tests like the SAT, and in your future career (whatever it may be)!

WHAT IS ALGEBRA NATION?

1. **Videos and Workbook**: Choose your Study Expert and watch them break down each topic as you follow along and mark up this workbook.
2. **Digital Practice:** Check your mastery of each topic online with the "Check Your Understanding" tool, and test your knowledge at the end of each section with the "Test Yourself!" practice tool.
3. **Algebra Wall**: Have questions? Want to chat about math with other students across Michigan in a safe, moderated, online environment? Go to the statewide Algebra Wall, where you can ask questions and receive help from other students, teachers, and our Study Experts. Study Experts will award Karma Points for helping other students. Top Karma Points earners will win prizes. Go to the Algebra Wall to learn more!
4. **Teacher Area**: Teachers can view data for their classes in the Teacher Area, access extra resources, and collaborate with colleagues through the Teacher Wall.
5. **On-Ramp Review Tools:** Use this adaptive tool to assess your understanding of pre-algebra using the On-Ramp to Algebra 1 review tool, and foundational math concepts using the On-Ramp to 6th Grade Math review tool.

Jump on Algebra Nation (by going to AlgebraNation.com or downloading the free Algebra Nation app from your phone or tablet's app store) and get started!

Ideas, questions, comments, or suggestions?
Just email help@AlgebraNation.com or call 1-888-608-MATH. We would love to hear from you!

TABLE OF CONTENTS

	PAGE NUMBER
Section 1: Expressions	1
Section 2: Equations and Inequalities	29
Section 3: Introduction to Functions	60
Section 4: Linear Equations, Functions, and Inequalities	91
Section 5: Quadratic Functions – Part 1	125
Section 6: Quadratic Functions – Part 2	151
Section 7: Exponential Functions	179
Section 8: Summary of Functions	200
Section 9: One-Variable Statistics	224
Section 10: Two-Variable Statistics	245
Index: Where Each Standard is Covered in Algebra Nation	266

All trademarks and product names referred to in this workbook are the property of their respective owners and used solely for educational purposes. Unless stated otherwise, Algebra Nation has no relationship with any of the companies or brands mentioned in this workbook, our videos, or our resources. Algebra Nation does not endorse or have preference for any of the companies or brands mentioned in this workbook.

Section 1: Expressions

Topic 1: Using Expressions to Represent Real-World Situations 3
Standards Covered: A-SSE.1, A-APR.1, N-Q.1
- ☐ I can write, interpret, and evaluate algebraic expressions in a real-world context.

Topic 2: Properties of Exponents 5
Standards Covered: N-RN.2
- ☐ I can apply the properties to rewrite expressions.

Topic 3: Operations with Rational and Irrational Numbers 8
Standards Covered: N-RN.3
- ☐ I can complete operations and proofs with rational and irrational numbers, and make generalizations on the relationships between rational and irrational numbers.

Topic 4: Radical Expressions and Expressions with Rational Exponents 11
Standards Covered: N-RN.1, N-RN.2
- ☐ I can rewrite expressions with radicals and rational exponents.

Topic 5: Adding Expressions with Radicals and Rational Exponents 13
Standards Covered: N-RN.2
- ☐ I can add expressions with radicals and rational exponents.

Topic 6: More Operations with Radicals and Rational Exponents 16
Standards Covered: N-RN.2
- ☐ I can find products and quotients of expressions with radicals and rational exponents.

Topic 7: Understanding Polynomial Expressions 18
Standards Covered: A-APR.1
- ☐ I can classify polynomials by number of terms and degree.
- ☐ I can identify the leading term and leading coefficient of a polynomial.

Topic 8: Operations with Polynomials – Part 1 21
Standards Covered: A-APR.1
- ☐ I can add and subtract polynomials.

Topic 9: Operations with Polynomials – Part 2 23
Standards Covered: A-APR.1
- ☐ I can multiply polynomials.

Topic 10: Complex Numbers 26
Standards Covered: N-CN.1
- ☐ I can define i as the square root of -1 or $i^2 = -1$.
- ☐ I can write complex numbers in the form of a + bi when a and b are real numbers.

Visit MathNation.com or search "Math Nation" in your phone or tablet's app store to watch the videos that go along with this workbook!

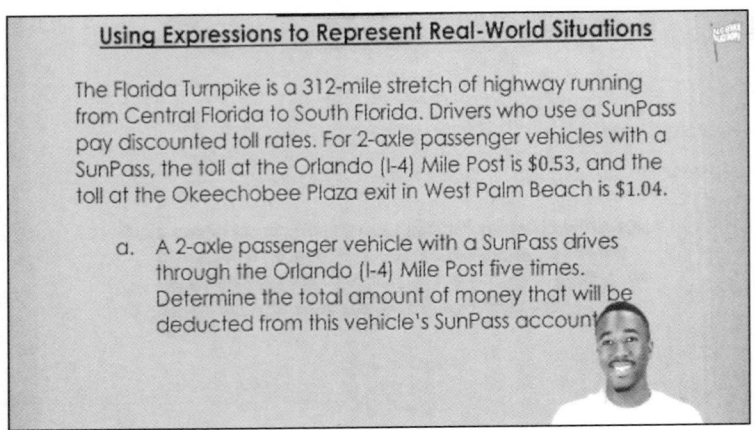

Using Expressions to Represent Real-World Situations

The Florida Turnpike is a 312-mile stretch of highway running from Central Florida to South Florida. Drivers who use a SunPass pay discounted toll rates. For 2-axle passenger vehicles with a SunPass, the toll at the Orlando (I-4) Mile Post is $0.53, and the toll at the Okeechobee Plaza exit in West Palm Beach is $1.04.

a. A 2-axle passenger vehicle with a SunPass drives through the Orlando (I-4) Mile Post five times. Determine the total amount of money that will be deducted from this vehicle's SunPass account.

The following Michigan Mathematics Standards will be covered in this section:
A-SSE.1 - Interpret expressions that represent a quantity in terms of its context. a. Interpret parts of an expression, such as terms, factors, and coefficients.
A-APR.1 - Understand that polynomials form a system analogous to the integers, namely, they are closed under the operations of addition, subtraction, and multiplication; add, subtract, and multiply polynomials.
N-Q.1 - Use units as a way to understand problems and to guide the solution of multi-step problems; choose and interpret units consistently in formulas; choose and interpret the scale and the origin in graphs and data displays.
N-RN.2 - Rewrite expressions involving radicals and rational exponents using the properties of exponents.
N-RN.3 - Explain why the sum or product of two rational numbers is rational; that the sum of a rational number and an irrational number is irrational; and that the product of a nonzero rational number and an irrational number is irrational.
N-RN.1 - Explain how the definition of the meaning of rational exponents follows from extending the properties of integer exponents to those values, allowing for a notation for radicals in terms of rational exponents.
N-CN.1 - Know there is a complex number I such that $i^2 = -1$, and every complex number has the form a + bi with a and b real.

Section 1: Expressions

Section 1: Expressions
Section 1 – Topic 1
Using Expressions to Represent Real-World Situations

The Arnold Mackinac Island Ferry completes 9 round trips each day. Shepler's Ferry completes 18 round trips each day. Let d represent any given number of days.

a. Write an algebraic expression to describe the Arnold Mackinac Island Ferry's total number of round trips after any given number of days.

b. Create an algebraic expression to describe Shepler's Ferry's total number of round trips after any given number of days.

c. Write an algebraic expression to describe the combined total number of round trips for the Arnold Mackinac Island Ferry and Shepler's Ferry after any given number of days.

d. After five days, how many round trips did both ferries complete altogether?

Let's Practice!

1. Mario and Luigi plan to buy a Nintendo Switch for $299.00. Nintendo Switch games cost $59.99 each. They plan to purchase one console.

    a. Write an algebraic expression to describe how much they will spend, before sales tax, based on purchasing the console and the number of games.

    b. If they purchase one console and three games, how much will they spend before sales tax?

    c. Mario and Luigi want to purchase some extra controllers for their friends. Each controller costs $29.99. Use an algebraic expression to describe how much they will spend in total, before sales tax, based on purchasing the console, the number of games, and the number of extra controllers.

    d. What will be the total cost, before sales tax, if Mario and Luigi purchase one console, three games, and two extra controllers?

STUDY EDGE TIP: When defining variables, choose variables that make sense to you, such as h for hours and d for days.

Try It!

2. Suppose Micah and Crystal purchase two tickets to the Detroit Red Wings game. Tickets cost $35.50 each, water bottles inside the stadium cost $3.50 each, and pretzels with cheese cost $5.00 each. Use an algebraic expression to describe how much they spend based on the number of tickets, water bottles, and pretzels they buy. Identify the parts of the expression by underlining the coefficient(s), circling the constant(s), and drawing a box around the variable(s).

3. Ramiro brought home ten pounds of rice to add to the 24 ounces of rice he had in the pantry. Let x represent the amount of rice Ramiro uses over the next few days.

   a. Write an algebraic expression to describe the amount of rice remaining in Ramiro's pantry.

   b. Determine if there are any constraints on x.

BEAT THE TEST!

1. José is going to have the exterior of his home painted. He will choose between Krystal Klean Painting and Elegance Home Painting. Krystal Klean Painting charges $175.00 to come out and evaluate the house plus $7.00 for every additional 30 minutes of work. Elegance Home Painting charges $23.00 per hour of work. Let h represent the number of hours for which José hires a painter. Which of the following statements are true? Select all that apply.

   ☐ The expression $14h$ represents the total charge for Krystal Klean Painting.
   ☐ The expression $23h$ represents the total charge for Elegance Home Painting.
   ☐ The expression $175 + 14h + 23h$ represents the total amount José will spend for the painters to paint the exterior of his home.
   ☐ If José hires the painters for 10 hours, then Elegance Home Painting will be cheaper.
   ☐ If José hires the painters for 20 hours, then Krystal Klean Painting will be cheaper.

Algebra Wall — Want some help? You can always ask questions on the Algebra Wall and receive help from other students, teachers, and Study Experts. You can also help others on the Algebra Wall and earn Karma Points for doing so. Go to AlgebraNation.com to learn more and get started!

Section 1: Expressions

2. During harvesting season at Florida Blue Farms, hand pickers collect about 200 pounds of blueberries per day with a 95% pack-out rate. The blueberry harvester machine collects about 22,000 pounds of blueberries per day with a 90% pack-out rate. The pack-out rate is the percentage of collected blueberries that can be packaged to be sold, based on Florida Blue Farms' quality standards.

Let h represent the number of days the hand pickers work and m represent the number of days the harvester machine is used. Which of the following algebraic expressions can be used to estimate the amount of collected blueberries that are packed at the Florida Blue Farms for fresh consumption this season?

Ⓐ $(0.95h + 200)(0.90m + 22000)$
Ⓑ $0.95(200h) + 0.90(22000m)$
Ⓒ $200.95h + 22000.90m$
Ⓓ $(200h + 0.95)(22000m + 0.90)$

Want to learn more about how Florida Blue Farms uses algebra to harvest blueberries? Visit the Student Area in Algebra Nation to see how people use algebra in the real world! You can find the video in the "Math in the Real World: Algebra at Work" folder.

Algebra Wall — Want some help? You can always ask questions on the Algebra Wall and receive help from other students, teachers, and Study Experts. You can also help others on the Algebra Wall and earn Karma Points for doing so. Go to AlgebraNation.com to learn more and get started!

Section 1 – Topic 2
Properties of Exponents

Let's review the properties of exponents.

$2^4 =$

$2^3 =$

$2^2 =$

$2^1 =$

What pattern do you notice?

Continuing the pattern, what does the following term equal?

$2^0 =$

➤ This is the **zero exponent property**: $a^0 =$ _____.

Continuing the pattern, what do the following terms equal?

$2^{-1} =$

$2^{-2} =$

➤ This is the **negative exponent property**: $a^{-n} =$ _____ and $\dfrac{1}{a^{-n}} =$ _____.

Section 1: Expressions

Let's explore multiplying terms with exponents and the same base.

$2^3 \cdot 2^4 =$

$2^5 \cdot 2^{-3} =$

$x^3 \cdot x^2 =$

> This is the **product property**: $a^m \cdot a^n =$ _____.

Let's explore dividing terms with exponents and the same base.

$\dfrac{4^5}{4^3} =$

$\dfrac{x^7}{x^8} =$

> This is the **quotient property**: $\dfrac{a^m}{a^n} =$ _____.

Let's explore raising powers to an exponent.

$(5^3)^2 =$

$(y^4)^3 =$

> This is the **power of a power property**: $(a^m)^n =$ _____.

Let's explore raising a product to an exponent.

$(2 \cdot 3)^2 =$

$(4 \cdot x)^3 =$

> This is the **power of a product property**: $(ab)^n =$ _____.

Let's explore a quotient raised to an exponent.

$\left(\dfrac{20}{3}\right)^2 =$

$\left(\dfrac{6}{y}\right)^3 =$

> This is the **power of a quotient property**: $\left(\dfrac{a}{b}\right)^n =$ _____.

Section 1: Expressions

Let's Practice!

1. Determine if the following equations are true or false. Justify your answers.

   a. $3^3 \cdot 3^4 = \dfrac{(3^9)}{(3^2)}$

   b. $(5 \cdot 4^2)^3 = 5^4 \cdot 5^0 \cdot \left(\dfrac{4^6}{5^{-1}}\right)^{-1}$

Try It!

2. Use the properties of exponents to match each of the following expressions with its equivalent expression.

   A. $\left(\dfrac{7}{2}\right)^4$ I. $7^3 \cdot 2^6$

   B. $(7 \cdot 2^2)^3$ II. $\dfrac{7^4}{2^4}$

   C. $(7^2)(7^2)$ III. $\dfrac{2^4}{7^4}$

   D. $(7^2)(7)^0$ IV. 7^4

   E. $\left(\dfrac{7}{2}\right)^{-4}$ V. 7^2

   F. $\dfrac{(7^6)}{(7^3)}$ VI. 7^3

Section 1: Expressions

BEAT THE TEST!

1. Crosby and Adam are working with exponents.

   Part A: Crosby claims that $3^3 \cdot 3^2 = 3^5$. Adam argues that $3^3 \cdot 3^2 = 3^6$. Which one of them is correct? Use the properties of exponents to justify your answer.

   Part B: Crosby claims that $\frac{3^8}{3^2} = 3^4$. Adam argues that $\frac{3^8}{3^2} = 3^6$. Which one of them is correct? Use the properties of exponents to justify your answer.

Algebra Wall

Want some help? You can always ask questions on the Algebra Wall and receive help from other students, teachers, and Study Experts. You can also help others on the Algebra Wall and earn Karma Points for doing so. Go to MathNation.com to learn more and get started!

Section 1 – Topic 3
Operations with Rational and Irrational Numbers

Let's review rational and irrational numbers.

> Numbers that can be represented as $\frac{a}{b}$, where a and b are integers and $b \neq 0$, are called _____ numbers.

> Numbers that cannot be represented in this form are called _____ numbers.

   o Radicals that cannot be rewritten as integers are examples of such numbers.

Determine whether the following numbers are rational or irrational.

	Rational	Irrational
$\sqrt{9}$	○	○
$\sqrt{8}$	○	○
π	○	○
$\frac{22}{7}$	○	○
$9.\overline{48}$	○	○
$\frac{33}{2}$	○	○
$2.23606...$	○	○
-25	○	○

Section 1: Expressions

Given two rational numbers, a and b, prove that the sum of a and b is rational.

Given a rational number, a, and an irrational number, b, prove that the sum of a and b is irrational.

Given two rational numbers, a and b, what can be said about the product of a and b?

Given a non-zero rational number, a, and an irrational number, b, what can be said about the product of a and b?

Section 1: Expressions

Let's Practice!

1. Consider the following expression.

    $$2 + \sqrt{3}$$

    The above expression represents the [ ] o sum / o product

    of a(n) [ ] o rational number / o irrational number   and a(n)

    [ ] o rational number / o irrational number   and is equivalent to a(n)

    [ ] o rational number. / o irrational number.

Try It!

2. María and her 6 best friends are applying to colleges. They find that Bard College accepts $\frac{1}{3}$ of its applicants. María and her friends write the expression below to represent how many of them would likely be accepted.

    $$7 \cdot \frac{1}{3}$$

    The above expression represents the [ ] o sum / o product

    of a(n) [ ] o rational number / o irrational number   and a(n)

    [ ] o rational number / o irrational number   and is equivalent to a(n)

    [ ] o rational number. / o irrational number.

10   Section 1: Expressions

BEAT THE TEST!

1. Let a and b be non-zero rational numbers and c be an irrational number. Consider the operations below and determine whether the result will be rational or irrational.

	Rational	Irrational
$a + b$	☐	☐
$a - c$	☐	☐
$a \cdot b$	☐	☐
$\dfrac{a}{b}$	☐	☐
$a \cdot b \cdot c$	☐	☐

2. Consider $x \cdot y = z$. If z is an irrational number, what can be said about x and y?

> Want some help? You can always ask questions on the Algebra Wall and receive help from other students, teachers, and Study Experts. You can also help others on the Algebra Wall and earn Karma Points for doing so. Go to MathNation.com to learn more and get started!

Section 1 – Topic 4
Radical Expressions and Expressions with Rational Exponents

Exponents are not always in the form of integers. Sometimes you will see them expressed as rational numbers.

Consider the following expressions with rational exponents. Use the property of exponents to rewrite them as radical expressions.

$9^{\frac{1}{2}} =$ $\qquad$ $8^{\frac{1}{3}} =$

Do you notice a pattern? If so, what pattern do you notice?

Consider the following expressions with rational exponents. Use the pattern above and the property of exponents to rewrite them as radical expressions.

$2^{\frac{2}{3}}$ $\qquad$ $5^{\frac{3}{2}}$

For exponents that are rational numbers, such as $\dfrac{a}{b}$, we have $x^{\frac{a}{b}} = $ _____ $=$ _____ .

Section 1: Expressions

Let's Practice!

1. Use the rational exponent property to write an equivalent expression for each of the following radical expressions.

   a. $\sqrt{x+2}$

   b. $\sqrt[3]{x-5}+2$

2. Use the rational exponent property to write each of the following expressions as integers.

   a. $9^{\frac{1}{2}}$

   b. $16^{\frac{1}{2}}$

   c. $8^{\frac{1}{3}}$

   d. $8^{\frac{2}{3}}$

   e. $125^{\frac{2}{3}}$

   f. $16^{\frac{3}{4}}$

Try It!

3. Use the rational exponent property to write an equivalent expression for each of the following radical expressions.

   a. $\sqrt{y}$

   b. $\sqrt[5]{y+6}-3$

4. Use the rational exponent property to write each of the following expressions as integers.

   a. $49^{\frac{1}{2}}$

   b. $27^{\frac{1}{3}}$

   c. $216^{\frac{2}{3}}$

BEAT THE TEST!

1. Match each of the following to its equivalent expression.

   A. $2^{\frac{1}{3}}$

   B. $\sqrt{m-3}$

   C. $2^{\frac{2}{3}}$

   D. $\sqrt{m}-3$

   E. $2^{\frac{1}{2}}$

   F. $\sqrt{3m}$

   I. $m^{\frac{1}{2}} - 3$

   II. $(3m)^{\frac{1}{2}}$

   III. $(m-3)^{\frac{1}{2}}$

   IV. $\sqrt{2}$

   V. $\sqrt[3]{4}$

   VI. $\sqrt[3]{2}$

Want some help? You can always ask questions on the Algebra Wall and receive help from other students, teachers, and Study Experts. You can also help others on the Algebra Wall and earn Karma Points for doing so. Go to MathNation.com to learn more and get started!

Algebra Wall

Section 1 – Topic 5
Adding Expressions with Radicals and Rational Exponents

Let's explore operations with radical expressions and expressions with rational exponents. For each expression, label approximately where the answer would be found on the number line.

$\sqrt{5} + \sqrt{2}$

$5^{\frac{1}{2}} + 2^{\frac{1}{2}}$

$\sqrt{5} + \sqrt{5}$

$5^{\frac{1}{2}} + 5^{\frac{1}{2}}$

$2\sqrt{3} - 8\sqrt{3}$

$2 \cdot 3^{\frac{1}{2}} - 8 \cdot 3^{\frac{1}{2}}$

STUDY EDGE TIP

To add radicals, the radicand of both radicals must be the same. To add expressions with rational exponents, the base and the exponent must be the same. In both cases, you add only the coefficients.

Section 1: Expressions

Let's Practice!

1. Perform the following operations.

   a. $\sqrt{12} + \sqrt{3}$

   b. $12^{\frac{1}{2}} + 3^{\frac{1}{2}}$

   c. $\sqrt{72} + \sqrt{15} + \sqrt{18}$

   d. $72^{\frac{1}{2}} + 15^{\frac{1}{2}} + 18^{\frac{1}{2}}$

   e. $\sqrt{32} + \sqrt[3]{16}$

   f. $32^{\frac{1}{2}} + 16^{\frac{1}{3}}$

Try It!

2. Perform the following operations.

   a. $\sqrt{6} + 3\sqrt{6}$

   b. $6^{\frac{1}{2}} + 3 \cdot 6^{\frac{1}{2}}$

   c. $\sqrt{50} + \sqrt{18} + \sqrt{10}$

   d. $50^{\frac{1}{2}} + 18^{\frac{1}{2}} + 10^{\frac{1}{2}}$

   e. $\sqrt[3]{2} + \sqrt[3]{8} + \sqrt[3]{16}$

   f. $2^{\frac{1}{3}} + 8^{\frac{1}{3}} + 16^{\frac{1}{3}}$

STUDY EDGE TIP: For radicals and expressions with rational exponents, always look for factors that are perfect squares when taking the square root (or perfect cubes when taking the cube root).

Section 1: Expressions

BEAT THE TEST!

1. Which of the following expressions are equivalent to $3\sqrt{2}$? Select all that apply.

   ☐ $3^{\frac{1}{2}} + 2^{\frac{1}{2}}$
   ☐ $8^{\frac{1}{2}} + 2^{\frac{1}{2}}$
   ☐ $3 \cdot 2^{\frac{1}{2}}$
   ☐ $\sqrt{18}$
   ☐ $2\sqrt{18}$
   ☐ $\sqrt{8} + \sqrt{2}$

2. Miguel completed a proof to show that $\sqrt{27} + \sqrt{3} = 4 \cdot 3^{\frac{1}{2}}$:

   $\sqrt{27} + \sqrt{3}$
   $= 27^{\frac{1}{2}} + 3^{\frac{1}{2}}$
   $= \underline{}$
   $= 3 \cdot 3^{\frac{1}{2}} + 3^{\frac{1}{2}}$
   $= 4 \cdot 3^{\frac{1}{2}}$

   Part A: Which expression can be placed in the blank to correctly complete Miguel's proof?

   Ⓐ $3^{\frac{1}{2}}\left(9^{\frac{1}{2}} + 3^{\frac{1}{2}}\right)$

   Ⓑ $(9 \cdot 3)^{\frac{1}{2}} + 3^{\frac{1}{2}}$

   Ⓒ $\left(9^{\frac{1}{2}} + 3^{\frac{1}{2}}\right) + 3^{\frac{1}{2}}$

   Ⓓ $(9)^{\frac{1}{2}} + 3^{\frac{1}{2}}$

Part B: Label and place $4 \cdot 3^{\frac{1}{2}}$ on the number line below.

$\longleftarrow\!\!+\!\!\rule{1cm}{0.4pt}\!\!+\!\!\rule{1cm}{0.4pt}\!\!+\!\!\rule{1cm}{0.4pt}\!\!+\!\!\rule{1cm}{0.4pt}\!\!+\!\!\longrightarrow$

Want some help? You can always ask questions on the Algebra Wall and receive help from other students, teachers, and Study Experts. You can also help others on the Algebra Wall and earn Karma Points for doing so. Go to MathNation.com to learn more and get started!

Section 1: Expressions

Section 1 – Topic 6
More Operations with Radicals and Rational Exponents

Let's explore multiplying and dividing expressions with radicals and rational exponents.

$\sqrt{10} \cdot \sqrt{2}$ $\qquad$ $10^{\frac{1}{2}} \cdot 2^{\frac{1}{2}}$

$\sqrt{2} \cdot \sqrt[3]{2}$ $\qquad$ $2^{\frac{1}{2}} \cdot 2^{\frac{1}{3}}$

$\dfrac{\sqrt{10}}{\sqrt{2}}$ $\qquad$ $\dfrac{10^{\frac{1}{2}}}{2^{\frac{1}{2}}}$

 **STUDY EDGE TIP** — The properties of exponents also apply to expressions with rational exponents.

Let's Practice!

1. Use the properties of exponents to perform the following operations.

   a. $\left(x^{\frac{1}{3}}\right)^{\frac{1}{2}}$

   b. $\left(\sqrt{7}\right)^{3}$

   c. $\left(a^{\frac{1}{2}} b^{\frac{2}{5}}\right) \cdot \left(a^{\frac{2}{3}} b^{\frac{1}{2}}\right)$

d. $\dfrac{\sqrt[4]{8}}{\sqrt{8}}$

c. $\sqrt[4]{4} \cdot \sqrt[3]{4}$

Try It!

2. Use the properties of exponents to perform the following operations.

    d. $(3 \cdot \sqrt[6]{27})^{\frac{1}{2}}$

    a. $(m^0 n^2)^{\frac{1}{5}}$

    b. $(\sqrt{8} \cdot \sqrt[3]{3})^{\frac{2}{3}}$

Section 1: Expressions

BEAT THE TEST!

1. Which of the following expressions are equivalent to $2^{\frac{1}{2}}$? Select all that apply.

   ☐ $\sqrt[3]{4}$
   ☐ $\sqrt[3]{8}$
   ☐ $\sqrt[4]{4}$
   ☐ $\sqrt[6]{8}$
   ☐ $\sqrt[6]{16}$

Want some help? You can always ask questions on the Algebra Wall and receive help from other students, teachers, and Study Experts. You can also help others on the Algebra Wall and earn Karma Points for doing so. Go to MathNation.com to learn more and get started!

Algebra Wall

Section 1 – Topic 7
Understanding Polynomial Expressions

A **term** is a constant, variable, or multiplicative combination of the two.

Consider $3x^2 + 2y - 4z + 5$.

How many terms do you see?

List each term.

This is an example of a **polynomial expression**. A polynomial can be one term or the sum of several terms. There are many different types of **polynomials**.

A monarchy has one leader. How many terms do you think a monomial has?

A bicycle has two wheels. How many terms do you think a binomial has?

A triceratops has three horns. How many terms do you think a trinomial has?

Let's recap:

Type of Polynomial	Number of Terms	Example
Monomial		
Binomial		
Trinomial		
Polynomial		

Some important facts:

- The **degree of a monomial** is the sum of the _____ of the variables.

- The **degree of a polynomial** is the degree of the monomial term with the _____ degree.

Sometimes, you will be asked to write polynomials in standard form.

- Write the monomial terms in _____ _____ order.

- The **leading term** of a polynomial is the term with the _____ _____.

- The **leading coefficient** is the coefficient of the _____ _____.

Let's Practice!

1. Are the following expressions polynomials? If so, name the type of polynomial and state the degree. If not, justify your reasoning.

   a. $8x^2y^3$

   b. $\dfrac{2a^2}{3b}$

   c. $\dfrac{3}{2}x^4 - 5x^3 + 9x^7$

   d. $10a^6b^2 + 17ab^3c - 5a^7$

   e. $2m + 3n^{-1} + 8m^2n$

Section 1: Expressions

Try It!

2. Are the following expressions polynomials?

   a. $\frac{1}{2}a + 2b^2$

   ○ polynomial
   ○ not a polynomial

   b. 34

   ○ polynomial
   ○ not a polynomial

   c. $\frac{xy}{y^2}$

   ○ polynomial
   ○ not a polynomial

   d. $2rs + s^4$

   ○ polynomial
   ○ not a polynomial

   e. $xy^2 + 3x - 4y^{-1}$

   ○ polynomial
   ○ not a polynomial

3. Consider the polynomial $3x^4 - 5x^3 + 9x^7$.

   a. Write the polynomial in standard form.

   b. What is the degree of the polynomial?

   c. How many terms are in the polynomial?

   d. What is the leading term?

   e. What is the leading coefficient?

BEAT THE TEST!

1. Match the polynomial in the left column with its descriptive feature in the right column.

   A. $x^3 + 4x^2 - 5x + 9$ I. Fifth-degree polynomial

   B. $5a^2b^3$ II. Constant term of -2

   C. $3x^4 - 9x^3 + 4x^9$ III. Seventh-degree polynomial

   D. $7a^6b^2 + 18ab^3c - 9a^7$ IV. Leading coefficient of 3

   E. $x^5 - 9x^3 + 2x^7$ V. Four terms

   F. $3x^3 + 7x^2 - 11$ VI. Eighth-degree polynomial

   G. $x^2 - 2$ VII. Equivalent to $4x^9 + 3x^4 - 9x^3$

Want some help? You can always ask questions on the Algebra Wall and receive help from other students, teachers, and Study Experts. You can also help others on the Algebra Wall and earn Karma Points for doing so. Go to MathNation.com to learn more and get started!

Algebra Wall

Section 1 – Topic 8
Operations with Polynomials – Part 1

Consider the expression $2(13 + 5x - x^2) - (x^2 - 4)$.

a. To write an equivalent expression, which operation(s) should be done before combining like terms?

b. Write an equivalent expression for the polynomial in standard form.

Consider the expression $-2x(4x - 9) + 3(7 - x)$.

a. To write an equivalent expression, which operation(s) should be done before combining like terms?

b. Write an equivalent expression for the polynomial in standard form.

Section 1: Expressions

Let's Practice!

1. For each of the following, write an equivalent expression in standard form.

   a. $-3(6x^2 - 10x + 9) + 8x(3x + 4)$

   b. $3a^2b^5(2a^4b + 5ab) - (9a^3b^3)^2$

   b. $4x(-9x + 5x^2 + 3) + 7(13 + 5x - x^2)$

   c. $(-4x^5y^3)^2 - 7xy^4(x^9y^2 - x^4y^2)$

Try It!

2. For each of the following, write an equivalent expression in standard form.

   a. $(8x^5 + 4x^3 - 7) - (11 - x^3 + 5x^5)$

Section 1 – Topic 9
Operations with Polynomials – Part 2

Algebra tiles can be used to visually represent multiplication. Find the area of each algebra tile below.

unit tile	x tile	x^2 tile
1 × 1	x × 1	x × x

a. Sketch a diagram of algebra tiles that represent $2x + 4$.

b. Sketch a diagram of algebra tiles that represent $3x - 5$.

Using algebra tiles, the area model below models the multiplication of two binomials.

The top row represents one of the binomial factors in the product. The first column represents the other binomial factor in the product.

Write an expression to represent the product of the two binomials.

In the diagram below, the area inside the black square represents the product of the two binomial factors.

Complete the table below with the number of tiles inside the black square.

x^2 tiles	x tiles	unit tiles

Find the polynomial that represents the product of the two binomial factors.

Section 1: Expressions

Why do you think we call this the area model?

It's not always practical to use algebra tiles to represent the area model with multiplication.

Why would it not be practical to use algebra tiles to represent the area model for the following polynomial expressions?

$(15x - 9)(3x + 24)$

$(3x + 2y)(4z + 3)$

In these cases, we can use the distributive property or use a diagram that models area. Note: the diagrams do not have to be to scale.

Use the distributive property to find the product of $(15x - 9)$ and $(3x + 24)$.

Use a diagram to find the product of $(3x + 2y)$ and $(4z + 3y)$.

Let's Practice!

For each of the following, write an equivalent expression in standard form. Remember, you can use area models or diagrams to help visualize your thinking.

1. $(x + 5)(x + 2)$

2. $(x - 7)^2$

3. $(3y + 2x)(5x - 6xy - 7y)$

Section 1: Expressions

Try It!

Write an equivalent expression for each in standard form.

4. $(9x - 7)(2x - 5)$

5. $(4x - 1)(-9x + 3) + 7(13 + 5x - x^2)$

BEAT THE TEST!

1. Which is equivalent to $(3x - 8)(4x + 2)$?

   Ⓐ $12x^2 + 16$
   Ⓑ $12x^2 - 16$
   Ⓒ $12x^2 - 6x + 16$
   Ⓓ $12x^2 - 26x - 16$

2. Select all of the expressions that are equivalent to $7x - 4x(2x - 5) + 9(2x^2 - 5x + 3)$.

   ☐ $10x^2 - 8x - 2$
   ☐ $10x^2 - 18x + 27$
   ☐ $24x^2 - 60x + 27$
   ☐ $2(5x^2 - 4x + 1)$
   ☐ $3x(2x - 5) + 18x^2 - 45x + 27$
   ☐ $5x(2x - 9) + 27(x + 1)$

Section 1: Expressions

Section 1 – Topic 10
Complex Numbers

Determine the following.

$\sqrt{49} =$

$\sqrt{81} =$

The square root of n (denoted $\sqrt{n}$) is a number that, when squared, equals n.

Consider the following.

$\sqrt{-49}$

$\sqrt{-81}$

Is there a real number that can be multiplied by itself to equal the number underneath the square root?

Consider $\sqrt{n}$, where $n < 0$.

Why does $\sqrt{n}$ not exist in this case?

To work with such radicals $\sqrt{n}$, where n is a negative number, the imaginary number has been defined as $i = \sqrt{-1}$.

Let's Practice!

1. $\sqrt{-49}$

2. $\sqrt{-81}$

Try It!

3. $\sqrt{-121}$

4. $\sqrt{-225}$

Complete the following imaginary number equations.

$i =$ $i^5 =$

$i^2 =$ $i^6 =$

$i^3 =$ $i^7 =$

$i^4 =$ $i^8 =$

Let's Practice!

5. i^{15}

6. i^{30}

Try It!

7. i^{24}

8. i^9

We can use imaginary numbers to write complex numbers.

A **complex number** is a number that can be expressed in the form $a + bi$.

> a and b are _____ numbers and i is the imaginary unit that satisfies the equation $i^2 = -1$.

> _____ is the real part.

> b is the _____ _____ part.

Let's Practice!

Consider the following complex numbers. Draw a box around the real part, circle the imaginary part, and underline the imaginary unit.

9. $2 - 3i$

10. $5 + 2i$

Try It!

11. Ms. Marquez at Bakers Academy High School asked her students to respond to a prompt. Gustavo turned in the following answer. Ms. Marquez returned the paper and told Gustavo it needed corrections. Identify problems with Gustavo's answer and give suggestions for what he should write.

> Describe the complex number $a + bi$.
> THE PURELY IMAGINARY PART IS i. THE REAL PARTS ARE A AND B.

Section 1: Expressions

BEAT THE TEST!

1. Classify the following numbers as real or pure imaginary, and write them as a complex number.

	Real	Pure Imaginary	Complex
$-2.1i^2$	○	○	
$2i$	○	○	
i^4	○	○	
$\sqrt{-16}$	○	○	
51.2	○	○	

Test Yourself! Practice Tool
Great job! You have reached the end of this section. Now it's time to try the "Test Yourself! Practice Tool," where you can practice all the skills and concepts you learned in this section. Log in to Math Nation and try out the "Test Yourself! Practice Tool" so you can see how well you know these topics!

Algebra Wall
Want some help? You can always ask questions on the Algebra Wall and receive help from other students, teachers, and Study Experts. You can also help others on the Algebra Wall and earn Karma Points for doing so. Go to AlgebraNation.com to learn more and get started!

Section 2: Equations and Inequalities

Topic 1: Equations: True or False?... 31
Standards Covered: A-REI.3
- ☐ I can determine if a value of a variable makes an equation a true statement.

Topic 2: Identifying Properties When Solving Equations 33
Standards Covered: A-REI.1
- ☐ I can justify the steps to solve an equation in one variable.

Topic 3: Solving Equations... 36
Standards Covered: A-REI.1, A-REI.3, A-CED.1
- ☐ I can create and solve equations that represent real-world situations.

Topic 4: Solving Equations Using the Zero Product Property 38
Standards Covered: A-APR.3
- ☐ I can use the zero product property to solve equations.

Topic 5: Solving Power Equations.. 40
Standards Covered: A-REI.3, A-CED.1
- ☐ I can use what I know about rules of exponents and rational exponents to solve power equations.

Topic 6: Solving Inequalities - Part 1 42
Standards Covered: A-REI.3, A-CED.1
- ☐ I can graph inequalities and apply the addition and subtraction properties of inequality.

Topic 7: Solving Inequalities - Part 2 44
Standards Covered: A-REI.3, A-CED.1
- ☐ I can use the properties of inequality to solve inequalities.

Topic 8: Solving Compound Inequalities... 47
Standards Covered: A-REI.3
- ☐ I can solve compound inequalities.
- ☐ I understand the differences between "and" and "or" compound inequalities.

Topic 9: Solving Absolute Value Equations and Inequalities 50
Standards Covered: A-REI.3
- ☐ I can solve absolute value equations and inequalities.

Topic 10: Rearranging Formulas 54
Standards Covered: A-CED.4
- ☐ I can solve equations for a specified variable.

Topic 11: Solution Sets to Equations with Two Variables... 57
Standards Covered: A-CED.2, A-REI.10
- ☐ I can represent a solution on a graph and determine if a function is discrete or continuous.

Visit MathNation.com or search "Math Nation" in your phone or tablet's app store to watch the videos that go along with this workbook!

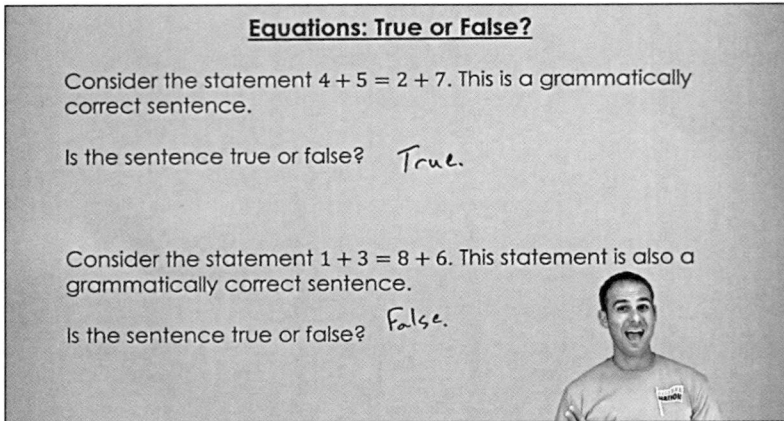

The following Michigan Mathematics Standards will be covered in this section:
A-REI.3 - Solve linear equations and inequalities in one variable, including equations with coefficients represented by letters.
A-REI.1 - Explain each step in solving a simple equation as following from the equality of numbers asserted at the previous step, starting from the assumption that they original equation has a solution. Construct a viable argument to justify a solution method.
A-CED.1 - Create equations and inequalities in one variable and use them to solve problems. Include equations arising from linear and quadratic functions, and simple rational, and exponential functions.
A-APR.3 - Identify zeros of polynomials when suitable factorizations are available, and use the zeros to construct a rough graph of the function defined by the polynomial.
A-CED.4 - Rearrange formulas to highlight a quantity of interest, using the same reasoning as in solving equations. For example, rearrange Ohm's law, $V = IR$, to highlight resistance, R.
A-CED.2 - Create equations in two or more variables to represent relationships between quantities; graph equations on coordinate axes with labels and scales.
A-REI.10 - Understand that the graph of an equation in two variables is the set of all its solutions plotted in the coordinate plane, often forming a curve (which could be a line).

Section 2: Equations and Inequalities
Section 2 – Topic 1
Equations: True or False?

Consider the statement $4 + 5 = 2 + 7$. This is a grammatically correct sentence.

Is the sentence true or false?

Consider the statement $1 + 3 = 8 + 6$. This statement is also a grammatically correct sentence.

Is the sentence true or false?

The previous statements are examples of **number sentences**.

> A number sentence is a statement of equality between two _____ expressions.

> A number sentence is said to be true if both numerical expressions are _____.

> If both numerical expressions don't equal the same number, we say the number sentence is _____.

> True and false statements are called **truth values**.

Let's Practice!

1. Determine whether the following number sentences are true or false. Justify your answer.

   a. $13 + 4 = 7 + 11$

   b. $\frac{1}{2} + \frac{5}{8} = 1.4 - 0.275$

Try It!

2. Determine whether the following number sentences are true or false. Justify your answer.

   a. $(83 \cdot 401) \cdot 638 = 401 \cdot (638 \cdot 83)$

   b. $(6 + 4)^2 = 6^2 + 4^2$

A number sentence is an example of an **algebraic equation**.

> An algebraic equation is a statement of equality between two _____.

> Algebraic equations can be number sentences (when both expressions contain only numbers), but often they contain _____ whose values have not been determined.

Consider the algebraic equation $4(x + 2) = 4x + 8$.

Are the expressions on each side of the equal sign equivalent? Justify your answer.

What does this tell you about the numbers we can substitute for x?

Let's Practice!

3. Consider the algebraic equation $x + 3 = 9$.

   a. What value can we substitute for x to make it a true number sentence?

   b. How many values could we substitute for x and have a true number sentence?

4. Consider the algebraic equation $x + 6 = x + 9$. What values could we substitute for x to make it a true number sentence?

Try It!

5. Complete the following sentences.

   a. $d^2 = 4$ is true for _____.

   b. $2m = m + m$ is true for _____.

   c. $d + 67 = d + 68$ is true for _____.

Section 2: Equations and Inequalities

BEAT THE TEST!

1. Which of the following equations have the correct solution? Select all that apply.

   ☐ $2x + 5 = 19; x = 7$

   ☐ $3 + x + 2 - x = 16; x = 3$

   ☐ $\dfrac{x+2}{5} = 2; x = 8$

   ☐ $6 = 2x - 8; x = 7$

   ☐ $14 = \dfrac{1}{3}x + 5; x = 18$

Section 2 – Topic 2
Identifying Properties When Solving Equations

The following equations are equivalent. Describe the operation that occurred in the second equation.

$3 + 5 = 8$ and $3 + 5 - 5 = 8 - 5$

$x - 3 = 7$ and $x - 3 + 3 = 7 + 3$

$2(4) = 8$ and $\dfrac{2(4)}{2} = \dfrac{8}{2}$

$\dfrac{x}{2} = 3$ and $2 \cdot \dfrac{x}{2} = 2 \cdot 3$

This brings us to some more properties that we can use to write equivalent equations.

Want some help? You can always ask questions on the Algebra Wall and receive help from other students, teachers, and Study Experts. You can also help others on the Algebra Wall and earn Karma Points for doing so. Go to AlgebraNation.com to learn more and get started!

Algebra Wall

Section 2: Equations and Inequalities

Properties of Equality

If x is a solution to an equation, then x will also be a solution to the new equation formed when the same number is added to each side of the original equation.

These are the **addition and subtraction properties of equality**.

- ➢ If $a = b$, then $a + c = b + c$ and $a - c = b - c$.

- ➢ Give examples of this property.

If x is a solution to an equation, x will also be a solution to the new equation formed when each side of the original equation is multiplied by the same number.

These are the **multiplication and division properties of equality**.

- ➢ If $a = b$, then $a \cdot c = b \cdot c$ and $\frac{a}{c} = \frac{b}{c}$.

- ➢ Give examples of this property.

Let's Practice!

1. The following equations are equivalent. Determine the property that was used to write the second equation.

   a. $x - 5 = 3x + 7$ and $x - 5 + 5 = 3x + 7 + 5$

   b. $x = 3x + 12$ and $x - 3x = 3x - 3x + 12$

   c. $-2x = 12$ and $\frac{-2x}{-2} = \frac{12}{-2}$

34

Section 2: Equations and Inequalities

Try It!

2. The following pairs of equations are equivalent. Determine the property that was used to write the second equation.

   a. $2(x + 4) = 14 - 6x$ and $2x + 8 = 14 - 6x$

   b. $2x + 8 = 14 - 6x$ and $2x + 8 + 6x = 14 - 6x + 6x$

   c. $2x + 8 + 6x = 14$ and $2x + 6x + 8 = 14$

   d. $8x + 8 = 14$ and $8x + 8 - 8 = 14 - 8$

   e. $8x = 6$ and $\frac{1}{8} \cdot 8x = \frac{1}{8} \cdot 6$

BEAT THE TEST!

1. For each algebraic equation, select the property or properties that could be used to solve it.

Algebraic Equation	Addition or Subtraction Property of Equality	Multiplication or Division Property of Equality	Distributive Property	Commutative Property
$\frac{x}{2} = 5$	☐	☐	☐	☐
$2x + 7 = 13$	☐	☐	☐	☐
$4x = 23$	☐	☐	☐	☐
$x - 3 = -4$	☐	☐	☐	☐
$4(x + 5) = 40$	☐	☐	☐	☐
$10 + x = 79$	☐	☐	☐	☐
$-8 - x = 19$	☐	☐	☐	☐
$2(x - 8) + 7x = 9$	☐	☐	☐	☐

Algebra Wall

Want some help? You can always ask questions on the Algebra Wall and receive help from other students, teachers, and Study Experts. You can also help others on the Algebra Wall and earn Karma Points for doing so. Go to AlgebraNation.com to learn more and get started!

Section 2: Equations and Inequalities

Section 2 – Topic 3
Solving Equations

Sometimes you will be required to justify the steps to solve an equation. The following equation is solved for x. Use the properties to justify the reason for each step in the chart below.

Statements	Reasons
a. $5(x + 3) - 2 = 2 - x + 9$	a. Given
b. $5x + 15 - 2 = 2 - x + 9$	b.
c. $5x + 15 - 2 = 2 + 9 - x$	c.
d. $5x + 13 = 11 - x$	d. Equivalent Equation
e. $5x + 13 - 13 = 11 - 13 - x$	e.
f. $5x = -2 - x$	f. Equivalent Equation
g. $5x + x = -2 - x + x$	g.
h. $6x = -2$	h. Equivalent Equation
i. $\frac{6x}{6} = \frac{-2}{6}$	i.
j. $x = -\frac{1}{3}$	j. Equivalent Equation

Other times, a word problem or situation may require you to write and solve an equation.

A class is raising funds to go ice skating at the Rink at Campus Martius in Detroit. The class plans to rent one bus. It costs $150.00 to rent a school bus for the day, plus $11.00 per student for admission to the rink, including skates.

What is the variable in this situation?

Write an expression to represent the amount of money the school needs to raise.

The class raised $500.00 for the trip. Write an equation to represent the number of students who can attend the trip.

Solve the equation to determine the number of students who can attend the trip.

Section 2: Equations and Inequalities

Let's Practice!

1. Consider the equation $2x - 3(2x - 1) = 3 - 4x$. Solve the equation for x. For each step, identify the property used to write an equivalent equation.

> **STUDY EDGE TIP:** Some equations, such as $2x = 2x$, have **all real numbers** as the solution. No matter what number we substitute for x, the equation will still be true.

Try It!

2. Consider the equation $3(4x + 1) = 3 + 12x - 5$. Solve the equation for x. For each step, identify the property used to convert the equation.

> **STUDY EDGE TIP:** Some equations, such as $2x + 5 = 2x - 1$, have **no solution**. There is no number that we could substitute for x that will make the equation true.

3. Brooklyn Technical High School surveyed its students about their favorite sports. The 487 students who listed soccer as their favorite sport represented 17 fewer students than three times the number of students who listed basketball as their favorite sport. Write and solve an equation to determine how many students listed basketball as their favorite sport.

Section 2: Equations and Inequalities

BEAT THE TEST!

1. The following equation is solved for x. Use the properties to justify the reason for each step in the chart below.

Statements	Reasons
a. $2(x + 5) - 3 = 15$	a. Given
b. $2x + 10 - 3 = 15$	b.
c. $2x + 7 = 15$	c. Equivalent Equation
d. $2x + 7 - 7 = 15 - 7$	d.
e. $2x = 8$	e. Equivalent Equation
f. $\frac{2x}{2} = \frac{8}{2}$	f.
g. $x = 4$	g. Equivalent Equation

Want some help? You can always ask questions on the Algebra Wall and receive help from other students, teachers, and Study Experts. You can also help others on the Algebra Wall and earn Karma Points for doing so. Go to AlgebraNation.com to learn more and get started!

Section 2 – Topic 4
Solving Equations Using the Zero Product Property

If someone told you that the product of two numbers is 10, what could you say about the two numbers?

If someone told you that the product of two numbers is zero, what could you say about the two numbers?

This is the **zero product property**.

➢ If $ab = 0$, then either $a = 0$ or $b = 0$.

Describe how to use the zero product property to solve the equation $(x - 3)(x + 9) = 0$. Then, identify the solutions.

Let's Practice!

1. Identify the solution(s) to $2x(x+4)(x+5) = 0$.

2. Identify the solution(s) to $(2x-5)(x+11) = 0$.

Try It!

3. Michael was given the equation $(x+7)(x-11) = 0$ and asked to find the zeros. His solution set was $\{-11, 7\}$. Explain whether you agree or disagree with Michael.

4. Identify the solution(s) to $2(y-3) \cdot 6(-y-3) = 0$.

Section 2: Equations and Inequalities

BEAT THE TEST!

1. Use the values below to determine the solutions for each equation.

0	2	3	$\frac{4}{5}$
$\frac{2}{7}$	$-\frac{1}{2}$	$-\frac{3}{4}$	-14
6	0	$-\frac{1}{4}$	-2

$(2y + 1)(y + 14) = 0$			

$(7n - 2)(5n - 4) = 0$			

$(4x + 3)(x - 6) = 0$			

$x(x + 2)(x - 3) = 0$			

$t(4t + 1)(t - 2) = 0$			

Section 2 – Topic 5
Solving Power Equations

We can use the rules of exponents and what we know about rational exponents to solve power equations.

Let's Practice!

1. $x^{\frac{1}{2}} = 4$

2. $\sqrt{x} = 4$

3. $x^{\frac{1}{2}} + 2 = 11$

4. $\sqrt{x} + 2 = 11$

Try It!

5. $x^{\frac{1}{2}} = 64$

6. $x^{\frac{1}{2}} + 2 = 27$

7. $(x + 2)^{\frac{1}{2}} = 6$

8. $(x - 3)^{\frac{2}{3}} = 9$

9. Zaira is taking a sail theory class with The Great Lakes Sailing Company. She determines that the hull speed, s, in nautical miles per hour, of a sailboat can be modeled by the formula $s = 1.34 \cdot l^{\frac{1}{2}}$, where l is the length in feet of the sailboat's waterline. Find the length of the sailboat's waterline if the speed of the boat is 4.2 nautical miles per hour.

BEAT THE TEST!

1. The average amount of bananas consumed by Americans (in pounds per person), y, can be modeled by the equation $y = (22x + 275)^{\frac{1}{2}}$, where x is the number of years since 1993. In which year were about 20 pounds of bananas consumed per person?

2. The average amount of sewage discharged by a factory, y, can be modeled by the equation $y = 235(2x + 0.75)^{\frac{1}{2}}$, where x is the number of years since 2000 and y is the average sewage discharged per month, in tons. In which year were approximately 610 tons of sewage discharged per month?

Section 2: Equations and Inequalities

Section 2 – Topic 6
Solving Inequalities – Part 1

Let's start by reviewing how to graph inequalities.

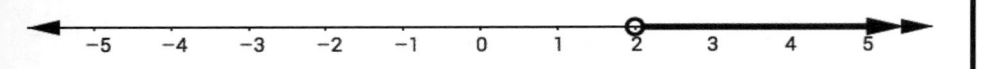

[Number line from -5 to 5 with an open circle at 2 and shading to the right]

➢ When the endpoint is a(n) _____ dot or circle, the number represented by the endpoint _____ _____ a part of the solution set.

Describe the numbers that are graphed in the example above.

Can you list all the numbers graphed in the example above? Explain your answer.

Write an inequality that represents the graph above.

Write the solution set that represents the graph above.

Consider the following graph.

[Number line from 4 to 15 with a closed dot at 10 and shading to the left]

➢ When the endpoint is a(n) _____ dot or circle, the number represented by the endpoint _____ a part of the solution set.

Write an inequality that represents the graph above.

Write the solution set that represents the graph above.

Why is "or equal to" included in the solution set?

Just like there are properties of equality, there are also **properties of inequality**.

If $x > 5$, is $x + 1 > 5 + 1$? Substitute values for x to justify your answer.

Section 2: Equations and Inequalities

Addition and Subtraction Property of Inequality

> If $a > b$, then $a + c > b + c$ and $a - c > b - c$ for any real number c.

Consider $(2x - 1) + 2 > x + 1$. Use the addition or subtraction property of inequality to solve for x.

Let's Practice!

1. Consider the inequality $(4 + x) - 5 \geq 10$. Use the addition or subtraction property of inequality to solve for x. Express the solution in set notation and graphically on a number line.

Try It!

2. Consider the inequality $4x + 8 < 1 + (2x - 5)$. Use the addition or subtraction property of inequality to solve for x. Express the solution in set notation and graphically on a number line.

3. Peter deposited $27 into his savings account, bringing the total to over $234. Write and solve an inequality to represent the amount of money in Peter's account before the $27 deposit.

Algebra Wall — Want some help? You can always ask questions on the Algebra Wall and receive help from other students, teachers, and Study Experts. You can also help others on the Algebra Wall and earn Karma Points for doing so. Go to AlgebraNation.com to learn more and get started!

Section 2: Equations and Inequalities

Section 2 – Topic 7
Solving Inequalities – Part 2

Consider $x > 5$ and $2 \cdot x > 2 \cdot 5$. Identify a solution to the first inequality. Show that this solution also makes the second inequality true.

Consider $x > 5$ and $-2 \cdot x > -2 \cdot 5$. Identify a solution to the first inequality. Show that this solution makes the second inequality false.

How can we change the second inequality so that the solution makes it true?

Consider $-q > 5$. Use the addition and/or subtraction property of inequality to solve.

Multiplication Property of Inequality

➢ If $a > b$, then for any positive real number k,
  ak _____ bk.

➢ If $a < b$, then for any positive real number k,
  ak _____ bk.

➢ If $a > b$, then for any negative real number k,
  ak _____ bk.

➢ If $a < b$, then for any negative real number k,
  ak _____ bk.

The same property is true when dealing with ≤ or ≥.

Let's Practice!

1. Find the solution set of each inequality. Express the solution in set notation and graphically on a number line.

    a. $-9y + 4 < -7y - 2$

b. $\dfrac{m}{3} + 8 \leq 9$

Try It!

3. Find the solution set to the inequality. Express the solution in set notation and graphically on a number line.

   a. $-6(x - 5) > 42$

2. At 5:00 PM in Atlanta, Georgia, Ethan noticed the temperature outside was 72°F. The temperature decreased at a steady rate of 2°F per hour. At what time was the temperature below 64°F?

   b. $4(x + 3) \geq 2(2x - 2)$

Section 2: Equations and Inequalities

BEAT THE TEST!

1. Ulysses is spending his vacation in South Carolina. He rents a car and is offered two different payment options. He can either pay $25.00 each day plus $0.15 per mile (option A) or pay $10.00 each day plus $0.40 per mile (option B). Ulysses rents the car for one day.

   Part A: Write an inequality representing the number of miles where option A will be the cheaper plan.

   Part B: How many miles will Ulysses have to drive for option A to be the cheaper option?

2. Stephanie has just been given a new job in the sales department of Frontier Electric Authority. She has two salary options. She can either receive a fixed salary of $500.00 per week or a salary of $200.00 per week plus a 5% commission on her weekly sales. The variable s represents Stephanie's weekly sales. Which solution set represents the dollar amount of sales that she must generate in a week in order for the option with commission to be the better choice?

   Ⓐ $\{s|s > \$300.00\}$
   Ⓑ $\{s|s > \$700.00\}$
   Ⓒ $\{s|s > \$3,000.00\}$
   Ⓓ $\{s|s > \$6,000.00\}$

Want some help? You can always ask questions on the Algebra Wall and receive help from other students, teachers, and Study Experts. You can also help others on the Algebra Wall and earn Karma Points for doing so. Go to AlgebraNation.com to learn more and get started!

Section 2 – Topic 8
Solving Compound Inequalities

Consider the following options.

   Option A: You get to play NBA 2K after you clean your room and do the dishes.

   Option B: You get to play NBA 2K after you clean your room or do the dishes.

What is the difference between Option A and B?

Circle the statements that are true.

$2 + 9 = 11$ and $10 < 5 + 6$

$4 + 5 \neq 9$ and $2 + 3 > 0$

$0 > 4 - 6$ or $3 + 2 = 6$

$15 - 20 > 0$ or $2.5 + 3.5 = 7$

These are called **compound equations** or **inequalities**.

➢ When the two statements in the previous sentences were joined by the word AND, the compound equation or inequality is true only if _____ statements are true.

➢ When the two statements in the previous sentences were joined by the word OR, the compound equation or inequality is true if at least _____ of the statements is true. Therefore, it is also considered true if _____ statements are true.

Let's graph $x < 6$ and $x > 1$.

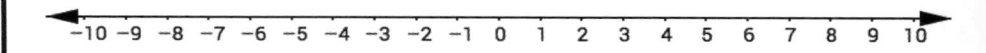

[number line from -10 to 10]

This is the _____ _____ to the compound inequality.

How many solutions does this inequality have?

Many times this is written as $1 < x < 6$. This notation denotes the conjunction "and."

We read this as "x is greater than one _____ less than six."

Section 2: Equations and Inequalities

47

Let's Practice!

1. Consider $x < 1$ or $x > 6$. Could we write the inequalities above as $1 > x > 6$? Explain your answer.

2. Graph the solution set to each compound inequality on a number line.

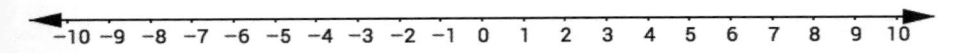

   a. $x = 2$ or $x > 5$

   b. $x > 6$ or $x < 6$

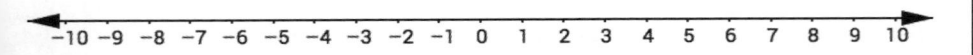

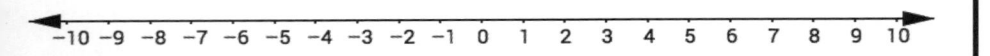

   c. $1 \leq -x \leq 7$

> **STUDY EDGE TIP:** Be on the lookout for negative coefficients. When solving inequalities, you will need to reverse the inequality symbol when you multiply or divide by a negative value.

3. Write a compound inequality for the following graphs.

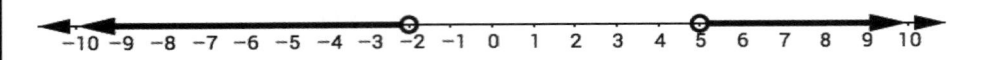

   a. Compound inequality: _____

   b. Compound inequality: _____

Section 2: Equations and Inequalities

Try It!

4. Graph the solution set to each compound inequality on a number line.

   a. $x < 1$ or $x > 8$

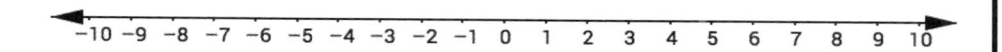

   b. $x \geq 6$ or $x < 4$

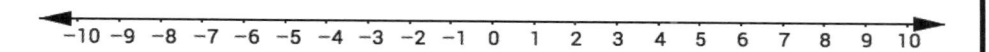

   c. $-6 \leq x \leq 4$

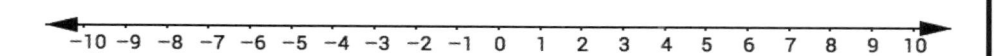

5. Write a compound inequality for the following graphs.

   a. Compound inequality: [ ]

   b. Compound inequality: [ ]

Section 2: Equations and Inequalities

BEAT THE TEST!

1. Use the terms and symbols in the table to write a compound inequality for each of the following graphs. You may only use each term once, but you do not have to use all of them.

$3x$	-14	-6	$\geq$	$-$	17	15	$<$
$7x$	$<$	2	or	$\leq$	$3x$	$+$	$>$

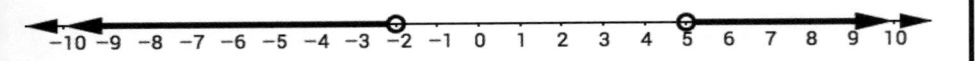

Compound Inequality: _____

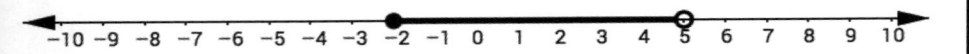

Compound Inequality: _____

Want some help? You can always ask questions on the Algebra Wall and receive help from other students, teachers, and Study Experts. You can also help others on the Algebra Wall and earn Karma Points for doing so. Go to AlgebraNation.com to learn more and get started!

Section 2 – Topic 9
Solving Absolute Value Equations and Inequalities

Absolute value represents the distance of a number from zero on a number line.

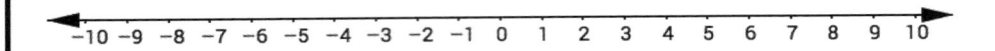

How far away is "9" from zero on the number line?

This is written as _____.

How far away is "-9" from zero on the number line?

This is written as _____.

This is the **absolute value** of a number.

➢ For any real numbers c and d, if $|c| = d$, then $c = d$ or $c = -d$.

For example, $|f| = 5$, so $f =$ ____ or $f =$ ____.

Consider $|c| < 5$.

Using our definition of absolute value, c represents all the numbers _____ _____ five units from zero on the number line.

What are some numbers that could be represented by c?

Graph all the numbers represented by c on a number line.

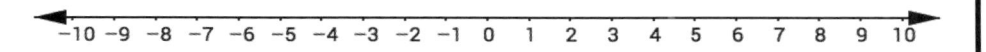

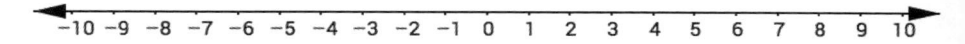

```
<---|---|---|---|---|---|---|---|---|---|---|---|---|---|---|---|---|---|---|---|---|--->
  -10 -9 -8 -7 -6 -5 -4 -3 -2 -1  0  1  2  3  4  5  6  7  8  9  10
```

What is the solution set for c?

> ➢ For any real numbers c and d, if $|c| < d$, then $-d < c < d$.
>
> ➢ For any real numbers c and d, if $|c| \leq d$, then $-d \leq c \leq d$.

Consider $|c| > 5$.

Using our definition of absolute value, c represents all the numbers _____ _____ five units from zero on the number line.

What are some numbers that could be represented by c?

Graph all the numbers represented by c on a number line.

```
<---|---|---|---|---|---|---|---|---|---|---|---|---|---|---|---|---|---|---|---|---|--->
  -10 -9 -8 -7 -6 -5 -4 -3 -2 -1  0  1  2  3  4  5  6  7  8  9  10
```

What is the solution set for c?

> ➢ For any real numbers c and d, if $|c| > d$, then $c > d$ or $c < -d$.
>
> ➢ For any real numbers c and d, if $|c| \geq d$, then $c \geq d$ or $c \leq -d$.

Let's Practice!

1. Solve each absolute value inequality and graph the solution set.

   a. $|n+5| < 7$

   b. $|a| + 3 > 9$

2. Tammy purchased a pH meter to measure the acidity of her freshwater aquarium. The ideal pH level for a freshwater aquarium is between 6.5 and 7.5 inclusive.

   a. Graph an inequality that represents the possible pH levels needed for Tammy's aquarium.

   b. Define the variable and write an absolute value inequality that represents the possible pH levels needed for Tammy's aquarium.

Section 2: Equations and Inequalities

Try It!

3. Solve each equation or inequality and graph the solution set.

   a. $|p + 7| = -13$

   b. $2|x| - 4 < 14$

   c. $|2m + 4| \geq 12$

4. Baseball fans often leave a baseball game if their team is ahead or behind by five runs or more. Toronto Blue Jays fans follow this pattern, and the Blue Jays have scored eight runs in a particular game.

   a. Graph an inequality that represents the possible runs, r, scored by the opposing team if Toronto fans are leaving the game.

   b. Write an absolute value inequality that represents the possible runs, r, scored by the opposing team if Toronto fans are leaving the game.

Section 2: Equations and Inequalities

BEAT THE TEST!

1. Match the following absolute value equations and inequalities to the graph that represents their solution set.

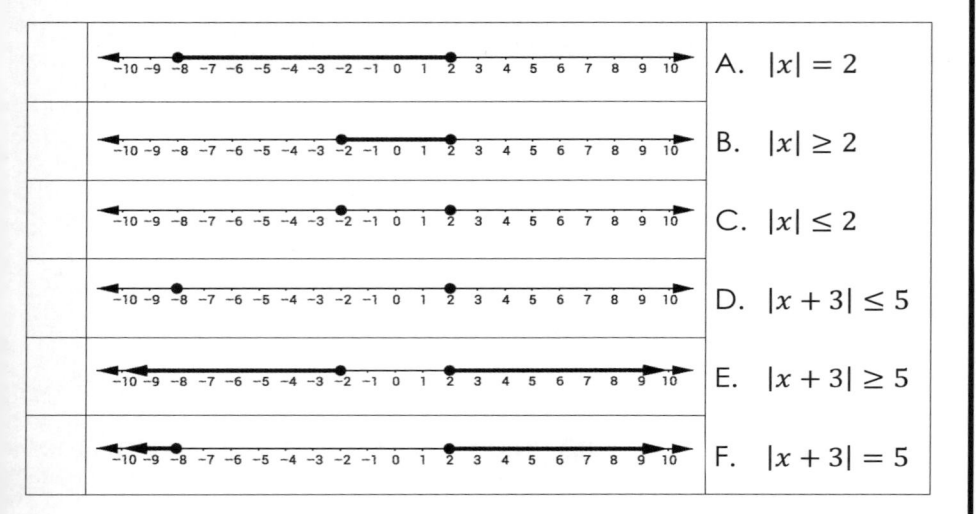

(number line with closed dots at -2 and 2, shading outside)	A. $|x| = 2$
(number line with closed dots at -2 and 2, shading between)	B. $|x| \geq 2$
(number line with closed dots at -2 and 2 only)	C. $|x| \leq 2$
(number line with closed dots at -8 and 2, shading outside)	D. $|x+3| \leq 5$
(number line with closed dots at -8 and 2, shading between)	E. $|x+3| \geq 5$
(number line with closed dots at -8 and 2 only)	F. $|x+3| = 5$

Section 2 – Topic 10
Rearranging Formulas

Solve each equation for x.

$2x + 4 = 12$ $\qquad\qquad 2x + y = z$

Did we use different properties when we solved the two equations?

Consider the formula for the perimeter of a rectangle: $P = 2l + 2w$.

Sometimes, we might need the formula solved for length.

STUDY EDGE TIP: When solving for a variable, it's helpful to circle that variable.

Let's Practice!

1. Consider the equation $rx - sx + y = z$; solve for x.

Try It!

2. Consider the equation $8c + 6j = 5p$; solve for c.

3. Consider the equation $\dfrac{x - c}{2} = d$; solve for c.

Section 2: Equations and Inequalities

BEAT THE TEST!

1. Isaiah planted a seedling in his garden and recorded its height every week. The equation shown can be used to estimate the height, h, of the seedling after w weeks since he planted the seedling.

$$h = \frac{3}{4}w + \frac{9}{4}$$

Solve the formula for w, the number of weeks since he planted the seedling.

2. Under the Brannock device method, shoe size and foot length for women are related by the formula $S = 3F - 21$, where S represents the shoe size and F represents the length of the foot in inches. Solve the formula for F.

Algebra Wall

Want some help? You can always ask questions on the Algebra Wall and receive help from other students, teachers, and Study Experts. You can also help others on the Algebra Wall and earn Karma Points for doing so. Go to AlgebraNation.com to learn more and get started!

Section 2 – Topic 11
Solution Sets to Equations with Two Variables

Consider $x + 2 = 5$. What is the only possible value of x that makes the equation a true statement?

Now consider $x + y = 5$. What are some solutions for x and y that would make the equation true?

Possible solutions can be listed as **ordered pairs**.

Graph each of the ordered pairs from the previous problem on the graph below.

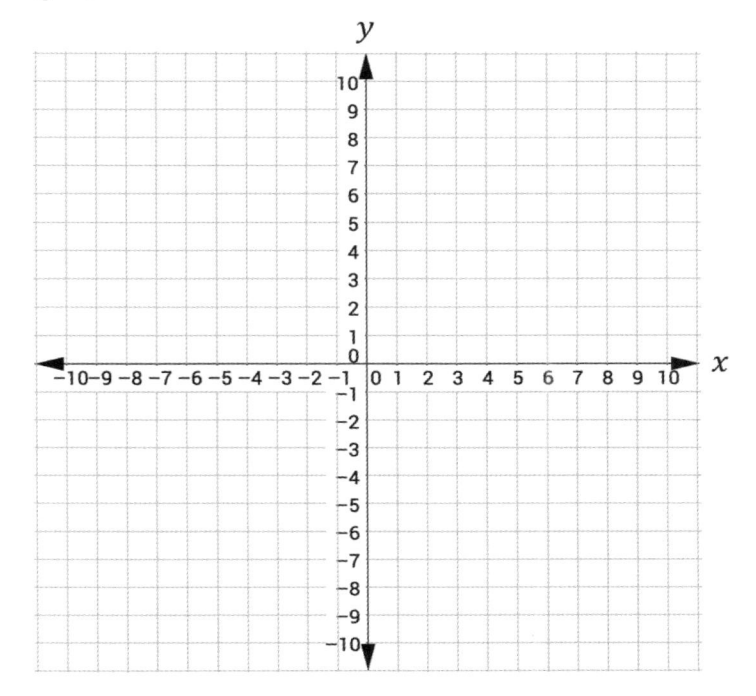

What do you notice about the points you graphed?

How many solutions are there to the equation $x + y = 5$?

Let's Practice!

1. Taylor has 10 songs on her phone's playlist. The playlist features songs from her two favorite artists, Beyoncé and Pharrell.

    a. Create an equation using two variables to represent this situation.

    b. List at least three solutions to the equation that you created.

    c. Does this equation have infinitely many solutions? Why or why not?

Section 2: Equations and Inequalities

> **STUDY EDGE TIP**
> In this case, our solutions must be natural numbers. This is called a **discrete function**. Notice that the solutions follow a linear pattern. However, they do not form a line.

d. Create a graph that represents the solution set to your equation.

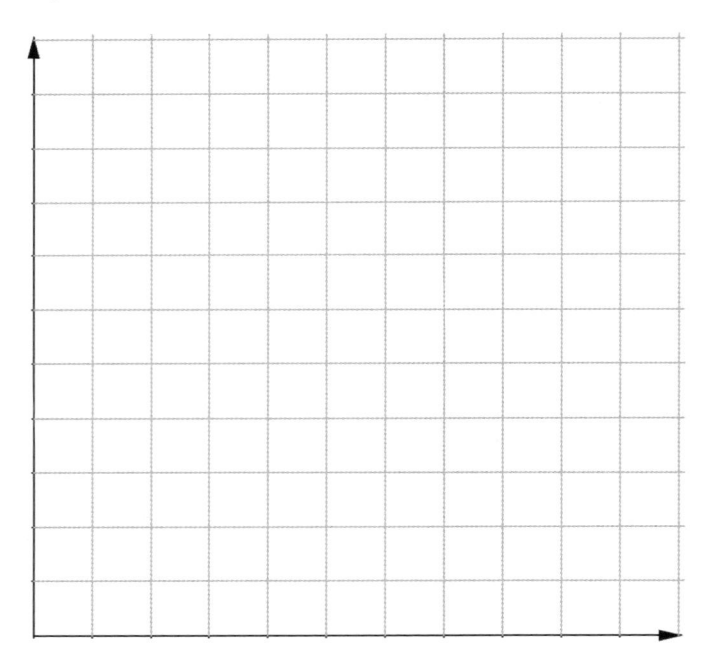

e. Why are there only positive values on this graph?

Try It!

2. The sum of two numbers is 15.

   a. Create an equation using two variables to represent this situation.

   b. List at least three possible solutions.

   c. How many solutions are there to this equation?

   d. Create a visual representation of all the possible solutions on the graph.

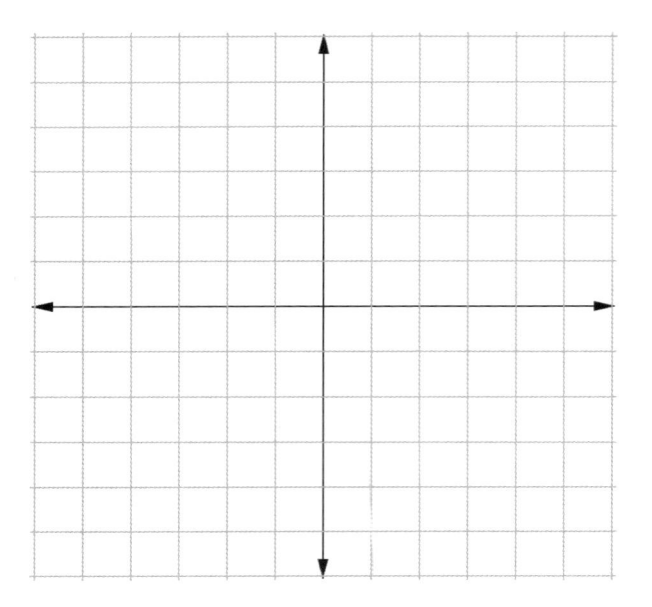

Section 2: Equations and Inequalities

> **STUDY EDGE TIP:** In this case, we have a **continuous function**. Notice the solutions are rational numbers and they form a line.

3. What if we changed the problem to say the sum of two integers is 15?

    a. Create an equation using two variables to represent this situation.

    b. Is this function discrete or continuous? Explain your answer.

    c. Represent the solution on the graph below.

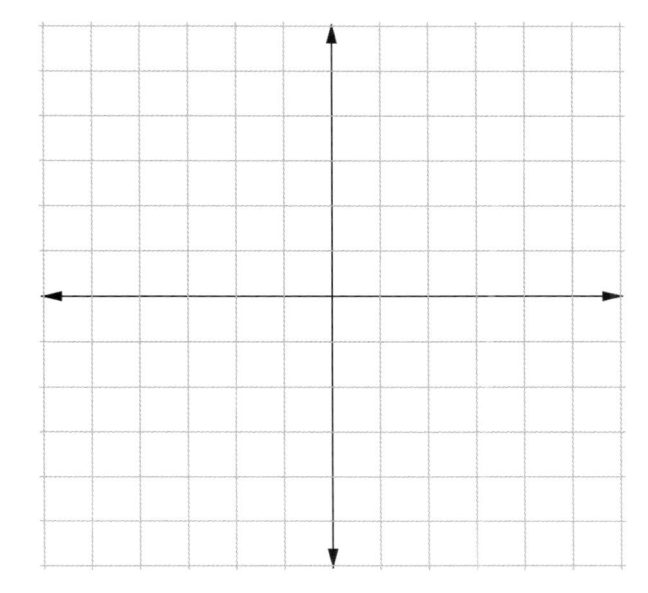

BEAT THE TEST!

1. Elizabeth's tablet has a combined total of 20 apps and movies. Let x represent the number of apps and y represent the number of movies. Which of the following could represent the number of apps and movies on Elizabeth's tablet? Select all that apply.

    ☐ $x + y = 20$
    ☐ 7 apps and 14 movies
    ☐ $x - y = 20$
    ☐ $y = -x + 20$
    ☐ 8 apps and 12 movies
    ☐ $xy = 20$

Test Yourself! Practice Tool — Great job! You have reached the end of this section. Now it's time to try the "Test Yourself! Practice Tool," where you can practice all the skills and concepts you learned in this section. Log in to Algebra Nation and try out the "Test Yourself! Practice Tool" so you can see how well you know these topics!

Section 2: Equations and Inequalities

Section 3: Introduction to Functions

Topic 1: What is a Function? 62
Standards Covered: F-IF.1, F-IF.2
    ☐ I can determine if a relationship is a function.

Topic 2: Representing, Naming, and Evaluating Functions 65
Standards Covered: F-IF.2, F-IF.5
    ☐ I can find the range and domain for a given function.
    ☐ I can write a function that represents a real-world situation and evaluate functions for specific values.

Topic 3: Adding and Subtracting Functions 67
Standards Covered: A-APR.1
    ☐ I can add and subtract polynomials written in function notation.

Topic 4: Multiplying Functions 69
Standards Covered: A-APR.1
    ☐ I can multiply polynomials using both modeling techniques and the distributive property.

Topic 5: Closure Property 73
Standards Covered: A-APR.1
    ☐ I can apply the closure property to operations on polynomials with integer coefficients.

Topic 6: Families of Functions 75
Standards Covered: F-IF.7
    ☐ I can identify the key features of different families of functions.

Topic 7: Key Features of Graphs of Functions – Part 1 78
Standards Covered: F.IF.4, F-IF.1
    ☐ I can determine key features of a function by examining its graph.

Topic 8: Key Features of Graphs of Functions – Part 2 82
Standards Covered: F-IF.4
    ☐ I can determine key features of a function by examining its graph.

Topic 9: Inverse Functions 84
Standards Covered: F-BF.4
    ☐ I can find the inverse function for anyone-to-one function.

Topic 10: Transformations of Functions 86
Standards Covered: F-BF.3
    ☐ I can apply a horizontal and vertical transformation to a function.

Visit MathNation.com or search "Math Nation" in your phone or tablet's app store to watch the videos that go along with this workbook!

What is a Function?

In mathematics, a collection of inputs and outputs is called a **relation**.

➤ **Domain** is the set of all possible __input__ values used for a relation or a function. In an ordered pair, the input is the *x*-value.

➤ **Range** is the set of all __output__ values that result from the input values of a relation or a function. In an ordered pair, the output is the *y*-value.

For a relation to be a **function**, every input value corresponds to <u>only</u> one output value.

Label input and output values. Determine whether shown here is a function.

The following Michigan Mathematics Standards will be covered in this section:
F-IF.1 - Understand that a function from one set (called the domain) to another set (called the range) assigns to each element of the domain exactly one element of the range. If f is a function and x is an element of its domain, then f(x) denotes the output of f corresponding to the input x. The graph of f is the graph of the equation y = f(x).
F-IF.2 - Use function notation, evaluate functions for inputs in their domains, and interpret statements that use function notation in terms of a context.
F-IF.5 - Relate the domain of a function to its graph and, where applicable, to the quantitative relationship it describes.
A-APR.1 - Understand that polynomials form a system analogous to the integers, namely, they are closed under the operations of addition, subtraction, and multiplication; add, subtract, and multiply polynomials.
F-IF.7 - Graph functions expressed symbolically and show key features of the graph, by hand in simple cases and using technology for more complicated cases.
F-IF.4 - For a function that models a relationship between two quantities, interpret key features of graphs and tables in terms of the quantities, and sketch graphs showing key features given a verbal description of the relationship. Key features include: intercepts; intervals where the function is increasing, decreasing, positive, or negative; relative maximums and minimums; symmetries; end behavior; and periodicity.
F-BF.4 - Find inverse functions.
F-BF.3 - Identify the effect on the graph of replacing f(x) by f(x) + k, k f(x), f(kx), and f(x + k) for specific values of k (both positive and negative); find the value of k given the graphs. Experiment with cases and illustrate an explanation of the effects on the graph using technology. Include recognizing even and odd functions from their graphs and algebraic expressions for them.

Section 3: Introduction to Functions

Section 3: Introduction to Functions
Section 3 – Topic 1
What is a Function?

In mathematics, a collection of inputs and outputs is called a **relation**.

- **Domain** is the set of all possible _____ values used for a relation or a function. In an ordered pair, the input is the x-value.

- **Range** is the set of all _____ values that result from the input values of a relation or a function. In an ordered pair, the output is the y-value.

For a relation to be a **function**, every input value corresponds to <u>only</u> one output value.

Label input and output values. Determine whether the relation shown here is a function.

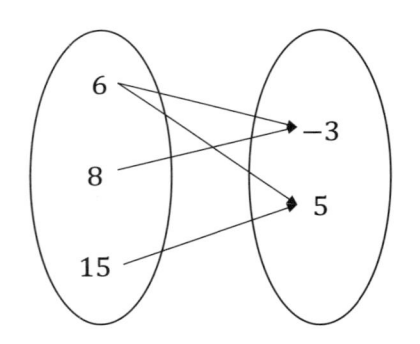

Relations and functions can be represented using a mapping diagram, a table of values, a set of ordered pairs, or a graph. The table shows each representation with an example of a relation and a function.

Relation	Function
Height of player (feet) → Points scored: 6→11, 5→11, $6\frac{5}{12}$→23, $6\frac{11}{12}$→23	Height of water bottle (inches) → Height of water bottle (centimeters): 12→30.48, 15→20.32, 8→38.1
x | y 2.3 | 7.4 2.7 | 6.5 1.6 | 5.2 2.3 | 6.8	x | y −4.7 | 7 2.4 | 4.7 −1.6 | 3.9 8.1 | 10.4
$\{(-6,5),(5,-6),(-4,1),(-4,5)\}$	$\{(-6,5),(5,5),(-2,5),(-4,5)\}$
graph	graph

As you looked at the table of representations, what did you notice?

The **vertical line test** can be used to determine if a relation represented by a graph is a function.

Using the graphs and the definition of a function, explain why the vertical line test can be used to determine if a relation represented by a graph is a function.

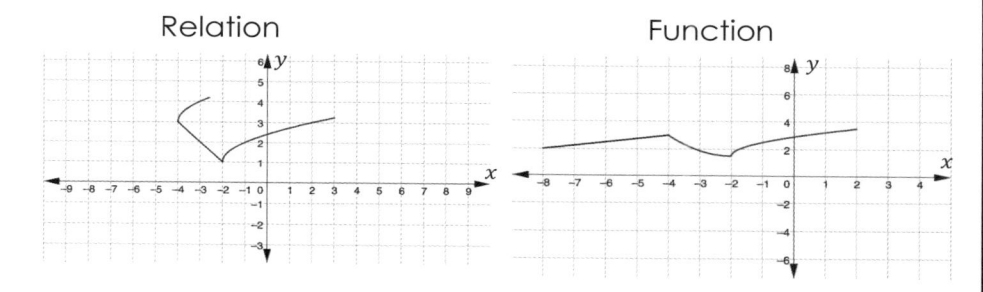

Relation

Function

We can represent functions using equations. The graph below is a linear function that can also be represented by an equation. In this case, the equation is $y = -\frac{1}{2}x + 2.3$.

The equation $y = -\frac{1}{2}x + 2.3$ can be written as _____ $= -\frac{1}{2}x + 2.3$.

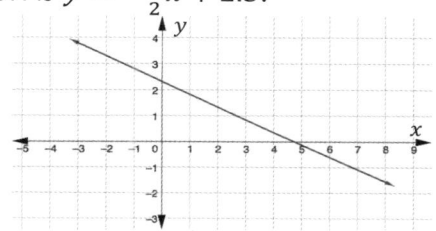

STUDY EDGE TIP: We can choose any letter to represent a function, such as $f(x)$ or $w(x)$, where x is the input value. By using different letters, we show that we are talking about different functions.

Let's Practice!

1. At sea level, the air presses down on our bodies at 14.7 pounds per square inch (psi). When diving in the ocean, the pressure increases. The equation $y = 0.445x + 14.7$, where x is the number of feet a diver descends, represents this situation.

   a. Explain using the definition how you know the relationship represented by the equation is a function.

   b. Write the equation $y = 0.445x + 14.7$ as function P.

   c. Find the value of y when $x = 2$ and write using function notation.

   d. Interpret $P(50) = 36.95$ for the given context.

Section 3: Introduction to Functions

Try It!

2. The table below gives the number of letters of the winning word of the Scripps National Spelling Bee and the number of people killed by venomous spiders for the years 1999-2009.

	1999	2000	2001	2002	2003	2004	2005	2006	2007	2008	2009
Letters in winning word of National Spelling Bee	9	8	11	12	11	13	12	9	9	7	9
People killed by venomous spider (CDC)	6	5	5	10	8	14	10	4	8	5	6

a. Use the data in the table to complete the mapping diagram.

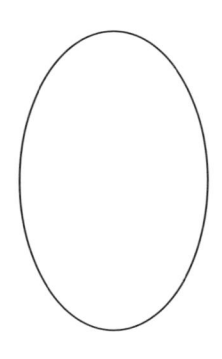

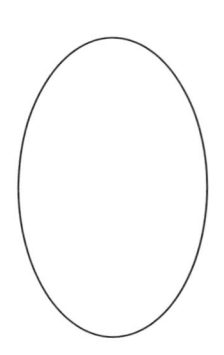

b. Is the relationship between the number of letters in a winning word and the number of people killed by venomous spiders a function? Use the definition of a function to explain.

BEAT THE TEST!

1. The tables shown represent data of honey-producing bee colonies in the US and marriage rate in Vermont for the years 1998-2002.

Year	Honey producing bee colonies in the US (thousands of colonies)	Year	Marriage rate in Vermont (marriages per 1000 people)
1998	2,652	1998	10
1999	2,622	1999	10
2000	2,550	2000	9.8
2001	2,574	2001	9.8
2002	2,599	2002	9.7

Which relationship of the data, honey-producing bee colonies in the US and the marriage rate in Vermont, is a function?

Ⓐ $\{(2652, 10), (2622, 10)(2550, 9.8), (2574, 9.8), (2599, 9.7)\}$

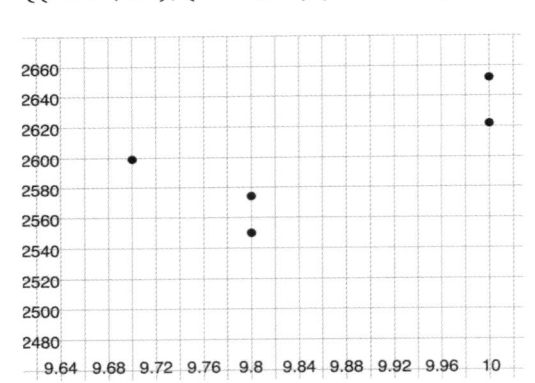

Ⓑ [scatter plot with axes marked 9.64–10 horizontally and 2480–2660 vertically]

Ⓒ [mapping diagram from Marriage rate in Vermont {10, 9.8, 9.7} to Honey-producing bee colonies {2,550, 2,574, 2,599, 2,622, 2,652}]

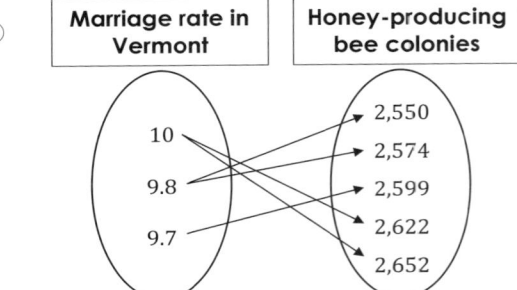

Ⓓ $M(9.7) = 2{,}599, M(9.8) = 2{,}550, M(9.8) = 2{,}574,$ $M(10) = 2{,}622, M(10) = 2{,}652$

Section 3: Introduction to Functions

2. The cost to manufacture x pairs of shoes can be represented by the function $C(x) = 63x$. Complete the statement about the function.

If $C(6) = 378$, then [0 / 6 / 63 / 378] pairs of shoes cost [$6. / $189. / $378. / $2,268.]

Section 3 – Topic 2
Representing, Naming, and Evaluating Functions

A ball is thrown into the air with an initial velocity of 15 meters per second. The quadratic function $h(t) = -4.9t^2 + 15t + 3$ represents the height of the ball above the ground, in meters, with respect to time t, in seconds.

Determine $h(2)$ and explain what it represents.

Is -3 a reasonable input for the function?

The graph below represents the height of the ball with respect to time.

Height of the Ball Over Time

What is a reasonable domain for the function?

What is a reasonable range for the function?

Want some help? You can always ask questions on the Algebra Wall and receive help from other students, teachers, and Study Experts. You can also help others on the Algebra Wall and earn Karma Points for doing so. Go to AlgebraNation.com to learn more and get started!

Section 3: Introduction to Functions

Let's Practice!

1. On the moon, the time, in seconds, it takes for an object to fall a distance, d, in feet, is given by the function $f(d) = 1.11\sqrt{d}$.

   a. Determine $f(5)$ and explain what it represents.

   b. The South Pole-Aitken basin on the moon is 42,768 feet deep. Determine a reasonable domain for a rock dropped from the rim of the basin.

2. Floyd drinks two Mountain Dew sodas in the morning. The function that represents the amount of caffeine, in milligrams, remaining in his body after drinking the sodas is given by $f(t) = 110(0.8855)^t$ where t is time in hours. Floyd says that in two days the caffeine is completely out of his system. Do you agree? Justify your answer.

Try It!

3. Medical professionals say that 98.6°F is the normal body temperature of an average person. Healthy individuals' temperatures should not vary more than 0.5°F from that temperature.

   a. Write an absolute value function $f(t)$ to describe an individual's variance from normal body temperature, where t is the individual's current temperature.

   b. Determine $f(101.5)$ and describe what that tells you about the individual.

   c. What is a reasonable domain for a healthy individual?

Section 3: Introduction to Functions

BEAT THE TEST!

1. The length of a shipping box is two inches longer than the width and four times the height.

   Part A: Write a function $V(w)$ that models the volume of the box, where w is the width, in inches.

   Part B: Evaluate $V(10)$. Describe what this tells you about the box.

Section 3 – Topic 3
Adding and Subtracting Functions

Let $h(x) = 2x^2 + x - 5$ and $g(x) = -3x^2 + 4x + 1$.

Find $h(x) + g(x)$.

Find $h(x) - g(x)$.

Let's Practice!

1. Consider the following functions.

$$f(x) = 3x^2 + x + 2$$
$$g(x) = 4x^2 + 2(3x - 4)$$
$$h(x) = 5(x^2 - 1)$$

a. Find $f(x) - g(x)$.

b. Find $g(x) - h(x)$.

Try It!

2. Recall the functions we used earlier.

$$f(x) = 3x^2 + x + 2$$
$$g(x) = 4x^2 + 2(3x - 4)$$
$$h(x) = 5(x^2 - 1)$$

a. Let $m(x)$ be $f(x) + g(x)$. Find $m(x)$.

b. Find $h(x) - m(x)$.

BEAT THE TEST!

1. Consider the functions below.

$$f(x) = 2x^2 + 3x - 5$$
$$g(x) = 5x^2 + 4x - 1$$

Which of the following is the resulting polynomial when $f(x)$ is subtracted from $g(x)$?

Ⓐ $-3x^2 - x - 4$
Ⓑ $-3x^2 + 7x - 6$
Ⓒ $3x^2 + x + 4$
Ⓓ $3x^2 + 7x - 6$

Want some help? You can always ask questions on the Algebra Wall and receive help from other students, teachers, and Study Experts. You can also help others on the Algebra Wall and earn Karma Points for doing so. Go to AlgebraNation.com to learn more and get started!

Section 3 – Topic 4
Multiplying Functions

Use the distributive property and modeling to perform the following function operations.

Let $f(x) = 3x^2 + 4x + 2$ and $g(x) = 2x + 3$.

Find $f(x) \cdot g(x)$.

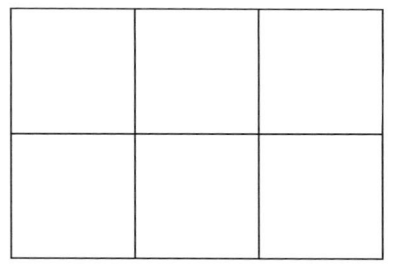

Section 3: Introduction to Functions

Let $m(y) = 3y^5 - 2y^2 + 8$ and $p(y) = y^2 - 2$.

Find $m(y) \cdot p(y)$.

Let's Practice!

1. Let $h(x) = x - 1$ and $g(x) = x^3 + 6x^2 - 5$.

   Find $h(x) \cdot g(x)$.

Section 3: Introduction to Functions

Try It!

2. The envelope below has a mailing label.

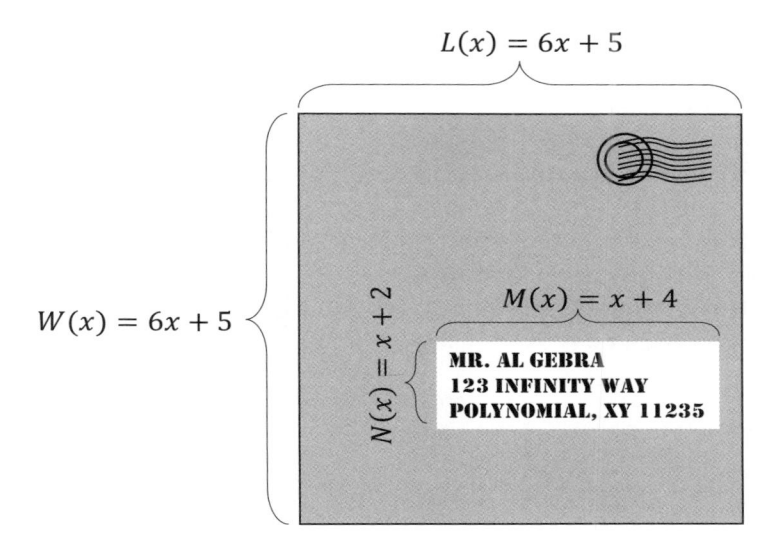

$L(x) = 6x + 5$

$W(x) = 6x + 5$

$N(x) = x + 2$

$M(x) = x + 4$

MR. AL GEBRA
123 INFINITY WAY
POLYNOMIAL, XY 11235

a. Let $A(x) = L(x) \cdot W(x) - M(x) \cdot N(x)$. Find $A(x)$.

b. What does the function $A(x)$ represent in this problem?

Section 3: Introduction to Functions

BEAT THE TEST!

1. The length of the sides of a square are s inches long. A rectangle is six inches shorter and eight inches wider than the square.

   Part A: Express both the length and the width of the rectangle as a function of a side of the square.

   Part B: Write a function to represent the area of the rectangle in terms of the sides of the square.

2. Felicia needs to find the area of a rectangular field in her backyard. The length is represented by the function $L(x) = 4x^4 - 3x^2 + 6$ and the width is represented by the function $W(x) = x + 1$. Which of the following statements is correct about the area, $A(x)$, of the rectangular field in Felicia's backyard? Select all that apply.

   ☐ $A(x) = 2[L(x) + W(x)]$
   ☐ The resulting expression for $A(x)$ is a fifth-degree polynomial.
   ☐ The resulting expression for $A(x)$ is a polynomial with a leading coefficient of 5.
   ☐ The resulting expression for $A(x)$ is a binomial with a constant of 6.
   ☐ $W(x) = \dfrac{A(x)}{L(x)}$

Section 3 – Topic 5
Closure Property

When we add two integers, what type of number is the sum?

When we multiply two irrational numbers, what type of numbers could the resulting product be?

A set is _____ for a specific operation if and only if the operation on two elements of the set **always** produces an element of the same set.

Are integers closed under addition? Justify your answer.

Are irrational numbers closed under multiplication? Justify your answer.

Let's apply the closure property to polynomials.

Are the following statements true or false? If false, give a counterexample.

Polynomials are closed under addition.

Polynomials are closed under subtraction.

Polynomials are closed under multiplication.

Let's Practice!

1. Check the boxes for the following sets that are closed under the given operations.

Set	+	−	×
$\{0, 1, 2, 3, 4, ...\}$	☐	☐	☐
$\{..., -4, -3, -2, -1\}$	☐	☐	☐
$\{..., -3, -2, -1, 0, 1, 2, 3, ...\}$	☐	☐	☐
{rational numbers}	☐	☐	☐
{polynomials}	☐	☐	☐

Try It!

2. Ms. Sanabria claims that the closure properties for polynomials are analogous to the closure properties for integers. Mr. Roberts claims that the closure properties for polynomials are analogous to the closure properties for whole numbers. Who is correct? Explain your answer.

BEAT THE TEST!

1. Choose from the following words and expressions to complete the statement below.

   $2x^5 + (3y)^{-2} - 2$ $(5y)^2 + 4x + 3y^3$

   $5y^{-1} + 7x^2 + 8y^2$

   | integers | variables | whole numbers |
   | coefficients | rational numbers | exponents |

   The product of $5x^4 - 3x^2 + 2$ and _____

   illustrates the closure property because the

   _____ of the product are _____,

   and the product is a polynomial.

Want some help? You can always ask questions on the Algebra Wall and receive help from other students, teachers, and Study Experts. You can also help others on the Algebra Wall and earn Karma Points for doing so. Go to AlgebraNation.com to learn more and get started!

Section 3 – Topic 6
Families of Functions

Let's consider three families of functions.

- Linear functions
- Quadratic functions
- Exponential functions

Linear functions have a _____ rate of change.

A real-world example of a linear function is the total cost to attend a Detroit Lions game based on the number of tickets purchased when tickets are $75 each. The rate of change is constant since each additional ticket costs the same amount.

Quadratic functions do not have a constant rate of change. We call the graph of a quadratic function a _____.

A real-world example of a quadratic function is the height of a ball dropped from the top of the Empire State Building, based on the number of seconds after it is dropped. Because gravity acts on the ball, the speed will increase as it gets closer to the ground, which means the rate of change is not constant.

Exponential functions do not have a constant rate of change. However, they increase by a common ratio.

A real-world example of an exponential function is the population of Grand Rapids, MI, which has increased by 0.4% every year since 2000.

Let's Practice!

1. Consider the linear function $f(x) = x$.

   Complete the table and sketch the graph of the function.

x	$f(x)$
-2	
-1	
0	
1	
2	

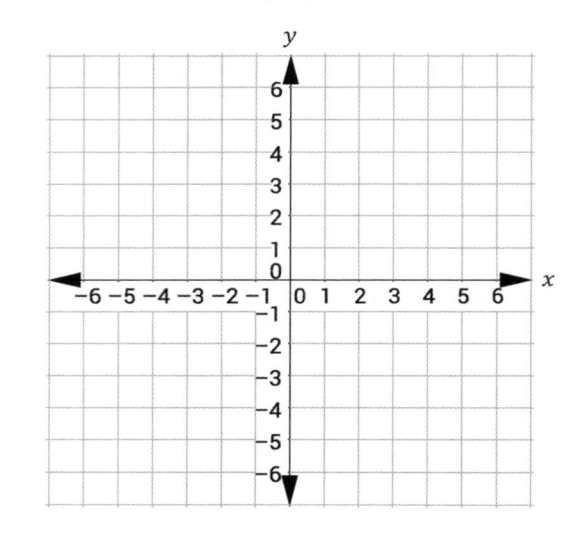

2. Consider the quadratic function $f(x) = x^2$.

   Complete the table and sketch the graph of the function.

x	$f(x)$
-2	
-1	
0	
1	
2	

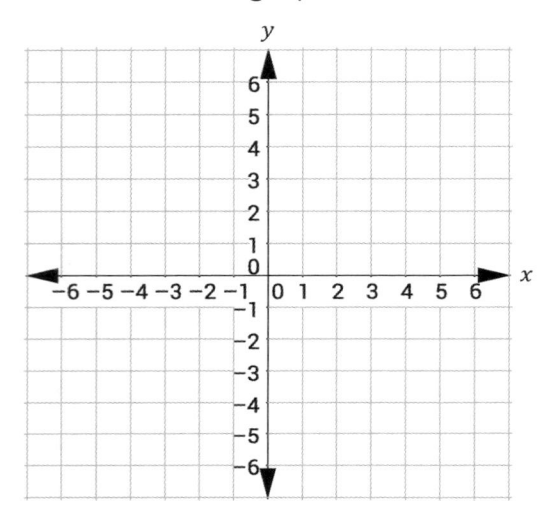

3. Consider the exponential function $f(x) = 2^x$.

   Complete the table and sketch the graph of the function.

x	$f(x)$
-2	
-1	
0	
1	
2	

Section 3: Introduction to Functions

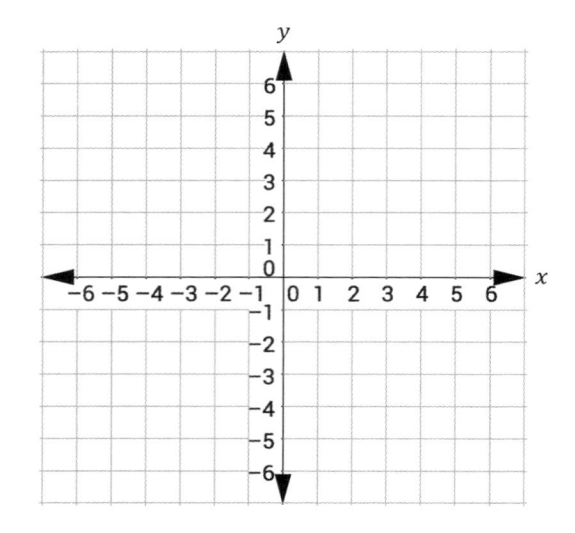

Try It!

4. Sketch the graphs of three different linear functions.

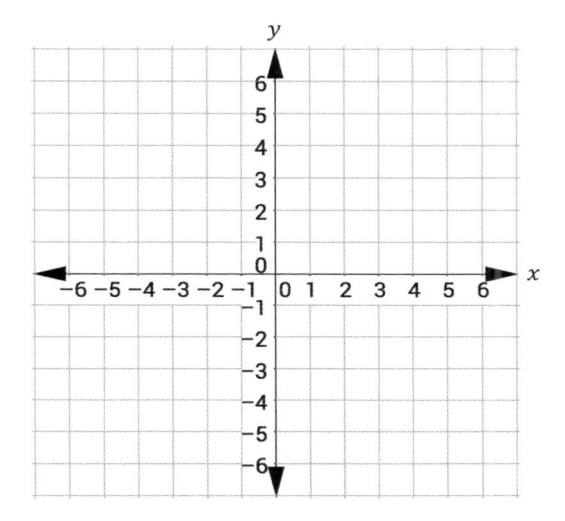

5. Sketch the graphs of three different quadratic functions.

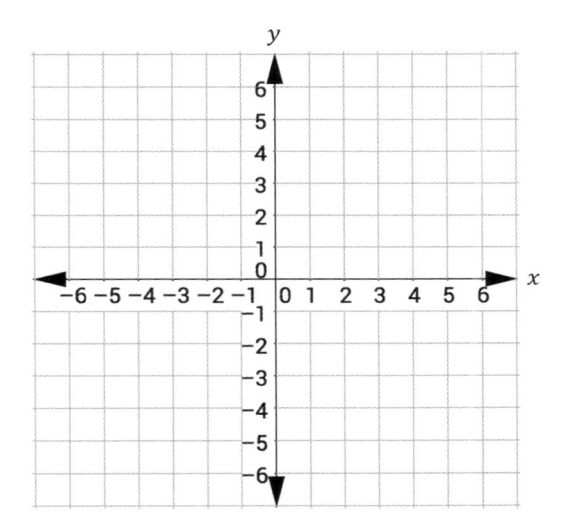

6. Sketch the graphs of three different exponential functions.

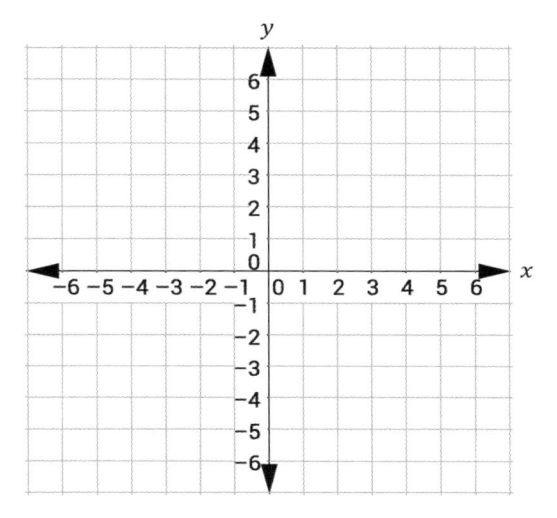

Section 3: Introduction to Functions

BEAT THE TEST!

1. Classify the following function characteristics or situations as linear, quadratic, or exponential. Select all that apply.

Distance traveled while driving 30 miles per hour	☐ Linear ☐ Quadratic ☐ Exponential
The number of people contracting a virus increasing each month by 300%	☐ Linear ☐ Quadratic ☐ Exponential
The shape of the graph of this function is a parabola.	☐ Linear ☐ Quadratic ☐ Exponential
A function that does not have a constant rate of change	☐ Linear ☐ Quadratic ☐ Exponential
The height of a stone dropped from a cliff, based on the number of seconds after it is dropped	☐ Linear ☐ Quadratic ☐ Exponential
A function that is increasing or decreasing by a common ratio	☐ Linear ☐ Quadratic ☐ Exponential

Algebra Wall — Want some help? You can always ask questions on the Algebra Wall and receive help from other students, teachers, and Study Experts. You can also help others on the Algebra Wall and earn Karma Points for doing so. Go to AlgebraNation.com to learn more and get started!

Section 3 – Topic 7
Key Features of Graphs of Functions – Part 1

Let's review the definition of a function.

Every input value (x) corresponds to _____ _____ output value (y).

Consider the following graph.

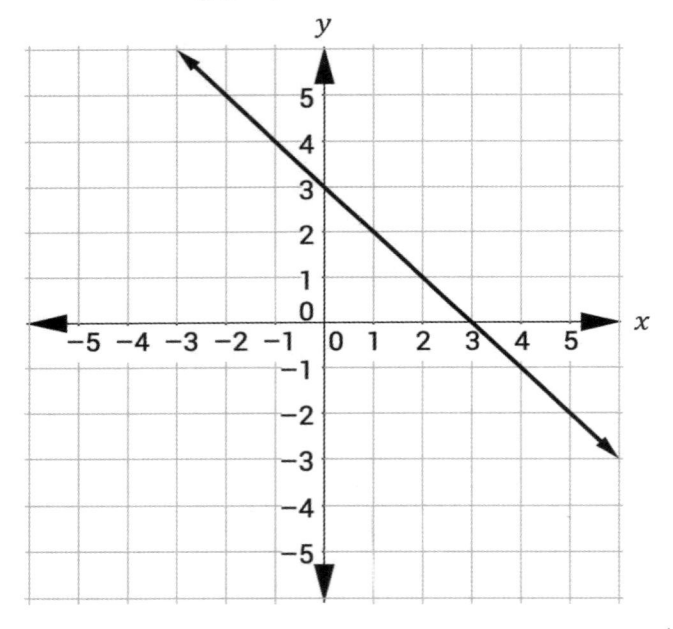

How can a vertical line help us quickly determine if a graph represents a function?

We call this the **vertical line test**. Use the vertical line test to determine if the graph above represents a function.

Important facts:

➢ Graphs of lines are not always functions. Can you describe a graph of a line that is not a function?

➢ Functions are not always linear.

Sketch a graph of a function that is not linear.

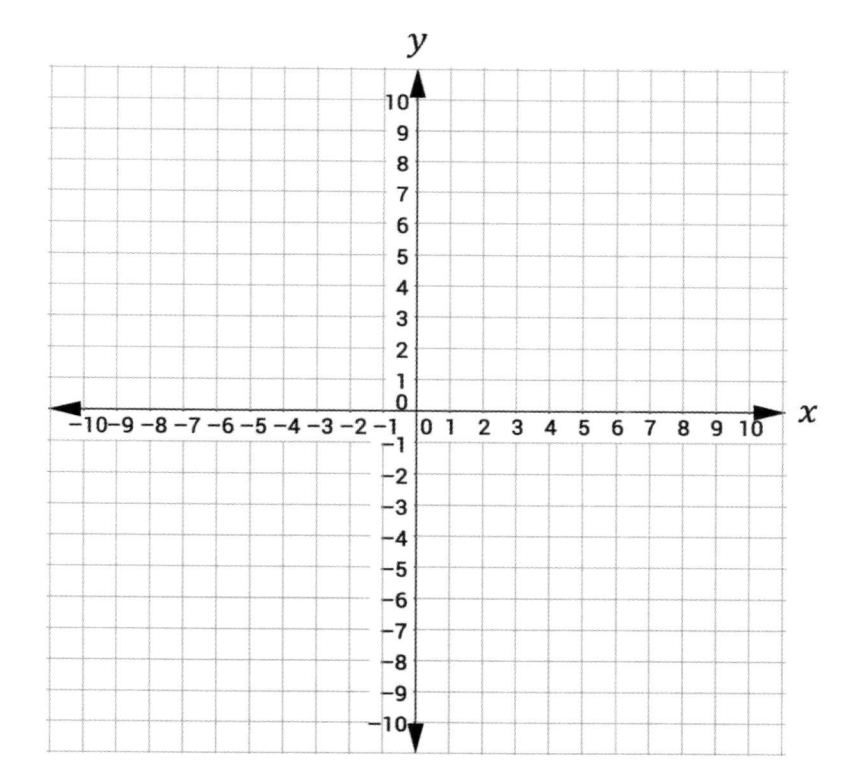

Let's Practice!

1. Use the vertical line test to determine if the following graphs are functions.

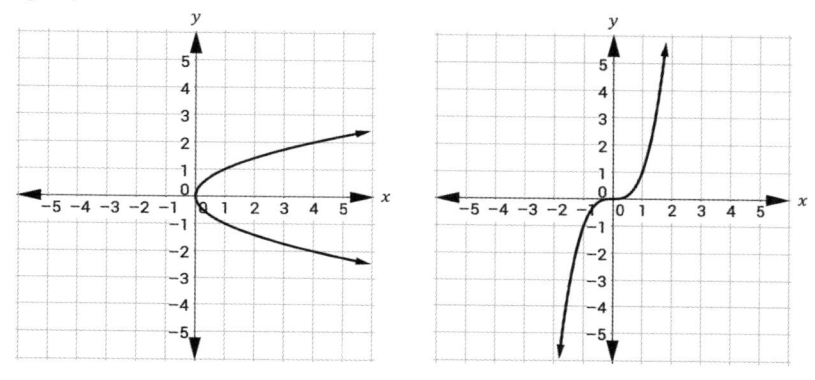

Try It!

2. Which of the following graphs represent functions? Select all that apply.

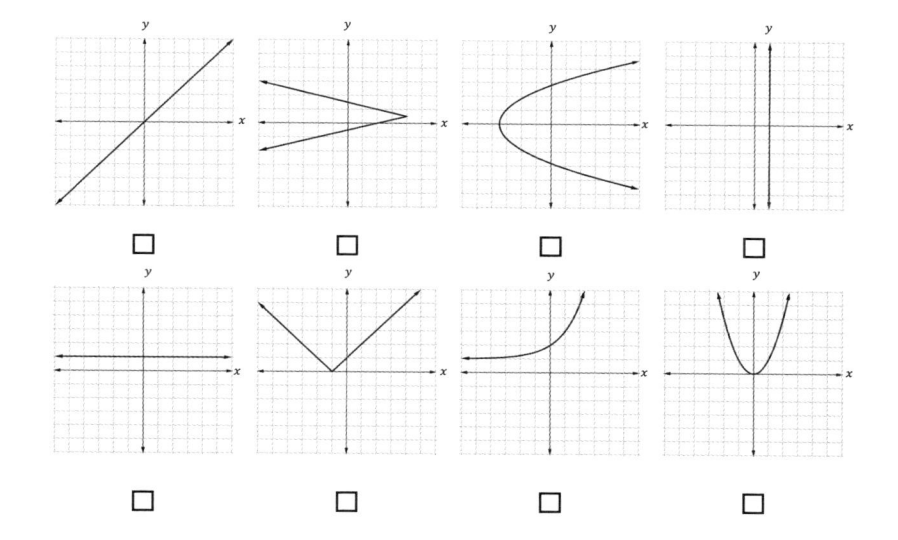

Section 3: Introduction to Functions

3. Consider the following scenarios. Determine if each one represents a function or not.

   a. An analyst takes a survey of people about their heights (in inches) and their ages. She then relates their heights to their ages (in years).

   b. A geometry student is dilating a circle and analyzes the area of the circle as it relates to the radius.

   c. A teacher has a roster of 32 students and relates the students' letter grades to the percent of points earned.

   d. A boy throws a tennis ball in the air and lets it fall to the ground. The boy relates the time passed to the height of the ball.

It's important to understand key features of graphs.

 ➢ An **x-intercept** of a graph is the location where the graph crosses the _____.

 ➢ The y-coordinate of the x-intercept is always _____.

 ➢ The **y-intercept** of a graph is the location where the graph crosses the _____.

 ➢ The x-coordinate of the y-intercept is always _____.

 ➢ The x-intercept is the _____ to $f(x) = 0$.

All of these features are very helpful in understanding real-world context.

Let's Practice!

4. Consider the following graph that represents the height, in feet, of a water balloon dropped from a 2nd story window after a given number of seconds.

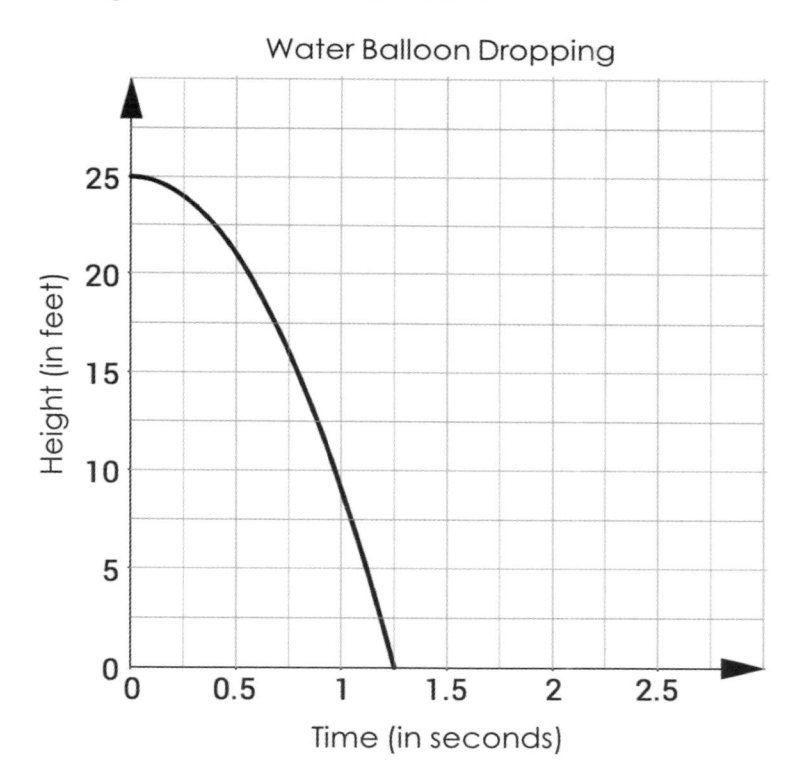

Water Balloon Dropping

[Graph showing height (in feet) on y-axis from 0 to 25, and Time (in seconds) on x-axis from 0 to 2.5. Curve starts at (0, 25) and decreases to approximately (1.25, 0).]

a. What is the x-intercept?

b. What is the y-intercept?

c. Label the intercepts on the graph.

Try It!

5. Refer to the previous problem for the following questions.

a. What does the y-intercept represent in this real-world context?

b. What does the x-intercept represent in this real-world context?

c. What is the solution to this situation?

> Want some help? You can always ask questions on the Algebra Wall and receive help from other students, teachers, and Study Experts. You can also help others on the Algebra Wall and earn Karma Points for doing so. Go to AlgebraNation.com to learn more and get started!

Section 3 – Topic 8
Key Features of Graphs of Functions – Part 2

Let's discuss other key features of graphs of functions.

➢ **Domain**: the input or the _____ values.

➢ **Range**: the _____ or the y-values.

➢ **Increasing intervals**: as the x-values _____, the y-values _____.

➢ **Decreasing intervals**: as the x-values _____, the y-values _____.

➢ **Relative maximum**: the point on a graph where the interval changes from _____ to _____.

➢ **Relative minimum**: the point on a graph where the interval changes from _____ to _____.

STUDY EDGE TIP: We read a graph from left to right to determine if it is increasing or decreasing, like reading a book.

Let's Practice!

1. Use the following graph of an *absolute value function* to answer the questions below.

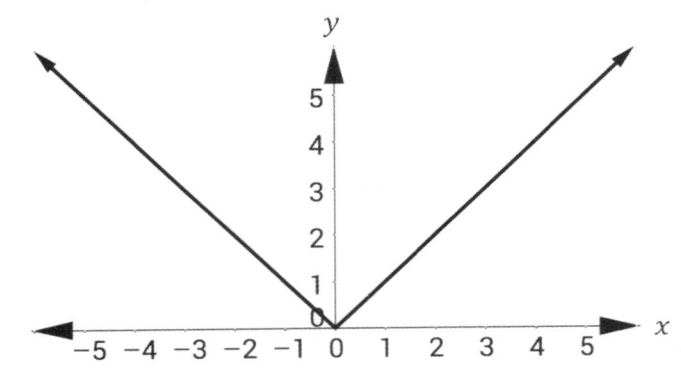

   a. Define the domain.

   b. Define the range.

   c. Where is the graph increasing?

   d. Where is the graph decreasing?

   e. Identify any relative maximums.

   f. Identify any relative minimums.

Section 3: Introduction to Functions

Try It!

2. Use the graph of the following **quadratic function** to answer the questions below.

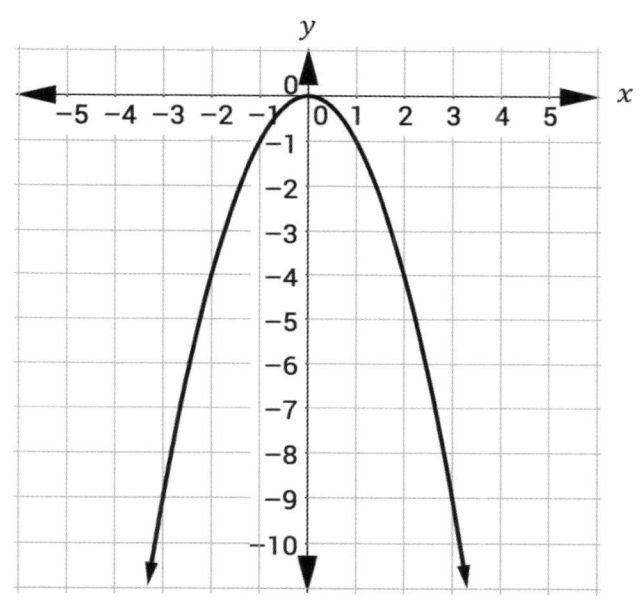

   a. Define the domain.

   b. Define the range.

   c. Where is the graph increasing?

   d. Where is the graph decreasing?

   e. Identify any relative maximums.

   f. Identify any relative minimums.

3. Describe everything you know about the key features of the following graph of an **exponential function**.

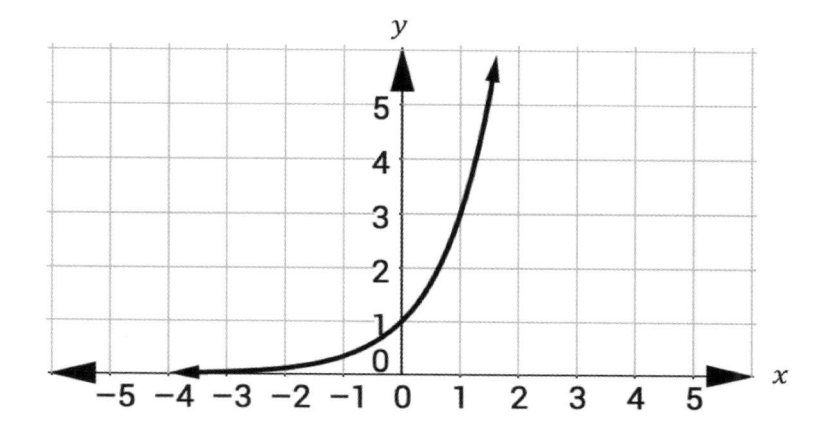

Section 3: Introduction to Functions

BEAT THE TEST!

1. The following graph is a *piecewise function*.

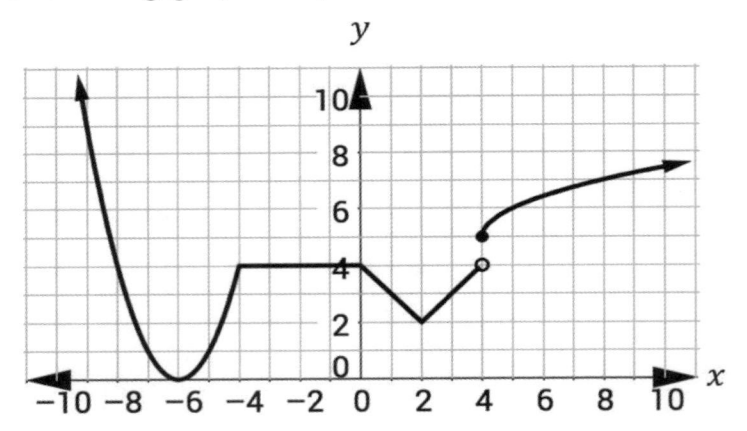

   [Graph showing piecewise function on coordinate plane]

   Which of the following statements are true about the graph? Select all that apply.

   ☐ The graph is increasing when the domain is $-6 < x < -4$.
   ☐ The graph has exactly one relative minimum.
   ☐ The graph is increasing when $-4 \leq x \leq 0$.
   ☐ The graph is increasing when $x > 4$.
   ☐ The graph is decreasing when the domain is $\{x | x < -6 \cup x > 2\}$.
   ☐ The range is $\{y | 0 \leq y < 4 \cup y \geq 5\}$.
   ☐ There is a relative minimum at $(2, 2)$.

   Want some help? You can always ask questions on the Algebra Wall and receive help from other students, teachers, and Study Experts. You can also help others on the Algebra Wall and earn Karma Points for doing so. Go to AlgebraNation.com to learn more and get started!

Section 3 – Topic 9
Inverse Functions

Remember that in a function, every input value corresponds to exactly one output value.

Consider the table below that represents the conversion of temperatures in degrees Fahrenheit to degrees Celsius.

Degrees Fahrenheit (Input)	−49	−22	14	122	167	212
Degrees Celsius (Output)	−45	−30	−10	50	75	100

This table defines a function since every input value corresponds to exactly one output value.

Notice that every output value corresponds to exactly one input value.

This is a special kind of function called a _____ function.

Are the following functions one-to-one?

$f = \{(-1, 6), (0, 5), (3, 2), (7, 10)\}$

$g = \{(-5, 4), (2, 6), (3, 5), (10, 4)\}$

We can use the vertical line test to determine if a graph represents a function. What type of line test could we use to determine if the function is one-to-one?

Are the following functions one-to-one?

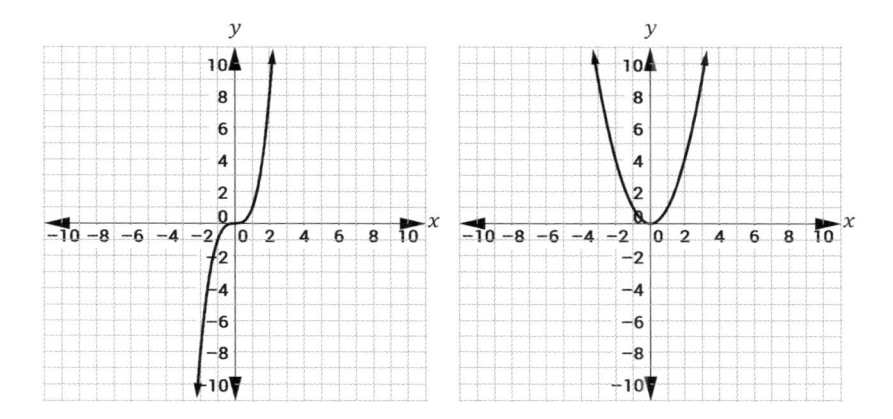

For every one-to-one function, we can find its **inverse function**. The output of the original function becomes the input of the inverse function.

The symbol f^{-1} is used to denote the inverse of the function _____.

We can find the inverse of a one-to-one function by switching the coordinates of the ordered pairs of the function.

Find the inverse of the following one-to-one function.

$f = \{(-1, 3), (0, 4), (2, -6), (3, 6), (7, -8)\}$

When given a function $f(x)$, we can find the inverse, $f^{-1}(x)$, by interchanging x and y and solving for y.

Let's Practice!

1. Find the inverse of $f(x) = 5x + 2$.

Try It!

2. Determine whether each function is a one-to-one function. If it is one-to-one, write the inverse function.

   a. $h = \{(11, 13), (4, 3), (3, 4), (8, 8)\}$

   b. $s = \{(2, 5), (3, -1), (7, 5), (6, 2)\}$

3. Find the inverse of the following functions.

   a. $f(x) = \frac{x-4}{7}$

   b. $g(x) = \sqrt[3]{x+1}$

Section 3: Introduction to Functions

BEAT THE TEST!

1. The graph of $f(x)$ is shown below.

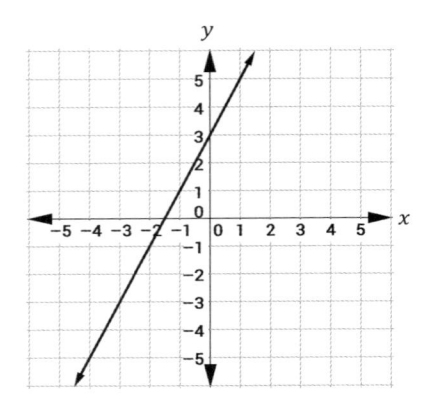

   Which of the following could represent $f^{-1}(x)$?

   Ⓐ $2x + 3$
   Ⓑ $-2x + 3$
   Ⓒ $\frac{1}{2}x - \frac{3}{2}$
   Ⓓ $\frac{1}{2}x - 3$

2. The function $h = \{(2,4), (3,5), (4,6), (5,2), (6,2)\}$. The inverse of h would be a function if the domain of h is restricted to

   Ⓐ $\{4, 5, 6\}$
   Ⓑ $\{2, 3, 4, 5\}$
   Ⓒ $\{2, 5, 6\}$
   Ⓓ $\{2, 3, 5, 6\}$

Section 3 – Topic 10
Transformations of Functions

The graph of $f(x)$ is shown below.

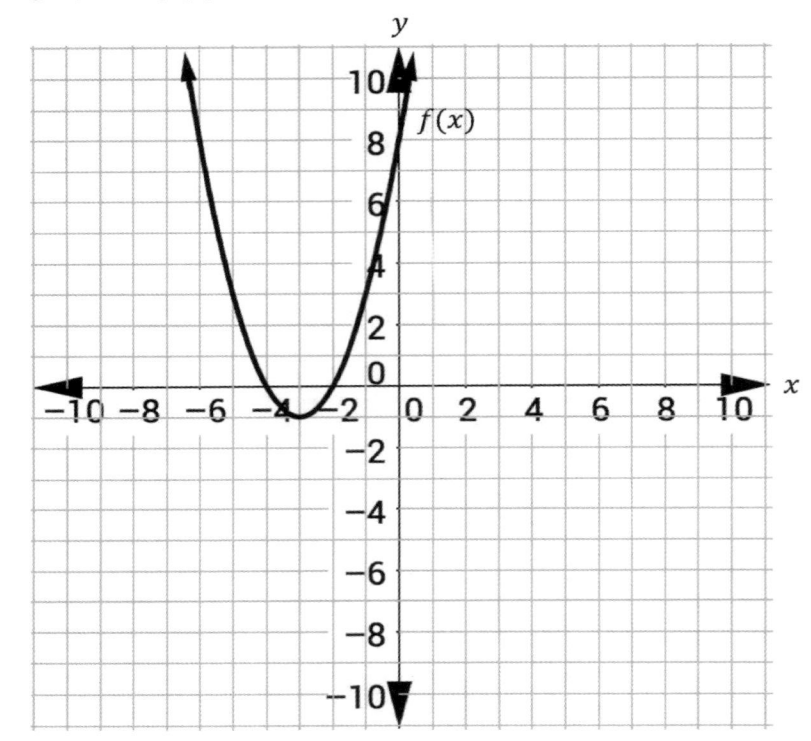

The following graphs are transformations of $f(x)$. Describe what happened in each graph.

$f(x) + 2$

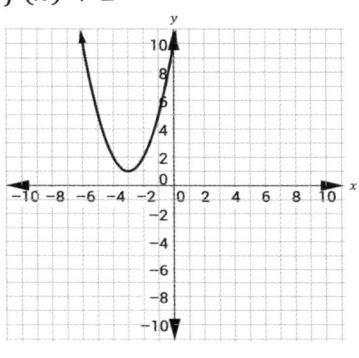

$f(x) - 1$

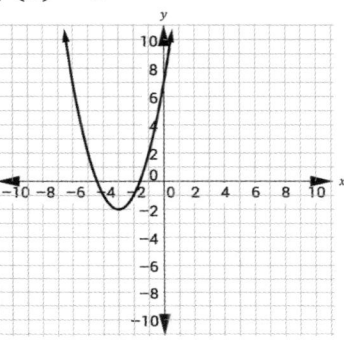

$f(x + 2)$

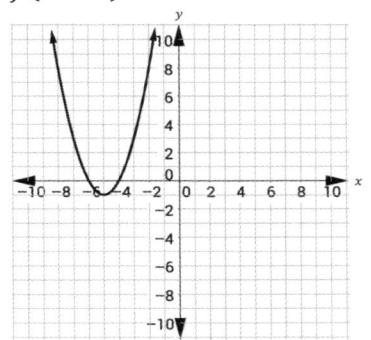

$f(x - 1)$

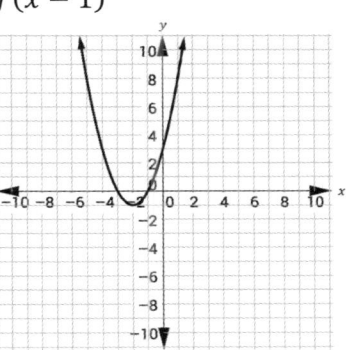

Which graphs transformed the independent variable?

Which graphs transformed the dependent variable?

Let's Practice!

1. For the following functions, state whether the independent or dependent variable is being transformed and describe the transformation (assume $k > 0$).

   a. $f(x) + k$

   b. $f(x) - k$

   c. $f(x + k)$

   d. $f(x - k)$

Section 3: Introduction to Functions

2. The following table represents the function $g(x)$.

x	$g(x)$
−2	0.25
−1	0.5
0	1
1	2
2	4

The function $h(x) = g(2x)$. Complete the table for $h(x)$.

x	$g(2x)$	$h(x)$
−1	$g(2(-1))$	
−0.5	$g(2(-0.5))$	
0		
0.5		
1		

Try It!

3. The table below shows the values for the function $f(x)$.

x	−2	−1	0	1	2
$f(x)$	4	2	0	2	4

Complete the table for the function $-\frac{1}{2}f(x)$.

x	$-\frac{1}{2}f(x)$
−2	
−1	
0	
1	
2	

Section 3: Introduction to Functions

4. The graph of $f(x)$ is shown below.

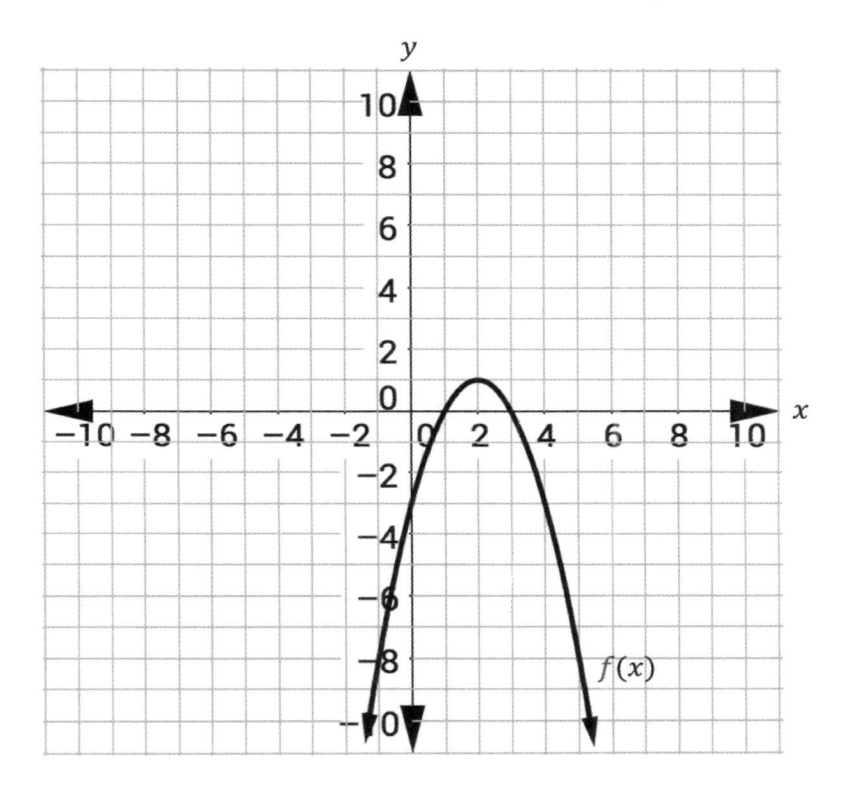

Let $g(x) = f(x+3) - 2$.

Graph $g(x)$ on the coordinate plane with $f(x)$.

BEAT THE TEST!

1. The graph of $f(x)$ is shown below.

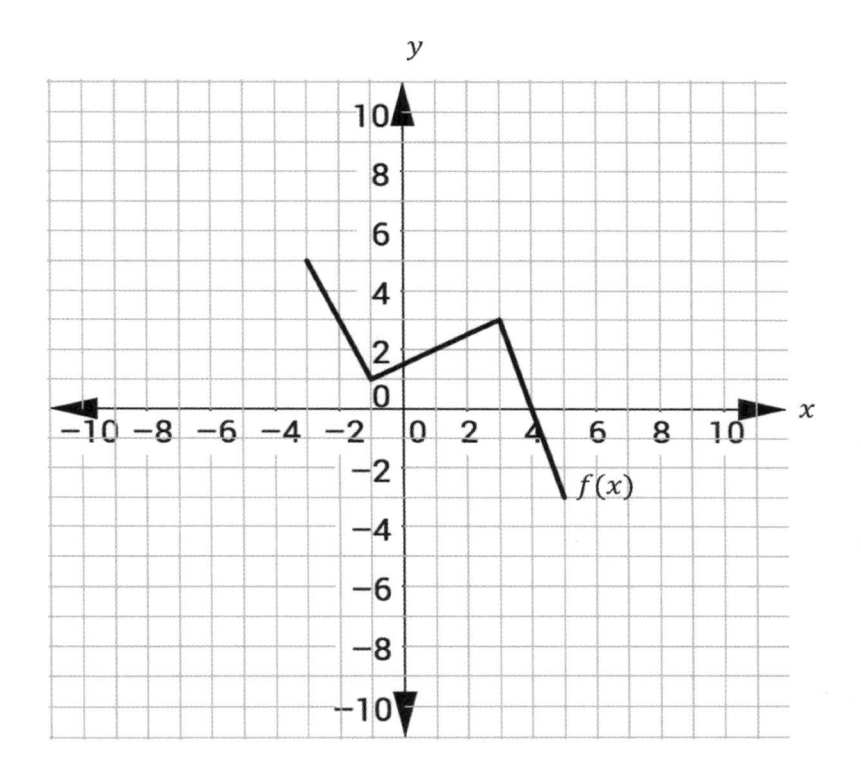

Let $g(x) = f(x-3)$ and $h(x) = f(x) - 3$.

Graph $g(x)$ and $h(x)$ on the coordinate plane with $f(x)$.

Section 3: Introduction to Functions

2. The table below shows the values for the function $p(x)$.

x	−4	−1	0	2	3
$p(x)$	12	6	4	8	10

Complete the table for the function $\frac{1}{2}p(x) - 3$.

x	$\frac{1}{2}p(x) - 3$
−4	3
−1	0
0	−1
2	1
3	2

> Great job! You have reached the end of this section. Now it's time to try the "Test Yourself! Practice Tool," where you can practice all the skills and concepts you learned in this section. Log in to Algebra Nation and try out the "Test Yourself! Practice Tool" so you can see how well you know these topics!

Section 4: Linear Equations, Functions, and Inequalities

Topic 1: Arithmetic Sequences 93
Standards Covered: F-IF.3, F-BF.1, F-BF.2, F-BF.1.a
☐ I can write recursive and explicit formulas when given a table of values.
☐ I understand the connection between arithmetic sequences and linear functions.

Topic 2: Rate of Change of Linear Functions 96
Standards Covered: F-LE.5, S-ID.7
☐ I can graph a linear function in real-world context and interpret the rate of change.

Topic 3: Interpreting Rate of Change and y-Intercept in a Real-World Context - Part 1 100
Standards Covered: F-LE.5, S-ID.7, A-CED.2
☐ I can interpret the slope and y-intercept of a linear function.
☐ I can write and graph a linear function that models a real-world context.

Topic 4: Interpreting Rate of Change and y-Intercept in a Real-World Context - Part 2 103
Standards Covered: F-IF.6, F-LE.5, S-ID.7, A-CED.2, A-CED.3, A-REI.10
☐ I can interpret the slope and y-intercept of a linear function.

Topic 5: Introduction to Systems of Equations 105
Standards Covered: A-REI.6, A-REI.11
☐ I can find a solution to a system of linear equations by graphing.

Topic 6: Finding Solution Sets to Systems of Equations Using Substitution and Graphing 109
Standards Covered: A-REI.6, A-REI.11, A-REI.10, A-CED.3
☐ I can solve systems of linear equations that represent real-world situations.

Topic 7: Using Equivalent Systems of Equations 112
Standards Covered: A-REI.5, A-REI.6
☐ I can find an equivalent system when given a system of linear equations.

Topic 8: Finding Solution Sets to Systems of Equations Using Elimination 116
Standards Covered: A-REI.6
☐ I can use elimination to find a solution to a system of linear equations.

Topic 9: Solution Sets to Inequalities with Two Variables 118
Standards Covered: A-REI.12, A-CED.3, N-Q.1
☐ I can create inequalities from real-world situations and then graph these inequalities on a coordinate plane.

Topic 10: Finding Solution Sets to Systems of Linear Inequalities 122
Standards Covered: A-CED.3, A-REI.12, F-LE.5
☐ I can write a system of linear inequalities, graph the system, and find various solution sets.

Visit MathNation.com or search "Math Nation" in your phone or tablet's app store to watch the videos that go along with this workbook!

Arithmetic Sequences

Let's look at the following sequence of numbers:
3, 8, 13, 18, 23, ...

- The "..." at the end means this <u>sequence</u> goes on forever.

- 3, 8, 13, 18, and 23 are the actual <u>terms</u> of this sequence.

- There are 5 terms in this sequence so far:
    - 3 is the 1st term.
    - 8 is the 2nd term.
    - 13 is the <u>3rd</u> term.
    - 18 is the <u>4th</u> term.

The following Michigan Mathematics Standards will be covered in this section:
F-IF.3 - Recognize that sequences are functions, sometimes defined recursively, whose domain is a subset of the integers. For example, the Fibonacci sequence is defined recursively by $f(0) = f(1) = 1$, $f(n+1) = f(n) + f(n-1)$ for $n \geq 1$.
F-BF.1 - Write a function that describes a relationship between two quantities.
F-BF.2 - Write arithmetic and geometric sequences both recursively and with an explicit formula, use them to model situations, and translate between the two forms.
F-BF.1.a - Write a function that describes a relationship between two quantities.   a. Determine an explicit expression, a recursive process, or steps for calculation from a context.
F-LE.5 - Interpret the parameters in a linear or exponential function in terms of a context.
S-ID.7 - Interpret the slope (rate of change) and the intercept (constant term) of a linear model in the context of the data
A-CED.2 - Create equations in two or more variables to represent relationships between quantities; graph equations on coordinate axes with labels and scales.
F-IF.6 - Calculate and interpret the average rate of change of a function (presented symbolically or as a table) over a specified interval. Estimate the rate of change from a graph.
A-CED.3 - Represent constraints by equations or inequalities and by systems of equations and/or inequalities, and interpret solutions as viable or nonviable options in a modeling context.
A-REI.10 - Understand that the graph of an equation in two variables is the set of all its solutions plotted in the coordinate plane, often forming a curve (which could be a line).
A-REI.6 - Solve systems of linear equations exactly and approximately (e.g., with graphs), focusing on pairs of linear equations in two variables.
A-REI.11 - Explain why the x-coordinates of the points where the graphs of the equations and intersect are the solutions of the equation; find the solutions approximately (e.g., using technology to graph the functions, make tables of values, or find successive approximations). Include cases were and/or are linear, polynomial, rational, absolute value, exponential, and logarithmic functions.
A-REI.5 - Prove that, given a system of two equations in two variables, replacing one equation by the sum of that equation and a multiple of the other produces a system with the same solutions.
A-REI.12 - Graph the solutions to a linear inequality in two variables as a half-plane (excluding the boundary in the case of a strict inequality), and graph the solution set to a system of linear inequalities in two variables as the intersection of the corresponding half-plane.
N-Q.1 - Use units as a way to understand problems and to guide the solution of multi-step problems; choose and interpret units consistently in formulas; choose and interpret the scale and the origin in graphs and data displays.

Section 4: Linear Equations, Functions, and Inequalities
Section 4 – Topic 1
Arithmetic Sequences

Let's look at the following sequence of numbers:
$3, 8, 13, 18, 23, \ldots$.

➢ The "..." at the end means that this _____ goes on forever.

➢ $3, 8, 13, 18,$ and 23 are the actual _____ of this sequence.

➢ There are 5 terms in this sequence so far:

- 3 is the 1st term.
- 8 is the 2nd term.
- 13 is the _____ term.
- 18 is the _____ term.
- 23 is the _____ term.

This is an example of an **arithmetic sequence**.

➢ This is a sequence where each term is the _____ of the previous term and a common difference, d.

We can represent this sequence in a table:

Term Number	Sequence Term	Term	Function Notation	
1	a_1	3	$f(1)$	a formula to find the 1st term
2	a_2	8		a formula to find the 2nd term
3	a_3	13	$f(3)$	a formula to find the ____ term
4	a_4		$f(4)$	a formula to find the ____ term
5	a_5			a formula to find the ____ term
...	...	...	...	...
n	a_n		$f(n)$	a formula to find the ____ term

How can we find the 9th term of this sequence?

One way is to start by finding the previous term:

Term Number	Sequence Term	Term	Function Notation	
1	a_1	3	$f(1)$	3
2	a_2	8 = 3 + ___	$f(2)$	3 + 5
3	a_3	13 = 8 + ___	$f(3)$	8 + 5
4	a_4	18 = 13 + ___	$f(4)$	13 + 5
5	a_5	23 = ___ + 5	$f(5)$	18 + 5
6	a_6		$f(6)$	23 + 5
7	a_7		$f(7)$	28 + 5
8	a_8		$f(8)$	33 + 5
9	a_9		$f(9)$	38 + 5

Write a general equation that we could use to find *any* term in the sequence.

This is a **recursive formula**.

> In order to solve for a term, you must know the value of its preceding term.

Can you think of a situation where the recursive formula would take a long time to use?

Let's look at another way to find unknown terms:

Term Number	Sequence Term	Term	Function Notation	
1	a_1	3	$f(1)$	3
2	a_2	8 = 3 + 5	$f(2)$	3 + 5(1)
3	a_3	13 = 8 + 5 = 3 + 5 + 5	$f(3)$	a_1 + 5(2)
4	a_4	18 = 13 + 5 = 3 + 5 + 5 + 5	$f(4)$	a_1 + 5(3)
5	a_5	23 = 18 + 5 = 3 + 5 + 5 + 5 + 5	$f(5)$	a_1 + 5(4)
6	a_6	28 = 23 + 5 = 3 + 5 + 5 + 5 + 5 + 5	$f(6)$	a_1 + 5(5)
7	a_7	33 = 28 + 5 = 3 + 5 + 5 + 5 + 5 + 5 + 5	$f(7)$	a_1 + 5(6)
8	a_8	38 = 33 + 5 = 3 + 5 + 5 + 5 + 5 + 5 + 5 + 5	$f(8)$	
9	a_9	43 = 38 + 5 = 3 + 5 + 5 + 5 + 5 + 5 + 5 + 5 + 5	$f(9)$	

Write a general equation that we could use to find *any* term in the sequence.

This is an **explicit formula**.

> To solve for a term, you need to know the first term of the sequence and the difference by which the sequence is increasing or decreasing.

Section 4: Linear Equations, Functions, and Inequalities

Let's Practice!

1. Consider the sequence 10, 4, −2, −8, ...

    a. Write a recursive formula for the sequence.

    b. Write an explicit formula for the sequence.

    c. Find the 42nd term of the sequence.

Try It!

2. Consider the sequence 7, 17, 27, 37, ...

    a. Find the next three terms of the sequence.

    b. Write a recursive formula for the sequence.

    c. Write an explicit formula for the sequence.

    d. Find the 33rd term of the sequence.

BEAT THE TEST!

1. Yohanna is conditioning all summer to prepare for her high school's varsity soccer team tryouts. She is incorporating walking planks into her daily training plan. Every day, she will complete four more walking planks than the day before.

    Part A: Yohanna starts with five walking planks on the first day. Write an explicit formula that can be used to find the number of walking planks she completes on any given day.

    Part B: How many walking planks will Yohanna do on the 12th day?

    Ⓐ 49
    Ⓑ 53
    Ⓒ 59
    Ⓓ 64

Section 4: Linear Equations, Functions, and Inequalities

2. The following figures were created with squares, where each side of the squares has a length of exactly one unit. A_1 represents the area of the first figure, A_2 represents the area of the second figure, and so on. Based on this pattern, what would be the rule for the area of the nth figure when $n > 1$?

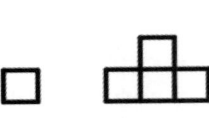

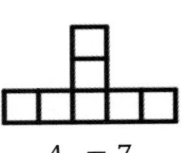

$A_1 = 1$ $A_2 = 4$ $A_3 = 7$
$n = 1$ $n = 2$ $n = 3$

- Ⓐ $A_n = 2A_{n-1} - 2$
- Ⓑ $A_n = 2A_{n-1} + 4$
- Ⓒ $A_n = A_{n-1} + 3$
- Ⓓ $A_n = A_{n-1} + 2$

Section 4 – Topic 2
Rate of Change of Linear Functions

Génesis reads 16 pages of *The Fault in Our Stars* every day.

Zully reads 8 pages every day of the same book.

Represent both situations on the graphs below using the same scales on the axes for both graphs.

Graph 1: Génesis's Reading Speed

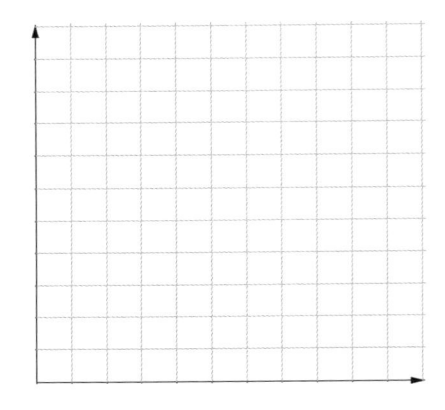

Graph 2: Zully's Reading Speed

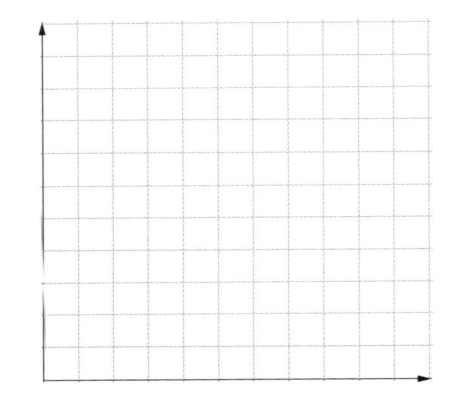

Aaron loves Cherry Coke. Each mini-can contains 100 calories.

Jacobe likes to munch on carrot snack packs. Each snack pack contains 40 calories.

Represent both situations on the graphs below using the same scales for both graphs.

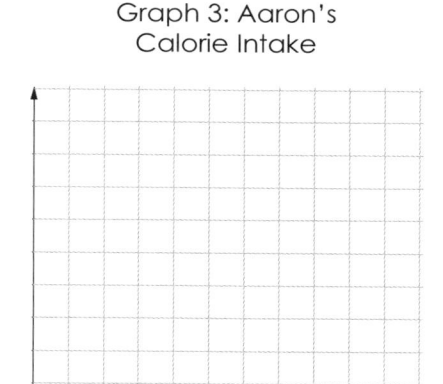

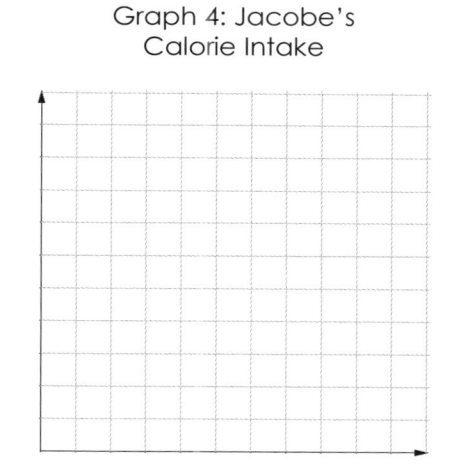

Graph 3: Aaron's Calorie Intake

Graph 4: Jacobe's Calorie Intake

In each of the graphs, we were finding the **rate of change** in the given situation.

What is the rate of change for each of the graphs?

Graph 1: _____ per _____

Graph 2: _____ per _____

Graph 3: _____ per _____

Graph 4: _____ per _____

This is also called the _____ of the line.

We can also find slope by looking at the $\frac{change\ in\ y}{change\ in\ x}$ or $\frac{rise}{run}$.

What is the slope of the following graph? What does the slope represent?

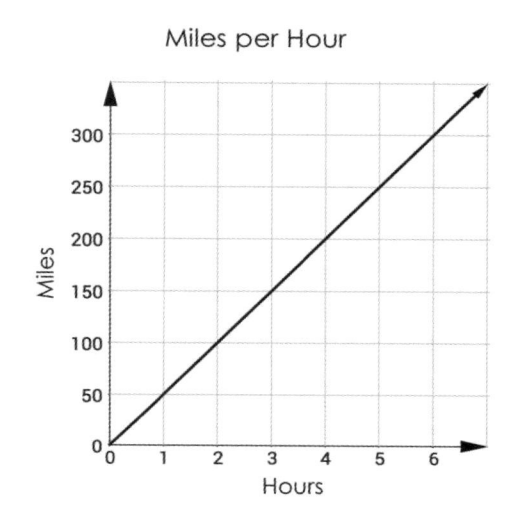

Miles per Hour

Section 4: Linear Equations, Functions, and Inequalities

Let's Practice!

1. Consider the following graph.

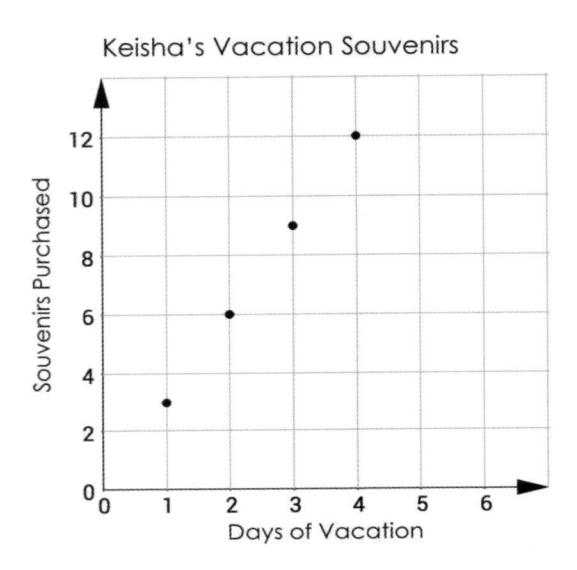

   Keisha's Vacation Souvenirs (scatterplot: Souvenirs Purchased vs. Days of Vacation)

   a. What is the rate of change of the graph?

   b. What does the rate of change represent?

2. Freedom High School collected data on the GPA of various students and the number of hours they spend studying each week. A scatterplot of the data is shown below with the line of best fit.

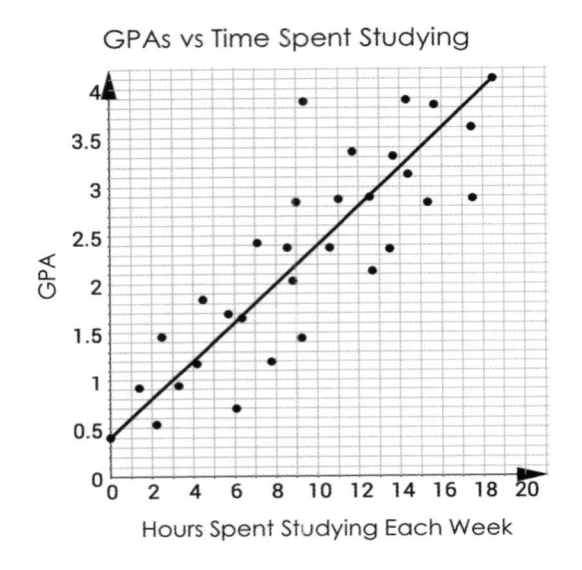

   GPAs vs Time Spent Studying (scatterplot: GPA vs. Hours Spent Studying Each Week)

   a. What is the slope of the line of best fit?

   b. What does the slope represent?

Section 4: Linear Equations, Functions, and Inequalities

Try It!

3. Sarah's parents give her a $100.00 allowance at the beginning of each month. Sarah spends her allowance on comic books. The graph below represents the amount of money Sarah spent on comic books last month.

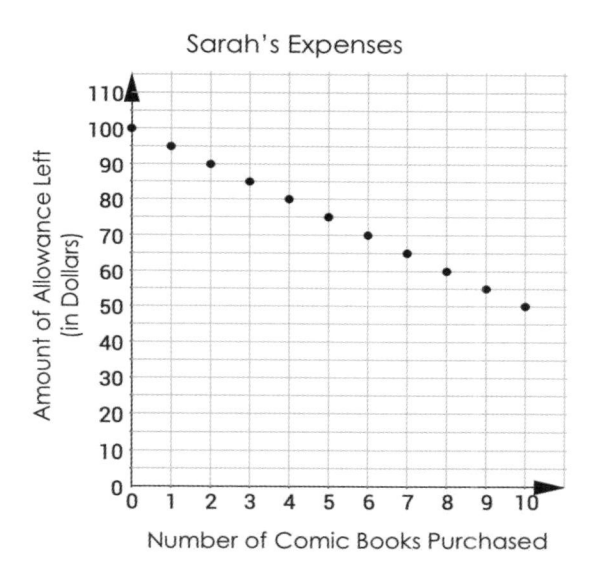

Sarah's Expenses

[Graph: Amount of Allowance Left (in Dollars) vs Number of Comic Books Purchased]

a. What is the rate of change?

b. What does the rate of change represent?

BEAT THE TEST!

1. A cleaning service cleans many apartments each day. The following table shows the number of hours the cleaners spend cleaning and the number of apartments they clean during that time.

Apartment Cleaning

Time (Hours)	1	2	3	4
Apartments Cleaned	2	4	6	8

Part A: Represent the situation on the graph below.

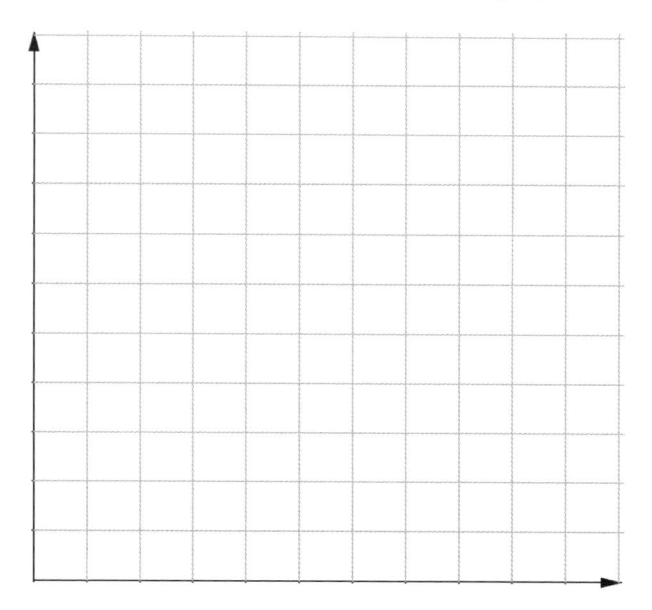

Section 4: Linear Equations, Functions, and Inequalities

Part B: The data suggest a linear relationship between the number of hours spent cleaning and the number of apartments cleaned. Assuming the relationship is linear, what does the rate of change represent in the context of this relationship?

  Ⓐ The number of apartments cleaned after one hour.
  Ⓑ The number of hours it took to clean one apartment.
  Ⓒ The number of apartments cleaned each hour.
  Ⓓ The number of apartments cleaned before the company started cleaning.

Part C: Which equation describes the relationship between the time elapsed and the number of apartments cleaned?

  Ⓐ $y = x$
  Ⓑ $y = x + 2$
  Ⓒ $y = 2x$
  Ⓓ $y = 2x + 2$

Want some help? You can always ask questions on the Algebra Wall and receive help from other students, teachers, and Study Experts. You can also help others on the Algebra Wall and earn Karma Points for doing so. Go to AlgebraNation.com to learn more and get started!

Section 4 – Topic 3
Interpreting Rate of Change and y-Intercept in a Real-World Context – Part 1

The T-Mobile ONE family plan includes four lines and unlimited data, calls, and texts for $160.00 per month, including taxes and fees. There is an activation fee of $80.00.

Define the variable and write a function that represents this situation.

Represent the situation on a graph.

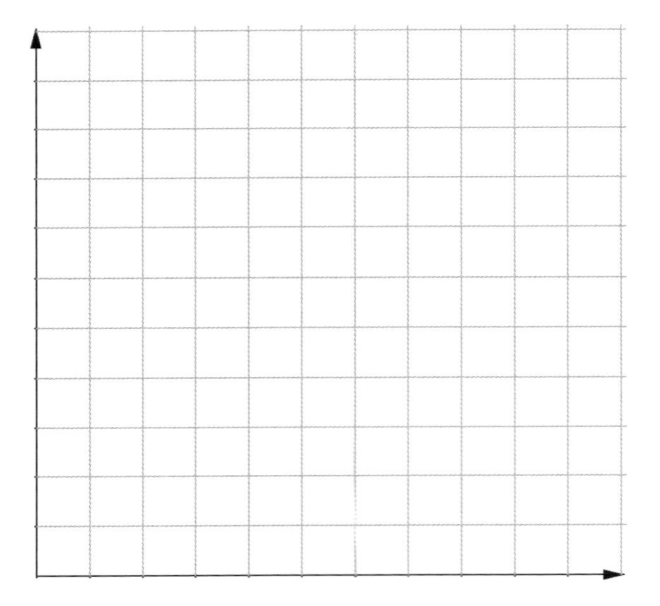

What is the slope of the line? What does the slope represent?

At what point does the line intersect the y-axis? What does this point represent?

The y-value of the point where the graph intersects the y-axis is the y-intercept.

Let's Practice!

1. You saved $250.00 to spend over the summer. You decide to budget $25.00 to spend each week.

   a. Define the variable and write a function that represents this situation.

   b. Represent the situation on a graph.

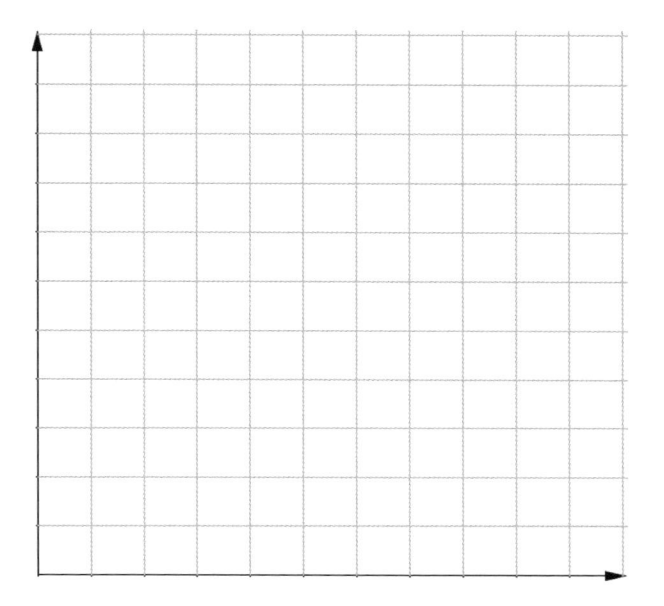

   c. What is the slope of the line? What does the slope represent?

   d. What is different about the slope of this line compared to our earlier problem? Why is it different?

   e. What is the y-intercept? What does this point represent?

Section 4: Linear Equations, Functions, and Inequalities

Try It!

2. Consider the following graph.

Cost of Visits to the Community Pool

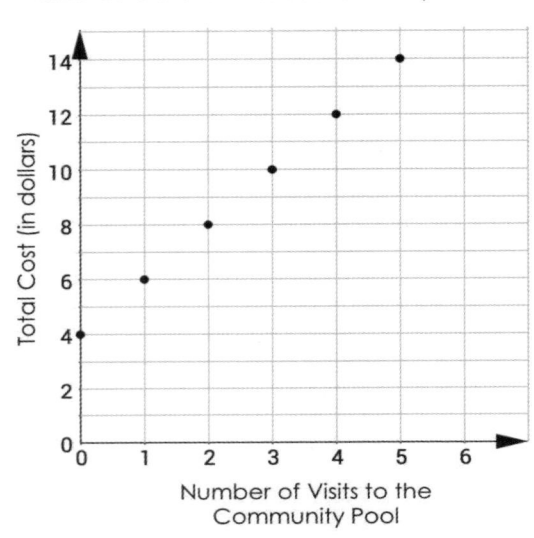

(Graph: Total Cost in dollars vs. Number of Visits to the Community Pool, with points at approximately (0,4), (1,6), (2,8), (3,10), (4,12), (5,14))

a. What is the slope of the line? What does the slope represent?

b. What is the y-intercept? What does the y-intercept represent?

c. Define the variables and write a function that represents this situation.

d. What does each point represent?

Consider the three functions that you wrote regarding the cell phone plan, summer spending habits, and the community pool membership. What do you notice about the constant term and the coefficient of the x term?

➢ The constant term is the _____.

➢ The coefficient of the x is the _____ or _____.

These functions are written in **slope-intercept** form.

We can use slope-intercept form to graph any linear equation.

> **STUDY EDGE TIP**
> The coefficient of x is the slope and the constant term is the y-intercept ONLY if the equation is in slope-intercept form, $y = mx + b$.

Algebra Wall
Want some help? You can always ask questions on the Algebra Wall and receive help from other students, teachers, and Study Experts. You can also help others on the Algebra Wall and earn Karma Points for doing so. Go to AlgebraNation.com to learn more and get started!

Section 4: Linear Equations, Functions, and Inequalities

Section 4 – Topic 4
Interpreting Rate of Change and y-Intercept in a Real-World Context – Part 2

Let's Practice!

1. Graph $y = 2x + 3$.

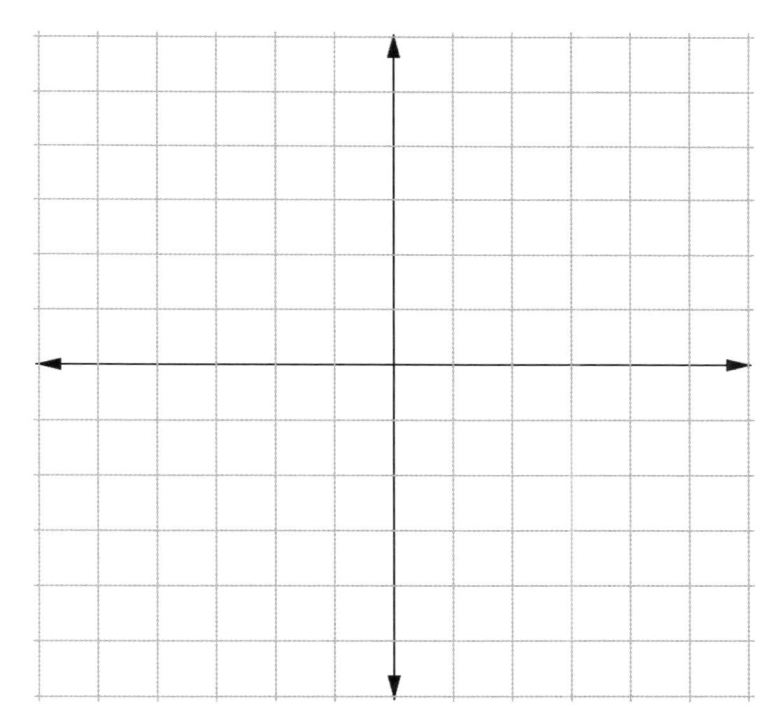

2. Consider the equation $2x + 5y = 10$.

   a. How does this equation look different from slope-intercept form of an equation?

   b. Rewrite the equation in slope-intercept form.

   c. Identify the slope and y-intercept.

   d. Graph the equation.

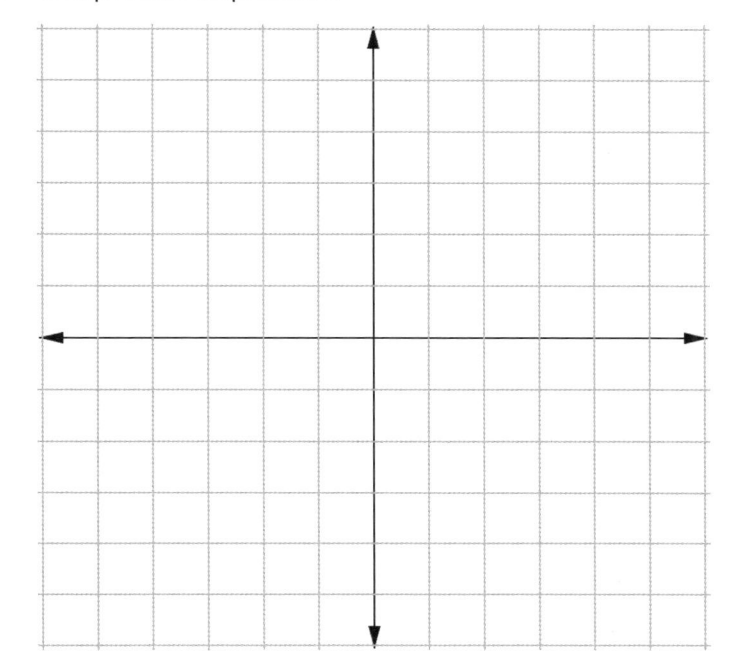

Section 4: Linear Equations, Functions, and Inequalities

Try It!

3. Graph the equation $-4x - 5y = -10$.

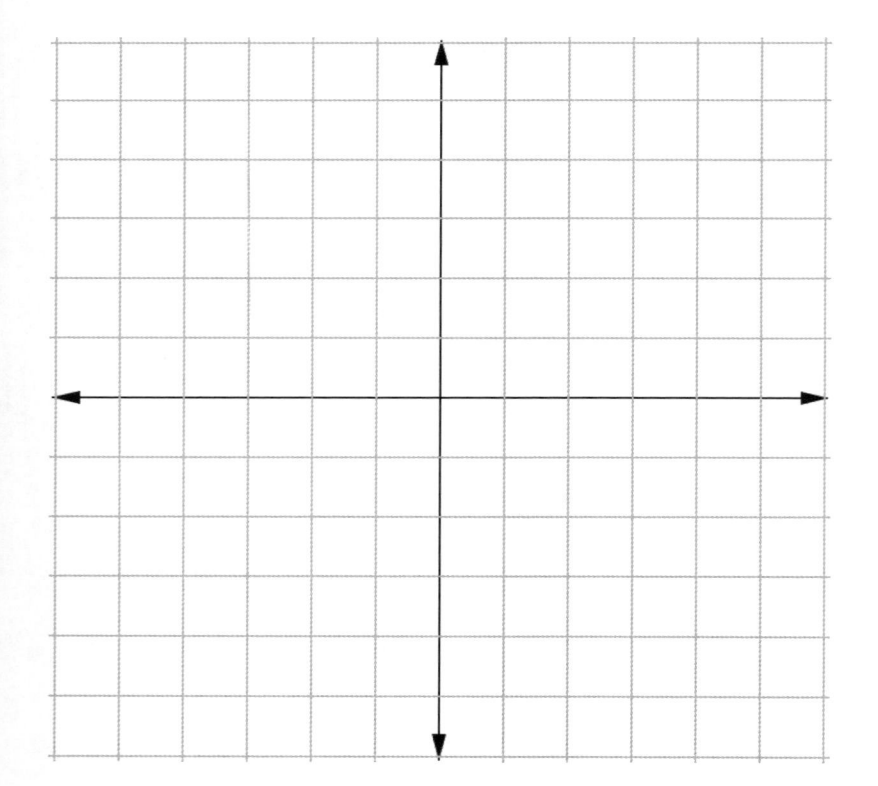

BEAT THE TEST!

1. Line t, $\triangle ECA$, and $\triangle FDB$ are shown on the coordinate grid below.

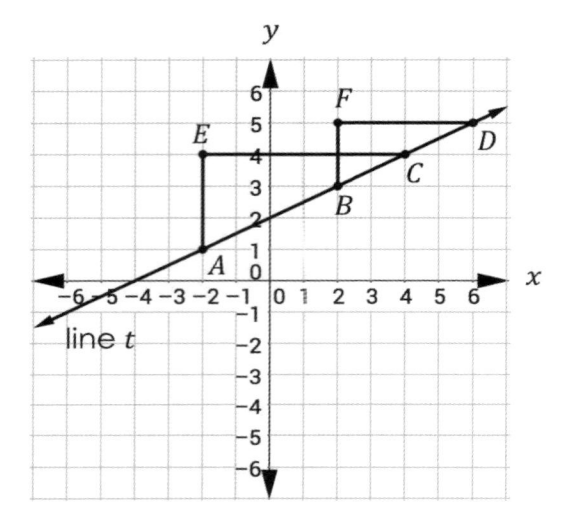

   Which of the following statements are true? Select all that apply.

   ☐ The slope of $\overline{AC}$ is equal to the slope of $\overline{BD}$.
   ☐ The slope of $\overline{AC}$ is equal to the slope of line t.
   ☐ The slope of line t is equal to $\dfrac{EC}{AE}$.
   ☐ The slope of line t is equal to $\dfrac{BF}{FD}$.
   ☐ The y-intercept of line t is $(0, 2)$.
   ☐ Line t represents a discrete function.

Section 4: Linear Equations, Functions, and Inequalities

2. The senior class at Elizabeth High School sold tickets to raise money for prom. The graph below represents the situation.

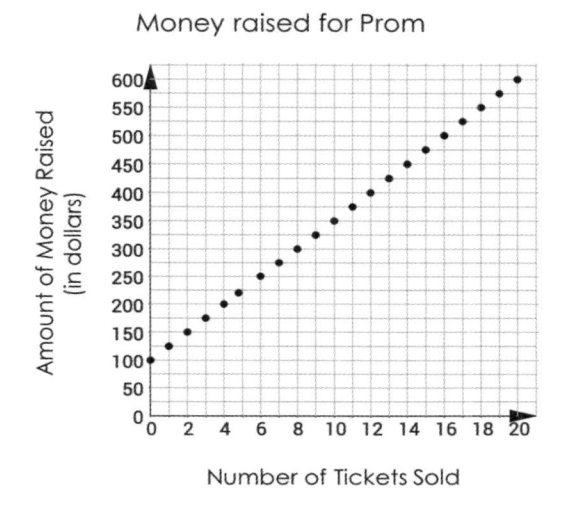

Money raised for Prom

Amount of Money Raised (in dollars) vs *Number of Tickets Sold*

Part A: How much did one ticket cost?

Part B: How much money did the senior class have at the start of the fundraiser?

Section 4 – Topic 5
Introduction to Systems of Equations

A system of equations is a set of two or more equations.

Consider the following system of equations.

$$\text{Line 1: } 2x - y = -5$$
$$\text{Line 2: } 2x + y = 1$$

Graph the system of equations on the coordinate plane below.

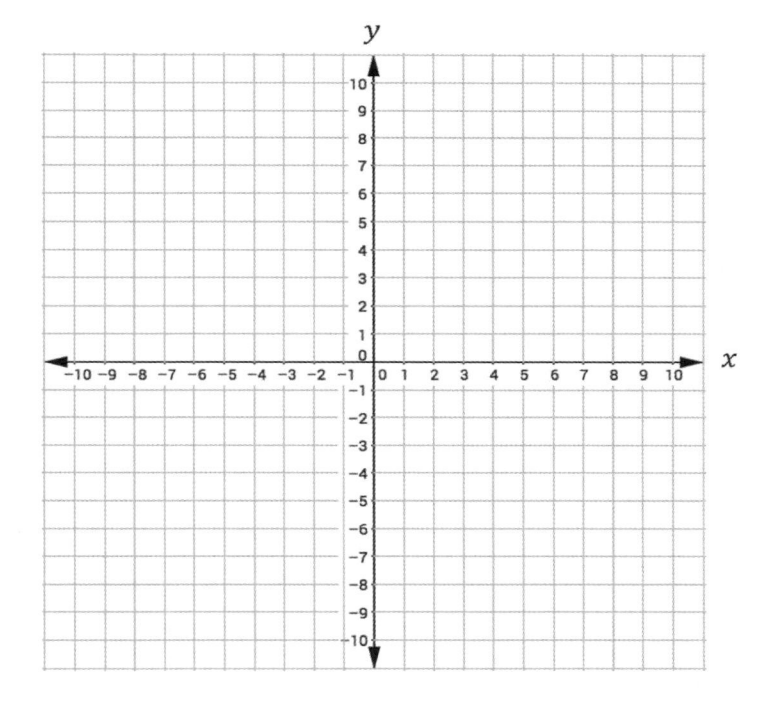

Recall that a solution to a linear equation is any ordered pair that makes that equation a true statement.

Section 4: Linear Equations, Functions, and Inequalities

What do you notice about the point $(-2, 5)$?

What do you notice about the point $(1, 7)$?

What do you notice about the point $(-1, 3)$?

What do you notice about the point $(1, 1)$?

Let's Practice!

1. Consider the following system of equations made up of Line 1 and Line 2.

$$\text{Line 1: } 5x + 2y = 8$$
$$\text{Line 2: } -3x - 2y = -4$$

Complete the following sentences.

a. The ordered pair $(-2, 5)$ is a solution to
- o line 1.
- o line 2.
- o the system of equations.

b. The ordered pair $(2, -1)$ is a solution to
- o line 1.
- o line 2.
- o the system of equations.

c. The ordered pair $(0, 4)$ is a solution to
- o line 1.
- o line 2.
- o the system of equations.

2. Is there ever a time when a system of equations will not have a solution? If so, sketch an example.

Try It!

3. Consider the following system of equations.

$$x - y = 3$$
$$-2x + 2y = -6$$

   a. Sketch the graph of the system of equations.

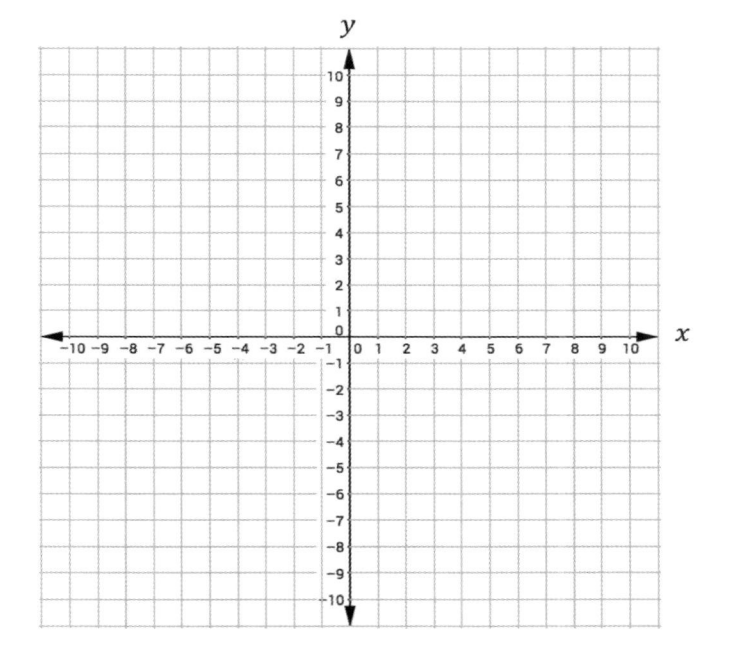

   b. What can be said about the solution to this system of equations?

4. Consider the following system of equations.

$$4x + 3y = 3$$
$$2x - 5y = -5$$

   a. Sketch the graph the system of equations.

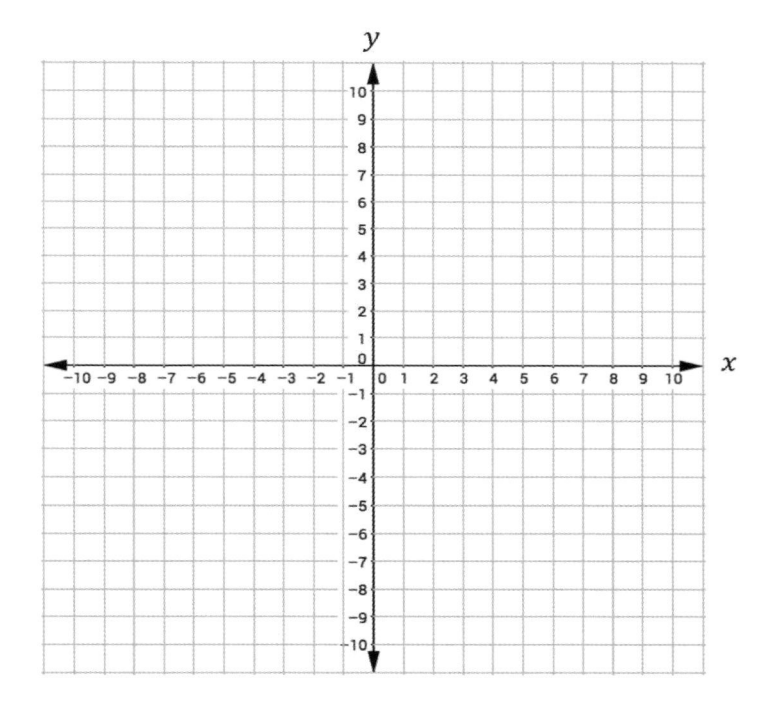

   b. What is the solution to the system?

Section 4: Linear Equations, Functions, and Inequalities

BEAT THE TEST!

1. Consider the following system of equations.

$$x + y = 5$$
$$2x - y = -2$$

   Part A: Sketch the graph of the system of equations.

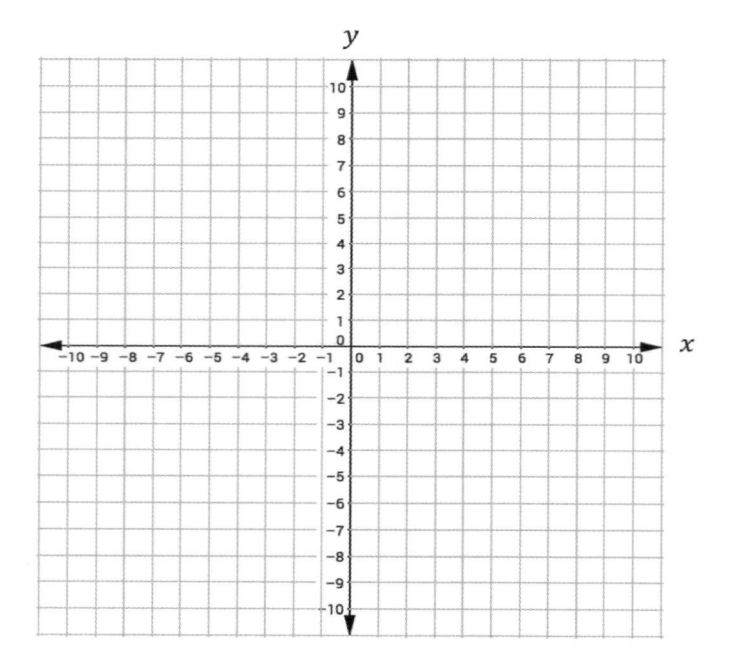

   Part B: Determine the solution to the system of equations.

   Part C: Create a third equation that could be added to the system so that the solution does not change. Graph the line on the coordinate plane above.

2. Two linear functions in a coordinate plane have no points of intersection. Which pair of functions does not intersect?

   Ⓐ $6x + 2y = 12$ and $20x + 10y = 14$

   Ⓑ $4x + 2y = 12$ and $20x + 10y = 30$

   Ⓒ $6x + 2y = 12$ and $y = 0.5x - 0.6$

   Ⓓ $10x + 10y = 6$ and $y = 0.5x - 0.6$

Section 4 – Topic 6
Finding Solution Sets to Systems of Equations Using Substitution and Graphing

We are able to use systems of equations to solve many real-world problems.

One method of solving systems of equations is by graphing like we did in the previous video.

Let's Practice!

1. Brianna's lacrosse coach suggested that she practice yoga to improve her flexibility. "Yoga-ta Try This!" Yoga Studio has two membership plans. Plan A costs $20.00 per month plus $10.00 per class. Plan B costs $100.00 per month for unlimited classes.

    a. Define the variables and write two functions to represent the monthly cost of each plan.

    b. Represent the two situations on the graph below.

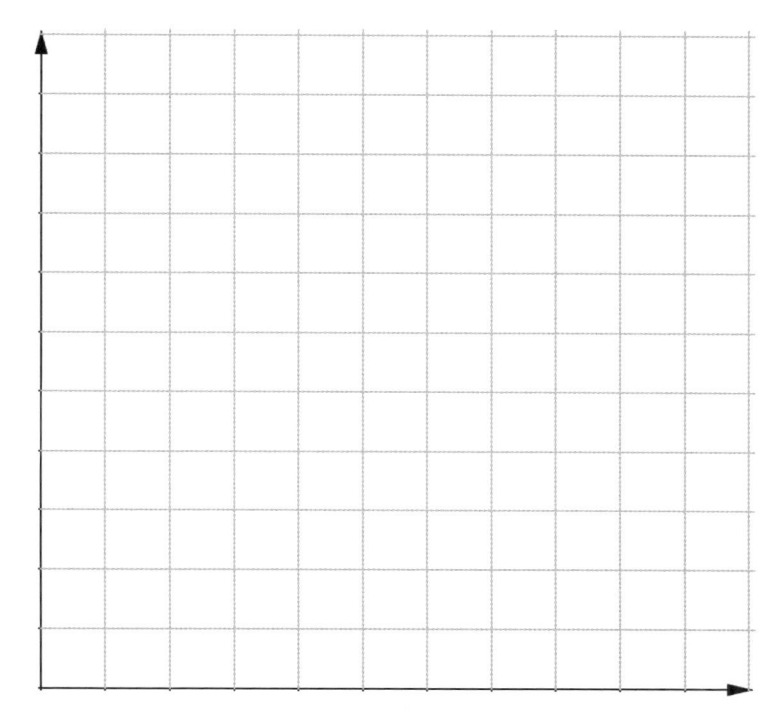

    c. What is the rate of change for each plan?

    d. What does the rate of change represent in this situation?

    e. What do the *y*-intercepts of the graphs represent?

Section 4: Linear Equations, Functions, and Inequalities

2. Brianna is trying to determine which plan is more appropriate for the number of classes she wants to attend.

   a. When will the two plans cost exactly the same?

   b. When is Plan A the better deal?

   c. When is Plan B the better deal?

We can also help Brianna determine the best plan for herself without graphing. Consider our two equations again.

We want to know when the total costs would be equal.

➢ Set the two plans equal to each other and solve for the number of visits.

➢ This method is called solving by _____.

Try It!

3. Vespa Scooter Rental rents scooters for $45.00 and $0.25 per mile. Scottie's Scooter Rental rents scooters for $35.00 and $0.30 per mile.

   a. Define the variables and write two functions to represent the situation.

   b. Represent the two situations on the graph below.

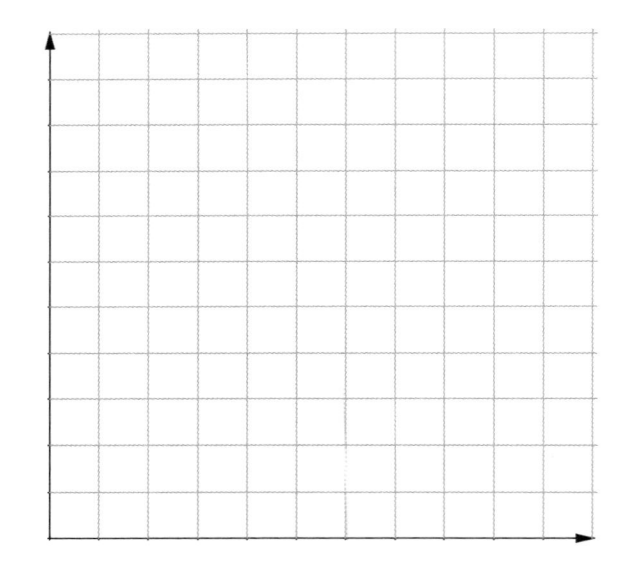

   c. What is the rate of change of each line? What do they represent?

   d. What do the y-intercepts of each line represent?

It's difficult to find the solution by looking at the graph. In such cases, it's better to use substitution to solve the problem.

4. Use the substitution method to help the renter determine when the two scooter rentals will cost the same amount.

   a. When will renting a scooter from Vespa Scooter Rental cost the same as renting a scooter from Scottie's Scooter Rental?

   b. Describe a situation when renting from Vespa Scooter Rental would be a better deal than renting from Scottie's Scooter Rental.

BEAT THE TEST!

1. Lyle and Shaun open savings accounts at the same time. Lyle deposits $100 initially and adds $20 per week. Shaun deposits $500 initially and adds $10 per week. Lyle wants to know when he will have the same amount in his savings account as Shaun.

   Part A: Write two equations to represent the amounts of money Lyle and Shaun have in their accounts.

   Part B: Which method would you use to solve the problem, substitution or graphing? Explain your answer.

   Part C: After how many weeks of making the additional deposits will Lyle have the same amount of money as Shaun?

   Want some help? You can always ask questions on the Algebra Wall and receive help from other students, teachers, and Study Experts. You can also help others on the Algebra Wall and earn Karma Points for doing so. Go to AlgebraNation.com to learn more and get started!

Section 4 – Topic 7
Using Equivalent Systems of Equations

An ordered pair that satisfies all equations in a system is called the _____ to that system.

If two systems of equations have the same solution, they are called _____ systems.

Let's explore how to write equivalent systems of equations.

Consider the following system of equations:

Equation A: $x + y = 4$
Equation B: $x - y = 6$

The solution to this system is $(5, -1)$. We can also see this when we graph the lines.

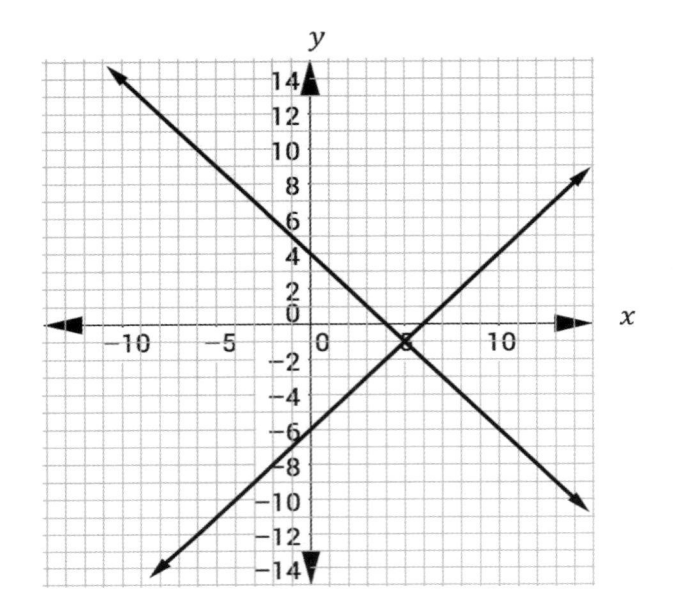

Describe the result when we multiply either of the equations by some factor.

Use this process to write an equivalent system.

Consider the original system of equations again.

$$\text{Equation A: } x + y = 4$$
$$\text{Equation B: } x - y = 6$$

What is the resulting equation when we add the two equations in the system together?

Graph the new equation on the same coordinate plane with our original system.

Algebraically, show that (5, −1) is also a solution to the sum of the two lines.

What is the resulting equation when we subtract the second equation from the first equation?

Graph the new equation on the same coordinate plane with our original system.

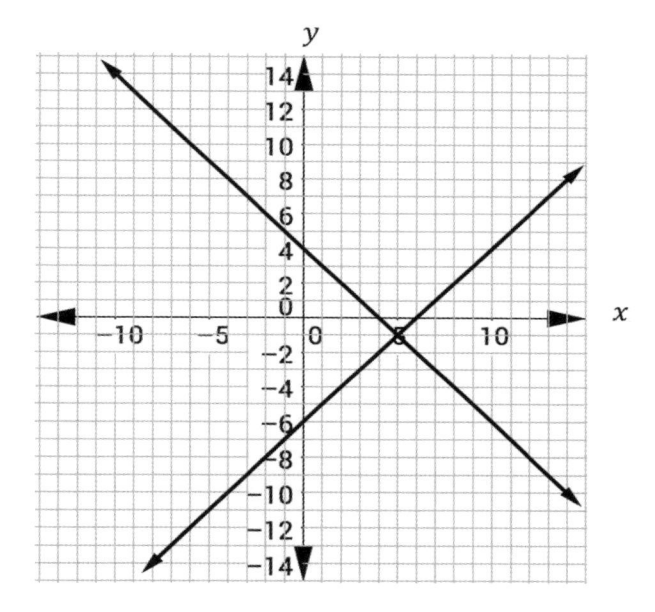

Algebraically, show that (5, −1) is also a solution to the difference of the two lines.

Section 4: Linear Equations, Functions, and Inequalities

Let's revisit the original system:

$$\text{Equation A: } x + y = 4$$
$$\text{Equation B: } x - y = 6$$

Complete the following steps to show that replacing one equation by the sum of that equation and a multiple of the other equation produces a system with the same solutions.

Create Equation C by multiplying Equation A by 2.

Create Equation D by finding the sum of Equation B and Equation C.

Graph Equation D on the same coordinate plane with our original system.

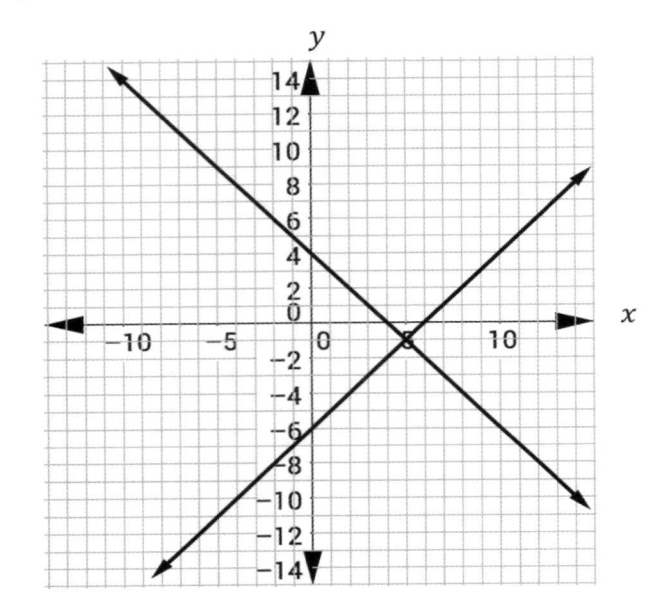

Algebraically, show that $(5, -1)$ is a solution to the Equation D.

Let's Practice!

1. Consider the following system, which has a solution of $(2, 5)$. $M, N, P, R, S,$ and T are non-zero real numbers.

$$Mx + Ny = P$$
$$Rx + Sy = T$$

Write two new equations that could be used to create an equivalent system of equations.

Try It!

2. List three ways to write new equations that can be used to create equivalent systems.

BEAT THE TEST!

1. The system $\begin{cases} Ax + By = C \\ Dx + Ey = F \end{cases}$ has the solution $(1, 3)$, where $A, B, C, D, E,$ and F are non-zero real numbers. Select all the systems of equations with the same solution.

   ☐ $(A - D)x + (B - E)y = C - F$
   $Dx + Ey = F$

   ☐ $(2A + D)x + (2B + E)y = C + 2F$
   $Dx + Ey = F$

   ☐ $Ax + By = C$
   $-3Dx - 3Ey = -3F$

   ☐ $(A - 5D)x + (B - 5E)y = C - 5F$
   $Dx + Ey = F$

   ☐ $Ax + (B + E)y = C$
   $(A + D)x + Ey = C + F$

Want some help? You can always ask questions on the Algebra Wall and receive help from other students, teachers, and Study Experts. You can also help others on the Algebra Wall and earn Karma Points for doing so. Go to AlgebraNation.com to learn more and get started!

Section 4: Linear Equations, Functions, and Inequalities

Section 4 – Topic 8
Finding Solution Sets to Systems of Equations Using Elimination

Consider the following system of equations:

$$2x + y = 8$$
$$x - 2y = -1$$

Write an equivalent system that will eliminate one of the variables when you add the equations.

Determine the solution to the system of equations.

Describe what the graph of the two systems would look like.

This method of solving a system is called _____.

Let's Practice!

1. Ruxin and Andre were invited to a Super Bowl party. They were asked to bring pizzas and sodas. Ruxin brought three pizzas and four bottles of soda and spent $48.05. Andre brought five pizzas and two bottles of soda and spent $67.25.

   a. Write a system of equations to represent the situation.

   b. Write an equivalent system that will eliminate one of the variables when you add the equations.

   c. Solve the system to determine the cost of one pizza and one bottle of soda.

Try It!

2. Jazmin and Justine went shopping for back to school clothes. Jazmin purchased three shirts and one pair of shorts and spent $38.00. Justine bought four shirts and three pairs of shorts and spent $71.50.

   a. Assuming all the shirts cost the same amount and all the shorts cost the same amount, write a system of equations to represent each girl's shopping spree.

   b. Use the elimination method to solve for the price of one pair of shorts.

BEAT THE TEST!

1. Complete the following table.

   Solve by Elimination: $\begin{cases} 2x - 3y = 8 \\ 3x + 4y = 46 \end{cases}$

Operations	Equations	Labels
	$2x - 3y = 8$ $3x + 4y = 46$	Equation 1 Equation 2
	$-6x + 9y = -24$	New Equation 1
Multiply Equation 2 by 2.		New Equation 2
	$-6x + 9y = -24$ $6x + 8y = 92$ $\overline{17y = 68}$	
Divide by 17.		
Solve for x.		
Write x and y as coordinates.	$(\square, \square)$	Solution to the system

Section 4: Linear Equations, Functions, and Inequalities

2. Which of the systems of equations below could not be used to solve the following system for x and y?

$$6x + 4y = 24$$
$$-2x + 4y = -10$$

Ⓐ $6x + 4y = 24$
    $2x - 4y = 10$

Ⓑ $6x + 4y = 24$
    $-4x + 8y = -20$

Ⓒ $18x + 12y = 72$
    $-6x + 12y = -30$

Ⓓ $12x + 8y = 48$
    $-4x + 8y = -10$

Section 4 – Topic 9
Solution Sets to Inequalities with Two Variables

Consider the following linear inequality.

$$y \geq 2x - 1$$

Underline each ordered pair that is a solution to the above inequality.

$(0, 5)$ $(-1, -1)$ $(1, 1)$ $(3, 0)$ $(4, 3)$ $(-1, -3)$

Plot each solution as a point in the coordinate plane.

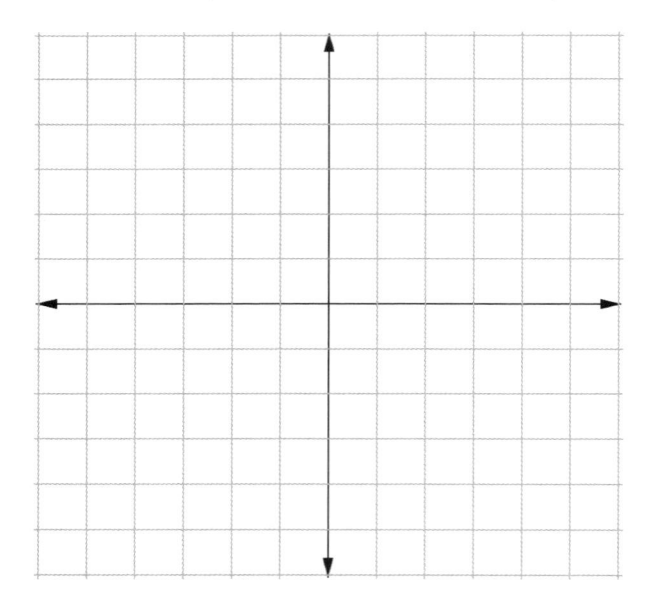

Graph the line $y = 2x - 1$ in the same coordinate plane. What do you notice about the solutions to the inequality $y \geq 2x - 1$ and the graph of the line $y = 2x - 1$?

Let's Practice!

1. The senior class is raising money for Grad Bash. The students' parents are donating cakes. The students plan to sell entire cakes for $20.00 each and slices of cake for $3.00 each. If they need at least $500.00, how many of each should they sell?

   a. List two possibilities for the number of whole cakes and cake slices students could sell to reach their goal of raising at least $500.00.

   b. Write an inequality to represent the situation.

   c. Graph the region of the solutions to the inequality.

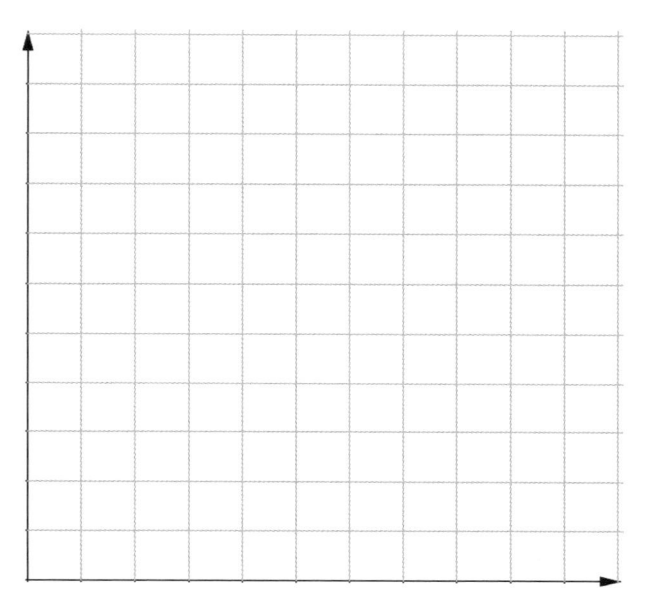

   d. What is the difference between the ordered pairs that fall on the line and the ones that fall in the shaded area?

   e. What does the x-intercept represent?

Section 4: Linear Equations, Functions, and Inequalities

Try It!

2. The freshman class wants to include at least 120 people in performances at a pep rally. Each skit will have 15 people, and each dance routine will feature 12 people.

   a. List two possible combinations of skits and dance routines.

   b. Write an inequality to represent the situation.

   c. Graph the region of the solutions to the inequality.

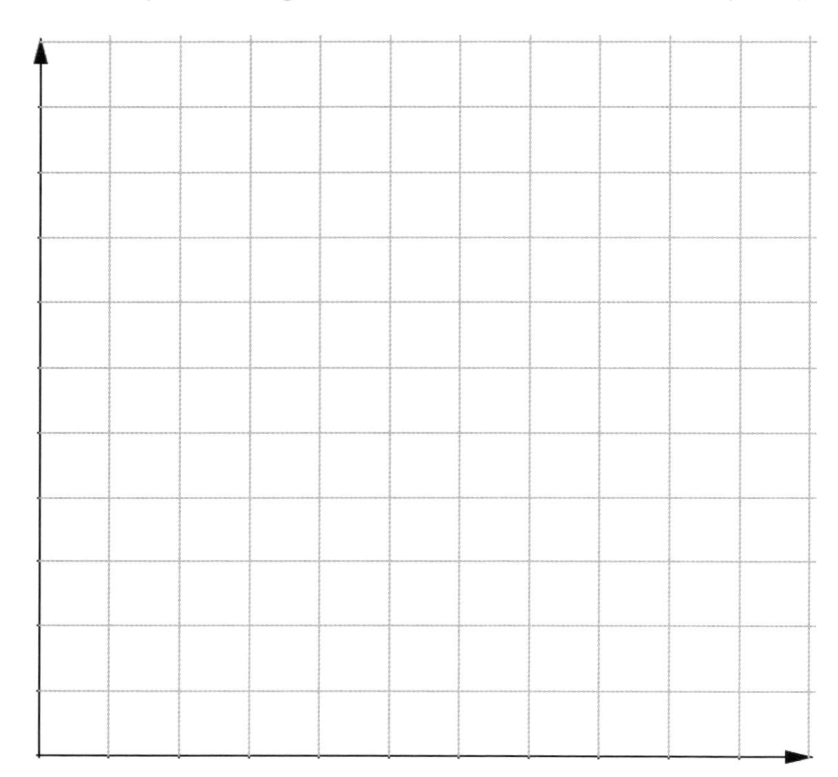

   d. What does the y-intercept represent?

Section 4: Linear Equations, Functions, and Inequalities

BEAT THE TEST!

1. Coach De Leon purchases sports equipment. Basketballs cost $20.00 each and soccer balls cost $18.00 each. He has a budget of $150.00. The graph shown below represents the number of basketballs and soccer balls he can buy given his budget constraint.

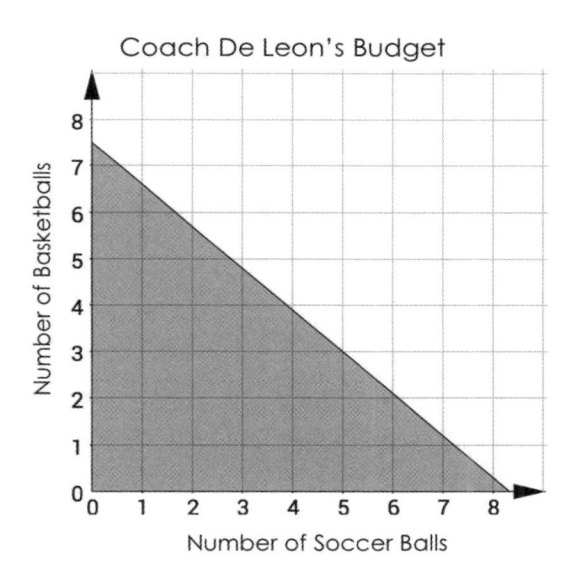

Coach De Leon's Budget

Number of Basketballs vs *Number of Soccer Balls*

Part A: Write an inequality to represent the situation.

Part B: Determine whether these combinations of basketballs, b, and soccer balls, s, can be purchased within the budget.

	$b = 5$ $s = 3$	$b = 2$ $s = 4$	$b = 0$ $s = 8$	$b = 8$ $s = 0$	$b = 4$ $s = 7$
Yes	○	○	○	○	○
No	○	○	○	○	○

Section 4: Linear Equations, Functions, and Inequalities

Section 4 – Topic 10
Finding Solution Sets to Systems of Linear Inequalities

Juan must purchase car insurance. He needs to earn at least $50.00 a week to cover the payments. The most he can work each week is 8 hours because of football practice. Juan can earn $10.00 per hour mowing yards and $12.00 per hour washing cars.

The system $\begin{cases} 10x + 12y \geq 50 \\ x + y \leq 8 \end{cases}$ represents Juan's situation.

Define the variables.

The graph below depicts Juan's situation. Interpret the graph and identify two different solutions.

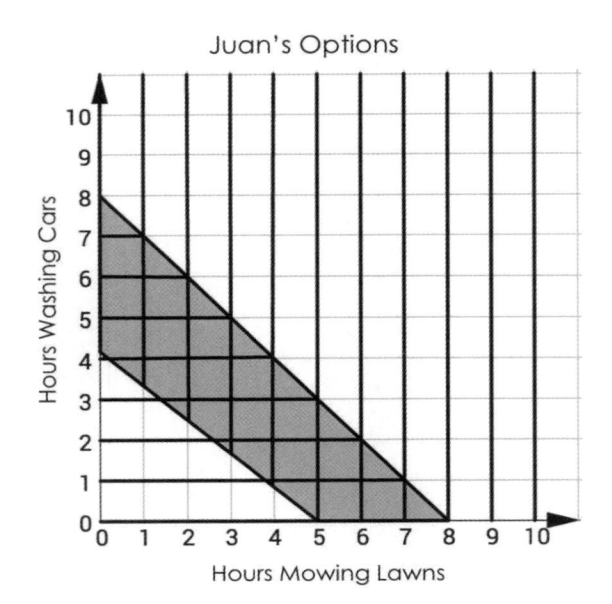

Juan's Options

(Graph with x-axis "Hours Mowing Lawns" from 0 to 10 and y-axis "Hours Washing Cars" from 0 to 10, showing shaded solution region)

Let's Practice!

1. Bristol is having a party and has invited 24 friends. She plans to purchase sodas that cost $5.00 for a 12-pack and chips that cost $3.00 per bag. She wants each friend to have at least two sodas. Bristol's budget is $35.00.

    a. Write a system of inequalities to represent the situation.

    b. Graph the region using boundary lines to show the solutions to the inequality.

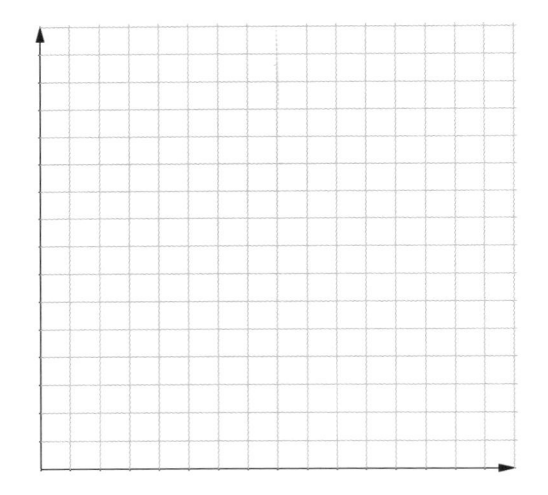

    c. Name two different solutions for Bristol's situation.

Section 4: Linear Equations, Functions, and Inequalities

Try It!

2. Anna is an avid reader. Her generous grandparents gave her money for her birthday, and she decided to spend at most $150.00 on books. *Reading Spot* is running a special: all paperback books are $8.00 and hardback books are $12.00. Anna wants to purchase at least 12 books.

   a. Write a system of inequalities to represent the situation.

   b. Graph the region of the solutions to the inequality.

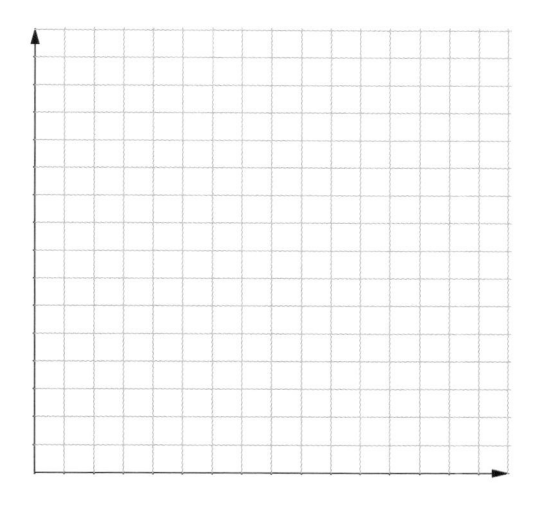

   c. Name two different solutions for Anna's situation.

BEAT THE TEST!

1. Tatiana is reviewing for the Algebra 1 final exam. She made this graph representing a system of inequalities:

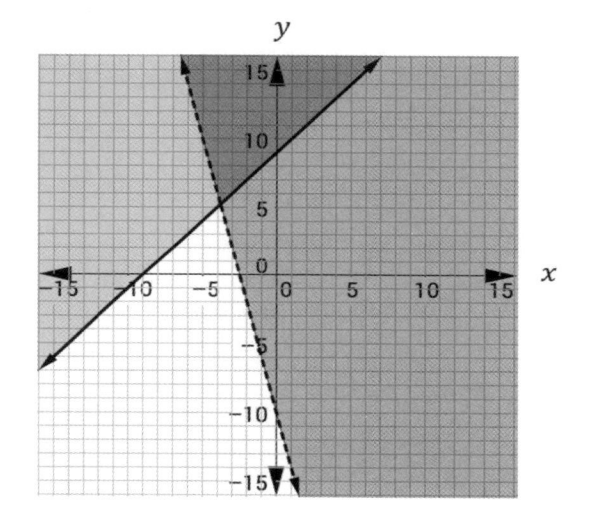

   Part A: Underline the ordered pairs below that represent solutions to the system of inequalities.

   $(-8, 3)$ $(-3, 8)$ $(-1, 9)$ $(-4, 9)$ $(9, 6)$ $(0, 9)$

   $(5, 5)$ $(-5, 10)$ $(-9, 1)$ $(-2, 7)$ $(1, 6)$ $(0, 0)$

   Part B: Derive the system of inequalities that describes the region of the graph Tatiana drew.

Section 4: Linear Equations, Functions, and Inequalities

2. Consider the system of inequalities below.

$$3y \leq -2x + 18$$
$$-4y \leq -x + 12$$

Which of the following points are in the solution set? Select all that apply.

- ☐ $(-4, -3)$
- ☐ $(1, 6)$
- ☐ $(2, 4)$
- ☐ $(5, -5)$
- ☐ $(3, 2)$

Test Yourself! Practice Tool

Great job! You have reached the end of this section. Now it's time to try the "Test Yourself! Practice Tool," where you can practice all the skills and concepts you learned in this section. Log in to Algebra Nation and try out the "Test Yourself! Practice Tool" so you can see how well you know these topics!

Section 5: Quadratic Functions – Part 1

Topic 1: Real-World Examples of Quadratic Functions 127
Standards Covered: F-IF.4
- ☐ I can determine the key features of a quadratic function.
- ☐ I can interpret the key features of a quadratic function to solve a real-world problem.

Topic 2: Factoring Quadratic Expressions 131
Standards Covered: A-SSE.3.a, A-SSE.2
- ☐ I can factor using an area model.
- ☐ I can factor by grouping and by using the distributive property.

Topic 3: Solving Quadratic Equations by Factoring 134
Standards Covered: A-SSE.3.a, A-REI.4.b, A-CED.1
- ☐ I can find the factors of a quadratic equation and use the zero product property to determine the solutions.

Topic 4: Solving Other Quadratic Equations by Factoring 136
Standards Covered: A-SSE.3.a, A-REI.4.b, A-SSE.2
- ☐ I can solve quadratic equations not in standard form and quadratic equations with the coefficient of the quadratic term that is not equal to one.

Topic 5: Solving Quadratic Equations by Factoring – Special Cases 138
Standards Covered: A-SSE.2, A-SSE.3.a, A-REI.4.b
- ☐ I can factor and solve a perfect square trinomial.
- ☐ I can factor and solve a quadratic equation using difference of squares.

Topic 6: Solving Quadratic Equations by Taking Square Roots 141
Standards Covered: A-REI.4.b
- ☐ I can solve quadratic equations by taking the square root.

Topic 7: Solving Quadratic Equations by Completing the Square 142
Standards Covered: A-REI.4a.b
- ☐ I can solve a quadratic equation by completing the square.

Topic 8: Deriving the Quadratic Formula 144
Standards Covered: A-REI.4.a, A-SSE.3
- ☐ I can derive the quadratic formula by completing the square.

Topic 9: Solving Quadratic Equations Using the Quadratic Formula 146
Standards Covered: A-REI.4.b
- ☐ I can use the quadratic formula to find solutions to quadratic equations.

Topic 10: Quadratic Functions in Action 148
Standards Covered: A-REI.4.b
- ☐ I can write a quadratic function to represent a real-world problem.
- ☐ I can interpret key features of a quadratic function in real-world context.

Visit MathNation.com or search "Math Nation" in your phone or tablet's app store to watch the videos that go along with this workbook!

Real-World Examples of Quadratic Functions

Let's revisit linear functions.

Imagine that you are driving down the road at a constant speed of 40 mph. This is a linear function.

We can represent the distance traveled versus time on a table (to the right).

Time (in hours)	Distance Traveled (in miles)
1	40
2	80
3	120
4	

We can represent the scenario on a graph:

The following Michigan Mathematics Standards will be covered in this section:
F-IF.4 - For a function that models a relationship between two quantities, interpret key features of graphs and tables in terms of the quantities, and sketch graphs showing key features given a verbal description of the relationship. Key features include: intercepts; intervals where the function is increasing, decreasing, positive, or negative; relative maximums and minimums; symmetries; end behavior; and periodicity.
A-SSE.3 - Choose and produce an equivalent form of an expression to reveal and explain properties of the quantity represented by the expression. a. Factor a quadratic expression to reveal the zeros of the function it defines.
A-SSE.2 - Use the structure of an expression to identify ways to rewrite it. For example, see x4 – y4 as (x2)2 – (y2)2, thus recognizing it as a difference of squares that can be factored as (x2 – y2)(x2 + y2).
A-REI.4.a.b - Solve quadratic equations in one variable. a. Use the method of completing the square to transform any quadratic equation in x into an equation of the form (x-p)^2=q that has the same solutions. Derive the quadratic formula from this form. b. Solve quadratic equations by inspection, taking square roots, completing the square, the quadratic formula, and factoring, as appropriate to the initial form of the equation. Recognize when the quadratic formula gives complex solutions.
A-CED.1 - Create equations and inequalities in one variable and use them to solve problems. Include equations arising from linear and quadratic functions, and simple rational and exponential functions.

Section 5: Quadratic Functions - Part 1

Section 5: Quadratic Functions – Part 1
Section 5 – Topic 1
Real-World Examples of Quadratic Functions

Let's revisit linear functions.

Imagine that you are driving down the road at a constant speed of 40 mph. This is a linear function.

We can represent the distance traveled versus time on a table (to the right).

Time (in hours)	Distance Traveled (in miles)
1	40
2	80
3	120
4	160

We can represent the scenario on a graph.

Distance Traveled

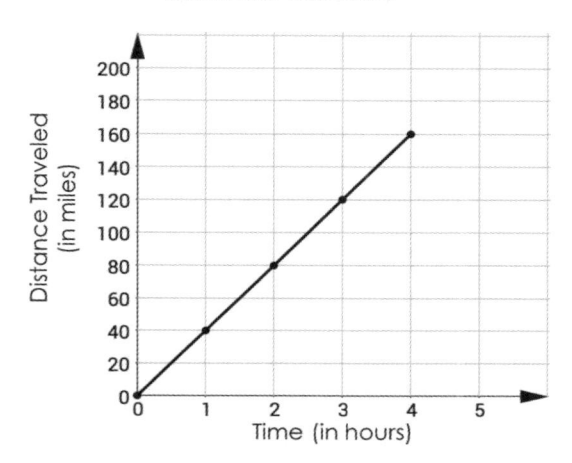

We can represent the distance traveled $d(t)$, in terms of time, t, with the equation $d(t) = 40t$.

Linear functions **always** have a constant rate of change. In this section, we are going to discover a type of non-linear function.

Consider the following situation.

Liam dropped a watermelon from the top of a 300 ft tall building. He wanted to know if the watermelon was falling at a constant rate over time. He filmed the watermelon's fall and then recorded his observations in the following table.

Time (in seconds)	Height (in feet)
0	300.0
1	283.9
2	235.6
3	155.1
4	42.4

What do you notice about the rate of change?

Why do you think that the rate of change is not constant?

Liam entered the data of the falling watermelon into his graphing calculator. The graph below displays the first quadrant of the graph.

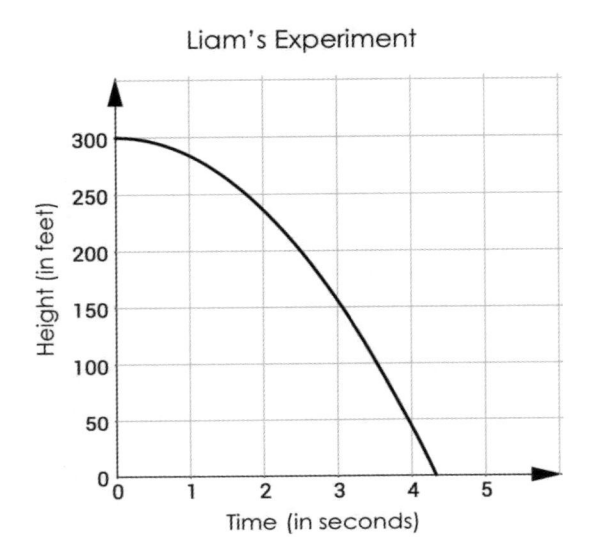

Liam's Experiment

What is the independent variable?

What is the dependent variable?

Liam then used his calculator to find the equation of the function, $h(t) = -16t^2 + 300$.

Important facts:

➢ We call this non-linear function a _____.

➢ The general form of the equation is _____.

The graph of $f(x) = x^2$ is shown below.

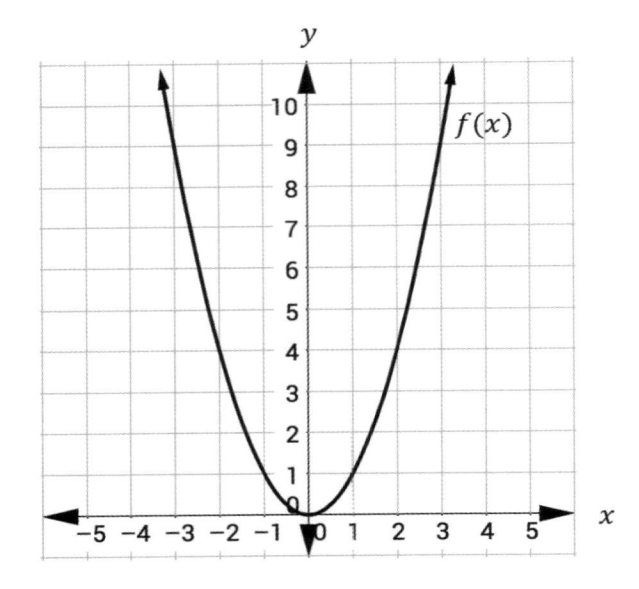

➢ This graph is called a _____.

Why did we only consider the first quadrant of Liam's graph?

Section 5: Quadratic Functions - Part 1

In Liam's graph, how long did it take for the watermelon to hit the ground?

This is also the x-intercept.

- The x-intercept is the _____ of the function.

- It is the solution of the function when it is set equal to zero.

There is only one zero to Liam's equation. Describe a situation where there could be two zeros.

What about no zeros?

To solve a quadratic equation using a graph:

- Look for the _____ of the graph.

- The zeros are the values where the graph intercepts the _____.

Let's Practice!

1. What are the zeros of the quadratic equation graphed below?

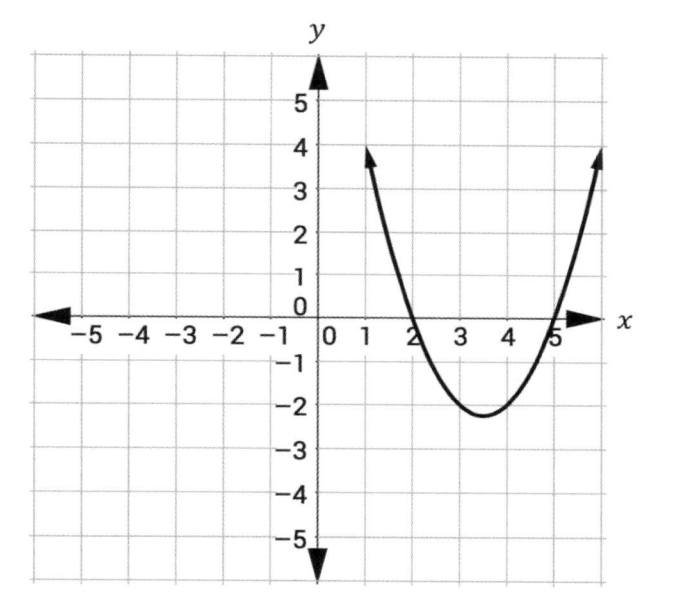

Section 5: Quadratic Functions - Part 1

Try It!

2. Aaron shot a water bottle rocket from the ground. A graph of height over time is shown below.

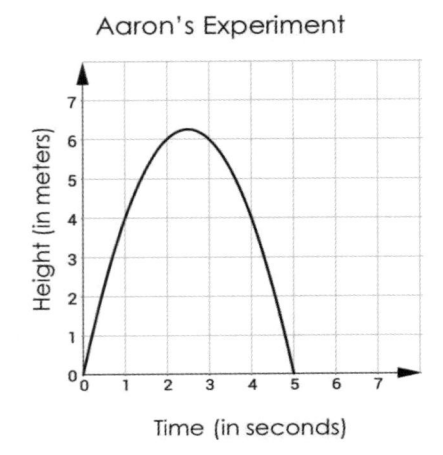

Aaron's Experiment

    a. What type of function best models the rocket's motion?

    b. After how many seconds did the rocket hit the ground?

    c. Estimate the maximum height of the rocket.

The maximum or minimum point of the parabola is called the _____.

BEAT THE TEST!

1. Jordan owns an electronics business. During her first year in the business, she collected data and created the following graph showing the relationship between the selling price of an item and the profit.

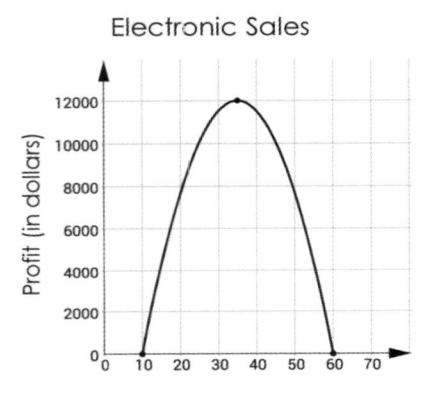

Electronic Sales

   Part A: Circle the zeros of the quadratic function graphed above.

   Part B: What do the zeros represent?

   Part C: Box the vertex of the graph.

   Part D: What does the vertex represent?

Algebra Wall

Want some help? You can always ask questions on the Algebra Wall and receive help from other students, teachers, and Study Experts. You can also help others on the Algebra Wall and earn Karma Points for doing so. Go to AlgebraNation.com to learn more and get started!

Section 5: Quadratic Functions - Part 1

Section 5 – Topic 2
Factoring Quadratic Expressions

Let's review the two methods we used for multiplying polynomials.

Area Model:

	x	$2y$	$-7z$
3			

Distributive Property:

$3(x + 2y - 7z)$

We can use these same methods to factor out the greatest common factor of an expression.

Area Model:

$10x^3$	$-14x^2$	$12x$

Distributive Property:

$10x^3 - 14x^2 + 12x$

Use the area model to write an equivalent expression for $(2x + 5)(x + 3)$.

	x	3
$2x$		
5		

We can use this same area model to factor a quadratic expression. Look at the resulting trinomial and notice the following four patterns:

➢ The first term of the trinomial can always be found in the _____ _____ rectangle.

➢ The last term of the trinomial can always be found in the _____ _____ rectangle.

➢ The second term of the trinomial is the _____ of the _____ and _____ _____ rectangles.

➢ The _____ of the _____ are always equal.

Section 5: Quadratic Functions - Part 1

Use the distributive property to write an equivalent expression for $(2x + 5)(x + 3)$.

We can also use the distributive property to factor a quadratic expression.

What are the two middle terms of the expanded form?

Consider the resulting trinomial.

$$2x^2 + 11x + 15$$

Notice that the product of the two middle terms of expanded form are equal to the product of the first and last term of the trinomial. The middle terms also sum to the middle term of the trinomial.

Let's consider how we can use this and the distributive property to factor a quadratic expression.

Factor $2x^2 + 3x - 5$ using the distributive property.

➢ Multiply the first term by the last term.

➢ Find two factors whose product is equal to $-10x^2$ and whose sum is equal to $3x$.

➢ Replace the middle term with these two factors.

➢ Factor the polynomial by grouping the first two terms and the last two terms.

Let's Practice!

1. Consider the quadratic expression $3x^2 + 4x - 4$.

   a. Factor using the area model.

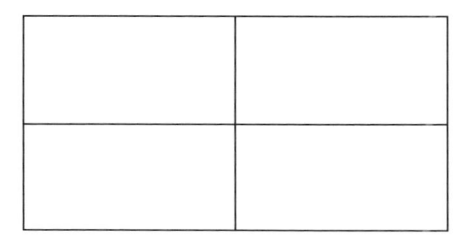

   b. Factor using the distributive property.

Try It!

2. Consider the quadratic expression $4w^2 - 21w + 20$.

   a. Factor using the area model.

   b. Factor using the distributive property.

> **STUDY EDGE TIP:** You can check your answer by using the distributive property. The product of the factors should always result in the original trinomial.

Section 5: Quadratic Functions - Part 1

BEAT THE TEST!

1. Identify all factors of the expression $18x^2 - 9x - 5$. Select all that apply.

   ☐ $2x + 5$
   ☐ $6x - 5$
   ☐ $18x - 5$
   ☐ $3x + 5$
   ☐ $3x + 1$

Section 5 – Topic 3
Solving Quadratic Equations by Factoring

Once a quadratic equation is factored, we can use the **zero product property** to solve the equation.

The zero product property states that if the product of two factors is zero, then one (or both) of the factors must be

_____.

➢ If $ab = 0$, then either $a = 0, b = 0$, or $a = b = 0$.

To solve a quadratic equation by factoring:

Step 1: Set the equation equal to zero.
Step 2: Factor the quadratic.
Step 3: Set each factor equal to zero and solve.
Step 4: Write the solution set.

Let's Practice!

1. Solve for b by factoring $b^2 + 8b + 15 = 0$.

2. Solve for f by factoring $10f^2 + 17f + 3 = 0$.

Try It!

3. Solve for j by factoring $6j^2 - 19j + 14 = 0$.

Section 5: Quadratic Functions - Part 1

BEAT THE TEST!

1. Tyra solved the quadratic equation $x^2 - 10x - 24 = 0$ by factoring. Her work is shown below:

   Step 1: $x^2 - 10x - 24 = 0$
   Step 2: $x^2 - 4x - 6x - 24 = 0$
   Step 3: $(x^2 - 4x) + (-6x - 24) = 0$
   Step 4: $x(x - 4) - 6(x - 4) = 0$
   Step 5: $(x - 4)(x - 6) = 0$
   Step 6: $x - 4 = 0, x - 6 = 0$
   Step 7: $x = 4$ or $x = 6$
   Step 8: $\{4, 6\}$

   Tyra did not find the correct solutions. Investigate the steps, decipher her mistakes, and explain how to correct Tyra's work.

Section 5 – Topic 4
Solving Other Quadratic Equations by Factoring

Many quadratic equations will not be in standard form.

- The equation won't always equal zero.

- There may be a greatest common factor (GCF) within all of the terms.

Let's Practice!

1. Solve for m: $3m^2 + 30m - 168 = 0$.

2. Solve for x: $(x + 4)(x - 5) = -8$.

Try It!

3. Solve for d: $6d^2 + 5d = 1$.

4. Solve for p: $p^2 + 36 = 13p$.

BEAT THE TEST!

1. What are the solutions to $40x^2 - 30x = 135$? Select all that apply.

   ☐ $-\frac{9}{2}$ ☐ $\frac{3}{4}$

   ☐ $-\frac{9}{4}$ ☐ $\frac{3}{2}$

   ☐ $-\frac{3}{2}$ ☐ $\frac{9}{4}$

   ☐ $-\frac{3}{4}$

> Want some help? You can always ask questions on the Algebra Wall and receive help from other students, teachers, and Study Experts. You can also help others on the Algebra Wall and earn Karma Points for doing so. Go to AlgebraNation.com to learn more and get started!

Section 5 – Topic 5
Solving Quadratic Equations by Factoring – Special Cases

There are a few special cases when solving quadratic equations by factoring.

Perfect Square Trinomials:

➢ $x^2 + 6x + 9$ is an example of a **perfect square trinomial**. We see this when we factor.

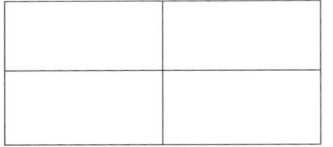

➢ A perfect square trinomial is created when you square a _____.

Recognizing a Perfect Square Trinomial:

A quadratic expression can be factored as a perfect square trinomial if it can be re-written in the form $a^2 + 2ab + b^2$.

Factoring a Perfect Square Trinomial:

➢ If $a^2 + 2ab + b^2$ is a perfect square trinomial, then $a^2 + 2ab + b^2 = (a + b)^2$.

➢ If $a^2 - 2ab + b^2$ is a perfect square trinomial, then $a^2 - 2ab + b^2 = (a - b)^2$.

Let's Practice!

1. Determine whether $16x^2 + 88x + 121$ is a perfect square trinomial. Justify your answer.

2. Solve for q: $q^2 - 10q + 25 = 0$.

Try It!

3. Determine whether $x^2 - 8x + 64$ is a perfect square trinomial. Justify your answer.

4. Solve for w: $4w^2 + 49 = -28w$.

5. What do you notice about the number of solutions to the perfect square quadratic equations?

6. Sketch the graph of a quadratic equation that is a perfect square trinomial.

Difference of Squares:

Use the distributive property to multiply the following binomials.

$(x + 5)(x - 5)$

$(5x + 3)(5x - 3)$

Describe any patterns you notice.

➤ When we have a binomial in the form $a^2 - b^2$, it is called the **difference of two squares**. We can factor this as $(a + b)(a - b)$.

Let's Practice!

7. Solve the equation $49k^2 = 64$ by factoring.

Try It!

8. Solve the equation $0 = 121p^2 - 100$.

BEAT THE TEST!

1. Which of the following expressions are equivalent to $8a^3 - 98a$? Select all that apply.

   ☐ $2(4a^3 - 49a)$
   ☐ $2a(4a^2 - 49)$
   ☐ $2a(4a^3 - 49a)$
   ☐ $(2a - 7)(2a + 7)$
   ☐ $2(2a - 7)(2a + 7)$
   ☐ $2a(2a - 7)(2a + 7)$

Want some help? You can always ask questions on the Algebra Wall and receive help from other students, teachers, and Study Experts. You can also help others on the Algebra Wall and earn Karma Points for doing so. Go to AlgebraNation.com to learn more and get started!

Section 5 – Topic 6
Solving Quadratic Equations by Taking Square Roots

Consider the following quadratic equation.

$$2x^2 - 36 = 0$$

When quadratic equations are in the form $ax^2 + c = 0$, solve by taking the square root.

Step 1: Get the variable on the left and the constant on the right.

Step 2: Take the square root of both sides of the equation. (Don't forget the negative root!)

Solve for x by taking the square root.

$2x^2 - 36 = 0$

Let's Practice!

1. Solve $x^2 - 121 = 0$.

Try It!

2. Solve $-5x^2 + 80 = 0$.

Section 5: Quadratic Functions - Part 1

BEAT THE TEST!

1. What is the smallest solution to the equation $2x^2 + 17 = 179$?

    Ⓐ -9
    Ⓑ -3
    Ⓒ 3
    Ⓓ 9

2. A rescuer on a helicopter that is 50 feet above the sea drops a lifebelt. The distance from the lifebelt to the sea can be modeled by the equation $h(t) = -16t^2 + s$, where t is the time, in seconds, after the lifebelt is dropped, and s is the initial height, in feet, of the lifebelt above the sea.

    How long will it take for the lifebelt to reach the sea? Round your answer to the nearest tenth of a second.

Section 5 – Topic 7
Solving Quadratic Equations by Completing the Square

Sometimes you won't be able to solve a quadratic equation by factoring. However, you can rewrite the quadratic equation so that you can **complete the square** to factor and solve.

Let's start by determining what number we can add to a quadratic expression to make it a perfect square trinomial.

What value could be added to the quadratic expression to make it a perfect square trinomial?

$x^2 + 6x +$ _____

$x^2 + 8x + 3 +$ _____

$x^2 - 22x - 71 +$ _____

Let's see how this can be used to find the zero(s) of quadratic equations.

Recall how we factored perfect square trinomials.
If $a^2 + 2ab + b^2$ is a perfect square trinomial, then
$a^2 + 2ab + b^2 = (a+b)^2$ and $a^2 - 2ab + b^2 = (a-b)^2$.

Solve $f(x) = ax^2 + bx + c$ by completing the square.

Step 1: Group ax^2 and bx together.

$$f(x) = (ax^2 + bx + \underline{\quad}) + c$$

Step 2: If $a \neq 1$, then factor out a.

$$f(x) = a(x^2 + \frac{b}{a}x + \underline{\quad}) + c$$

Step 3: Divide $\frac{b}{a}$ by two and square the result. Add that number to the grouped terms. Subtract the product of that number and a from c so that you have not changed the equation.

$$f(x) = a(x^2 + \frac{b}{a}x + \frac{b^2}{4a^2}) + c - \frac{b^2}{4a}$$

Step 4: Factor the trinomial.

$$f(x) = a\left(x + \frac{b}{2a}\right)^2 + \frac{4ac - b^2}{4a}$$

Step 5: This is vertex form. Now we can find the zero(s) of the equation by setting the function equal to zero, moving the constant to the opposite side, and taking the square root of both sides.

Let's Practice!

1. Consider the following quadratic expression $2x^2 - 8x + 5$.

    a. Complete the square to write the quadratic expression in vertex form.

    b. If the expression represents a function, find the zero(s) of the quadratic function.

Try It!

2. Consider the quadratic expression $3x^2 + 12x + 31$.

    a. Complete the square to write the quadratic expression in vertex form.

    b. If the expression represents a function, find the zero(s) of the quadratic function.

BEAT THE TEST!

1. The equations shown below are steps to find the zeros of the function $g(x) = 2x^2 + 24x - 29$ by completing the square.

A. $g(x) = 2(x^2 + 12x + 36) - 29 - 72$
B. $x + 6 = \pm\sqrt{50.5}$
C. $g(x) = 2(x^2 + 12x + \_\_\_) - 29$
D. $x = -6 \pm \sqrt{50.5}$
E. $2(x + 6)^2 - 101 = 0$
F. $(x + 6)^2 = 50.5$
G. $\sqrt{(x + 6)^2} = \pm\sqrt{50.5}$
H. $g(x) = 2(x + 6)^2 - 101$

   Place the equations in the correct order by writing the letter corresponding to each step in the boxes below.

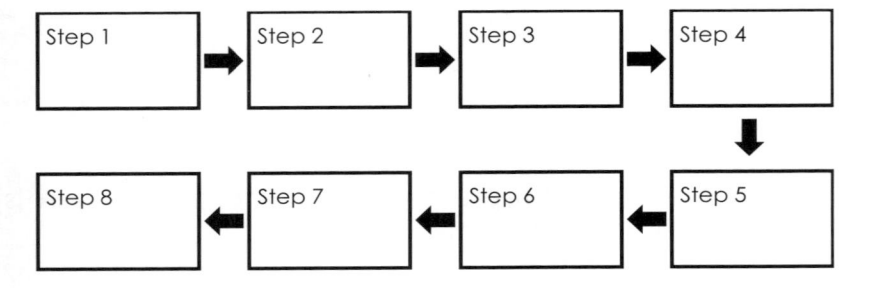

   Step 1 → Step 2 → Step 3 → Step 4

   Step 8 ← Step 7 ← Step 6 ← Step 5

Algebra Wall

Want some help? You can always ask questions on the Algebra Wall and receive help from other students, teachers, and Study Experts. You can also help others on the Algebra Wall and earn Karma Points for doing so. Go to AlgebraNation.com to learn more and get started!

Section 5 – Topic 8
Deriving the Quadratic Formula

We can use the process of completing the square to derive a formula to find the zero(s) of any quadratic equation.

Consider the quadratic equation, $f(x) = ax^2 + bx + c$, where $a \neq 0$. Recall our steps for completing the square as a method for solving $f(x) = 0$.

Step 1: Group ax^2 and bx together.

Step 2: If $a \neq 1$, then factor out a.

Step 3: Divide $\frac{b}{a}$ by two and square the result. Add that number to the grouped terms. Subtract the product of that number and a from c so that you have not changed the equation.

Step 4: Factor the trinomial.

Step 5: Solve the equation for $f(x) = 0$.

BEAT THE TEST!

1. Complete the missing steps in the derivation of the quadratic formula:

   $f(x) = ax^2 + bx + c$

   $$$$

   $f(x) = a\left(x^2 + \dfrac{b}{a}x + \dfrac{b^2}{4a^2}\right) + c - \dfrac{b^2}{4a}$

   $f(x) = a\left(x + \dfrac{b}{2a}\right)^2 + \dfrac{4ac - b^2}{4a}$

   $a\left(x + \dfrac{b}{2a}\right)^2 + \dfrac{4ac - b^2}{4a} = 0$

   $\left(x + \dfrac{b}{2a}\right)^2 = \dfrac{b^2 - 4ac}{4a^2}$

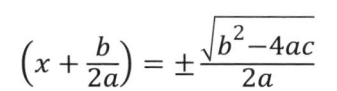

   $$$$

   $\left(x + \dfrac{b}{2a}\right) = \pm \dfrac{\sqrt{b^2 - 4ac}}{2a}$

   $$$$

Algebra Wall — Want some help? You can always ask questions on the Algebra Wall and receive help from other students, teachers, and Study Experts. You can also help others on the Algebra Wall and earn Karma Points for doing so. Go to AlgebraNation.com to learn more and get started!

Section 5 – Topic 9
Solving Quadratic Equations Using the Quadratic Formula

For any quadratic equation $ax^2 + bx + c = 0$, where $a \neq 0$,

$$x = \frac{-b \pm \sqrt{b^2 - 4ac}}{2a}$$

To use the quadratic formula:

Step 1: Set the quadratic equation equal to zero.

Step 2: Identify a, b, and c.

Step 3: Substitute a, b, and c into the quadratic formula and evaluate to find the zeros.

Let's Practice!

1. Use the quadratic formula to solve $x^2 - 4x + 3 = 0$.

2. Consider the graph of the quadratic equation $y = x^2 - 4x + 3$.

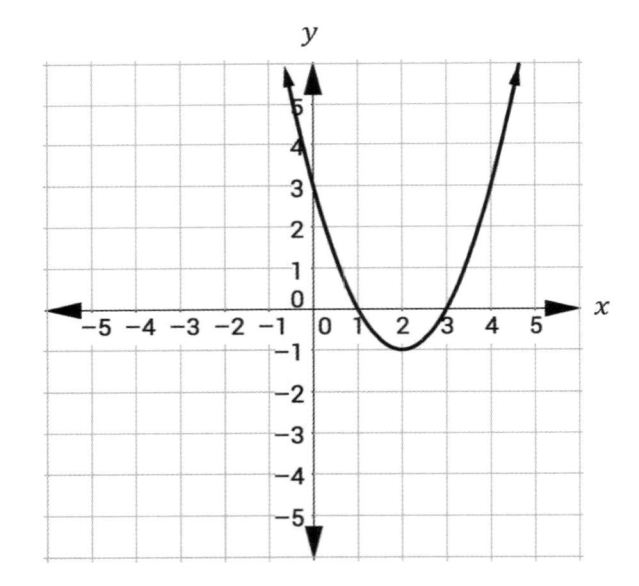

Does the graph verify the solutions we found using the quadratic formula?

3. Use the quadratic formula to solve $2w^2 + w = 5$.

Try It!

4. Use the quadratic formula to solve $3q^2 - 11 = 20q$.

BEAT THE TEST!

1. Your neighbor's garden measures 12 meters by 16 meters. He plans to install a pedestrian pathway all around it, increasing the total area to 285 square meters. The new area can be represented by $4w^2 + 56w + 192$. Use the quadratic formula to find the width, w, of the pathway.

   Part A: Write an equation that can be used to solve for the width of the pathway.

   Part B: Use the quadratic formula to solve for the width of the pathway.

Algebra Wall

Want some help? You can always ask questions on the Algebra Wall and receive help from other students, teachers, and Study Experts. You can also help others on the Algebra Wall and earn Karma Points for doing so. Go to AlgebraNation.com to learn more and get started!

Section 5 – Topic 10
Quadratic Functions in Action

Let's consider solving real-world situations that involve quadratic functions.

Consider an object being launched into the air. We compare the height versus time elapsed.

Object's Height Over Time

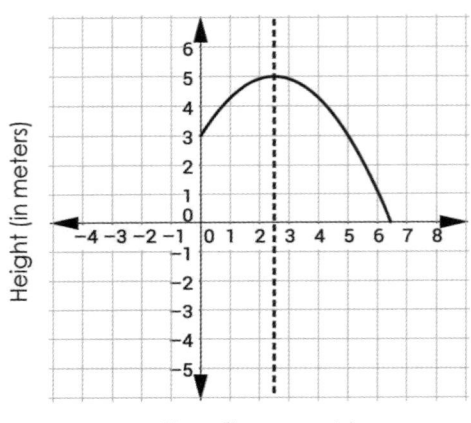

From what height is the object launched?

Once the object is launched, how long does it take to reach its maximum height?

What is the maximum height?

Once the object is launched, how long does it take for it to hit the ground?

Once the object is launched, when does it return to a height of three meters?

	Question	How to Answer it
1.	From what height is the object launched?	This is the y-intercept. In the standard form, $ax^2 + bx + c$, c is the y-intercept.
2.	How long does it take for the object to reach its maximum height?	This is the x-coordinate of the vertex, $x = \frac{-b}{2a}$, where values of a and b come from the standard form of a quadratic equation. $x = \frac{-b}{2a}$ is also the equation that represents the axis of symmetry.
3.	What is the maximum height?	This is the y-coordinate of the vertex. Substitute the x-coordinate from the step above and evaluate to find y. In vertex form, the height is k and the vertex is (h, k).
4.	How long does it take for the object to hit the ground?	The x-intercept(s) are the solution(s), or zero(s), of the quadratic function. Solve by factoring, using the quadratic formula, or by completing the square. In a graph, look at the x-intercept(s).
5.	When does the object return to a height of three meters?	In function $H(t) = at^2 + bt + c$, if height is given, then substitute the value for $H(t)$. If time is given, then substitute for t.

Section 5: Quadratic Functions - Part 1

Let's Practice!

1. Ferdinand is playing golf. He hits a shot off the tee box that has a height modeled by the function $h(t) = -16t^2 + 80t$, where $h(t)$ is the height of the ball, in feet, and t is the time in seconds it has been in the air. The graph that models the golf ball's height over time is shown below.

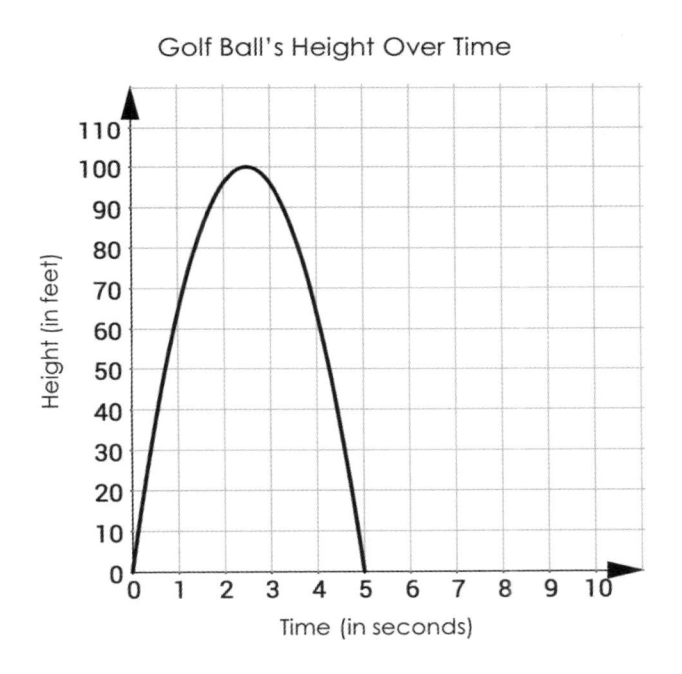

   Golf Ball's Height Over Time

   a. When does the ball reach its maximum height?

   b. What is the maximum height of the ball?

   c. What is the height of the ball at 3 seconds? When is the ball at the same height?

Try It!

2. Recall exercise 1.

   a. When is the ball 65 feet in the air? Explain.

   b. How long does it take until the ball hits the ground?

Section 5: Quadratic Functions - Part 1

BEAT THE TEST!

1. A neighborhood threw a fireworks celebration for the 4th of July. A bottle rocket was launched upward from the ground with an initial velocity of 160 feet per second. The formula for vertical motion of an object is $h(t) = 0.5at^2 + vt + s$, where the gravitational constant, a, is −32 feet per square second, v is the initial velocity, s is the initial height, and $h(t)$ is the height in feet modeled as a function of time, t.

    Part A: What function describes the height, h, of the bottle rocket after t seconds have elapsed?

    Part B: What was the maximum height of the bottle rocket?

Great job! You have reached the end of this section. Now it's time to try the "Test Yourself! Practice Tool," where you can practice all the skills and concepts you learned in this section. Log in to Algebra Nation and try out the "Test Yourself! Practice Tool" so you can see how well you know these topics!

Section 6: Quadratic Functions – Part 2

Topic 1: Observations from a Graph of a Quadratic Function... 153
Standards Covered: F-IF.4
    ☐ I can use the vertex form of a quadratic function and can create equations from the graph of a function.

Topic 2: Nature of the Solutions of Quadratic Equations and Functions 156
Standards Covered: A-REI.4.b, N-CN.7
    ☐ I can use the discriminant to determine the nature of the zeros of a quadratic equation.

Topic 3: Graphing Quadratic Functions Using a Table.. 159
Standards Covered: F-IF.7.a, F-IF.8.a
    ☐ I can graph quadratic functions using a table of values.

Topic 4: Graphing Quadratic Functions Using the Vertex and Intercepts.. 162
Standards Covered: F-IF.7.a, F-IF.8.a
    ☐ I can find the vertex and the intercepts and use the axis of symmetry to graph quadratic functions.

Topic 5: Graphing Quadratic Functions Using Vertex Form - Part 1... 165
Standards Covered: F-IF.7.a, A-SSE.1.a
    ☐ I can rewrite a quadratic function in vertex form.
    ☐ I can graph quadratic functions using vertex form.

Topic 6: Graphing Quadratic Functions Using Vertex Form - Part 2... 167
Standards Covered: F-IF.7.a, F-IF.9
    ☐ I can rewrite a quadratic function in vertex form.
    ☐ I can graph quadratic functions using vertex form.

Topic 7: Transformations of the Dependent Variable of Quadratic Functions 170
Standards Covered: F-BF.3
    ☐ I can apply vertical shifts, reflections, stretching, and compressing to a quadratic function.

Topic 8: Transformations of the Independent Variable of Quadratic Functions 172
Standards Covered: F-BF.3
    ☐ I can apply horizontal shifts, stretching, and compressing to a quadratic function.

Topic 9: Finding Solution Sets to Systems of Equations Using Tables of Values and Successive Approximations 175
Standards Covered: A-REI.11
    ☐ I can use a graph to find the solution to a system of linear and quadratic equations.
    ☐ I can use a table to find the solution to a system of linear and quadratic equations.

Visit MathNation.com or search "Math Nation" in your phone or tablet's app store to watch the videos that go along with this workbook!

Observations from a Graph of a Quadratic Function

Let's review some things we learned earlier about the information we can gather from the graph of a quadratic.

Vertex: $(1, -1)$

Axis of symmetry: $x = 1$

x-intercept(s): $(0, 0)$ and $($? $)$

y-intercept: $(0,$? $)$

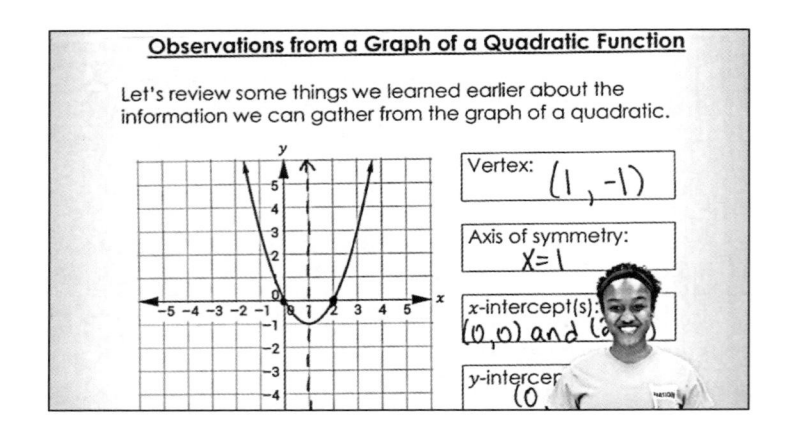

The following Michigan Mathematics Standards will be covered in this section:
F-IF.4 - For a function that models a relationship between two quantities, interpret key features of graphs and tables in terms of the quantities, and sketch graphs showing key features given a verbal description of the relationship. Key features include: intercepts; intervals where the function is increasing, decreasing, positive, or negative; relative maximums and minimums; symmetries; end behavior; and periodicity.
A-REI.4.b - Solve quadratic equations in one variable. b. Solve quadratic equations by inspection, taking square roots, completing the square, the quadratic formula and factoring, as appropriate to the initial form of the equation. Recognize when the quadratic formula gives complex solutions and write them as $a \pm bi$ for real numbers a and b.
N-CN.7 - Solve quadratic equations with real coefficients that have complex solutions.
F-IF.7.a - Graph functions expressed symbolically and show key features of the graph, by hand in simple cases and using technology in more complicated cases. a. Graph linear and quadratic functions and show intercepts, maxima, and minima.
F-IF.8.a - Write a function defined by an expression in different but equivalent forms to reveal and explain different properties of the function. a. Use the process of factoring and completing the square in a quadratic function to show zeros, extreme values, and symmetry of the graph, and interpret these in terms of a context.
A-SSE.1.a - Interpret expressions that represent a quantity in terms of its context. a. Interpret parts of an expression, such as terms, factors, and coefficients.
F-IF.9 - Compare properties of two functions each represented in a different way (algebraically, graphically, numerically in tables, or by verbal descriptions).
F-BF.3 - Identify the effect on the graph of replacing $f(x)$ by $f(x) + k$, $kf(x)$, $f(kx)$, and $f(x + k)$ for specific values of k (both positive and negative); find the value of k given the graphs. Experiment with cases and illustrate an explanation of the effects on the graph using technology. Include recognizing even and odd functions from their graphs and algebraic expressions for them.
A-REI.11 - Explain why the x-coordinates of the points where the graphs of the equations and intersect are the solutions of the equation; find the solutions approximately (e.g., using technology to graph the functions, make tables of values, or find successive approximations). Include cases were and/or are linear, polynomial, rational, absolute value, exponential, and logarithmic functions.

Section 6: Quadratic Functions – Part 2
Section 6 – Topic 1
Observations from a Graph of a Quadratic Function

Let's review some things we learned earlier about the information we can gather from the graph of a quadratic function.

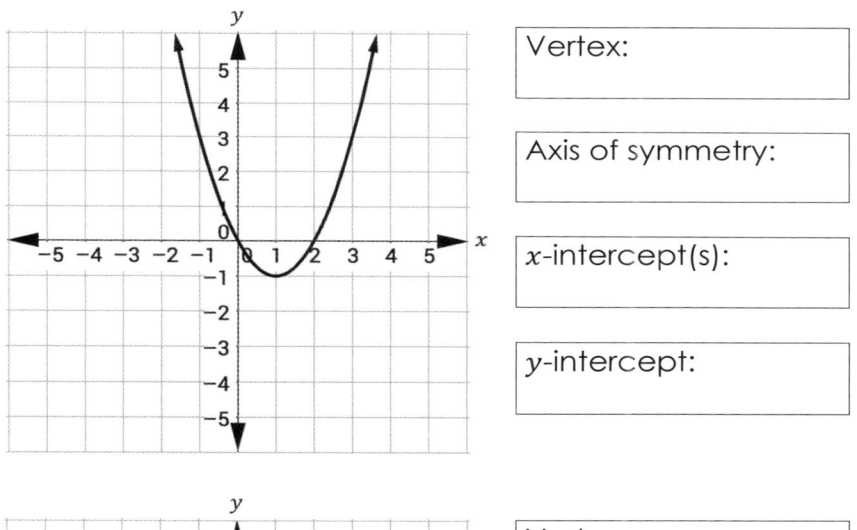

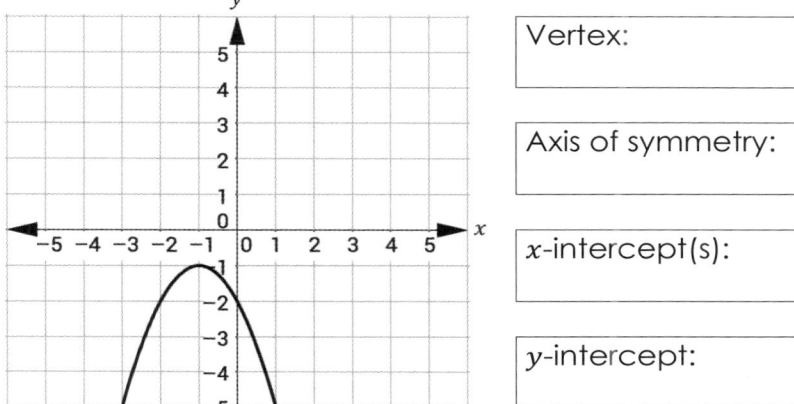

Vertex:

Axis of symmetry:

x-intercept(s):

y-intercept:

Vertex:

Axis of symmetry:

x-intercept(s):

y-intercept:

Let's Practice!

1. The graph shows the height of a rocket from the time it was launched from the ground. Use the graph to answer the questions below.

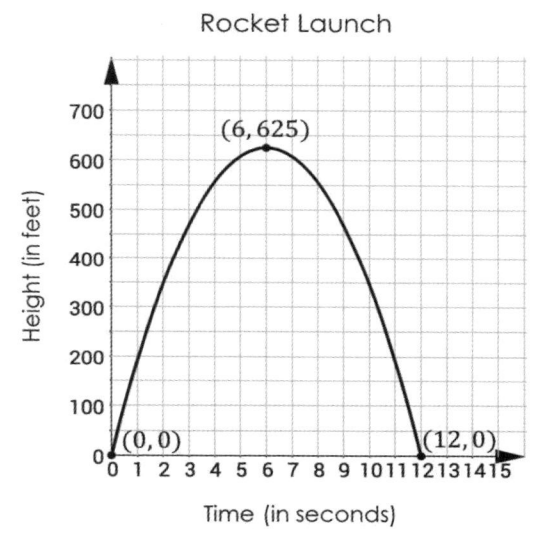

   Rocket Launch

   Vertex at (6, 625); x-intercepts at (0, 0) and (12, 0).
   Height (in feet) vs Time (in seconds)

   a. What is the y-intercept?

   b. What does the y-intercept represent?

153

Section 6: Quadratic Functions - Part 2

c. What are the x-intercepts?

d. What do the x-intercepts represent?

e. What is the maximum height of the rocket?

f. When will the rocket reach its maximum height?

g. When is the graph increasing?

h. When is the graph decreasing?

i. What is the domain of the graph?

j. What is the range of the graph?

We can also use the graph to write the equation of the quadratic function.

Recall the standard form of a quadratic equation.

$$f(x) = ax^2 + bx + c$$

There is another form of the quadratic equation called **vertex form**.

Vertex Form: $f(x) = a(x - h)^2 + k$

- (h, k) is the vertex of the graph.
- a determines if the graph opens up or down.
- a also determines if the parabola is vertically compressed or stretched.

To write an equation in vertex form from a graph, follow these steps:

Step 1: Substitute the vertex, (h, k), and the coordinates of another point on the graph, $(x, f(x))$, into $f(x) = a(x - h)^2 + k$.

Step 2: Solve for a.

Step 3: Substitute (h, k) and a into vertex form.

2. Recall our graph from exercise 1.

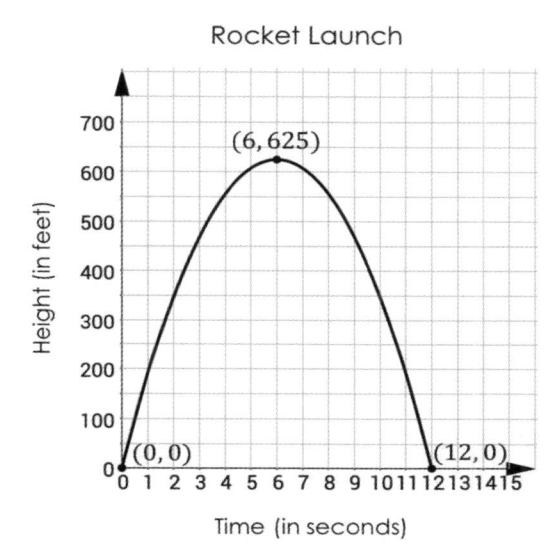

Rocket Launch

Vertex: (6, 625); points (0, 0) and (12, 0) on the graph. Time (in seconds) on the x-axis, Height (in feet) on the y-axis.

a. Substitute the vertex, (h, k), and the coordinates of another point on the graph, $(x, f(x))$, into $f(x) = a(x - h)^2 + k$ and solve for a.

b. Write the function for the graph in vertex form.

Try It!

3. Consider the graph below.

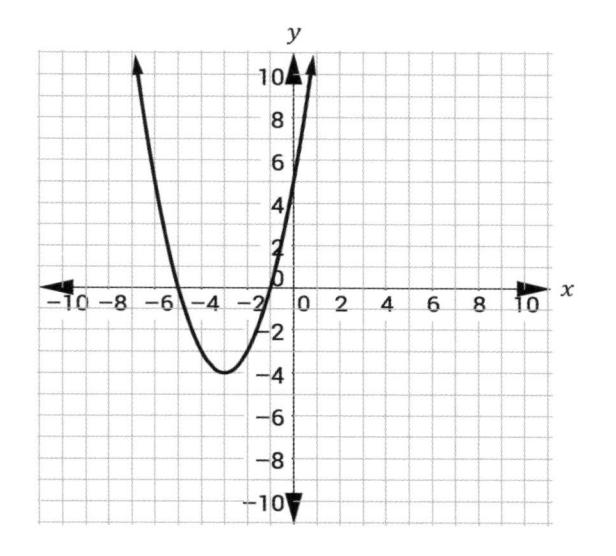

a. State five observations about the graph.

b. Write the equation of the graph.

Section 6: Quadratic Functions - Part 2

BEAT THE TEST!

1. The graph of a quadratic function is shown below.

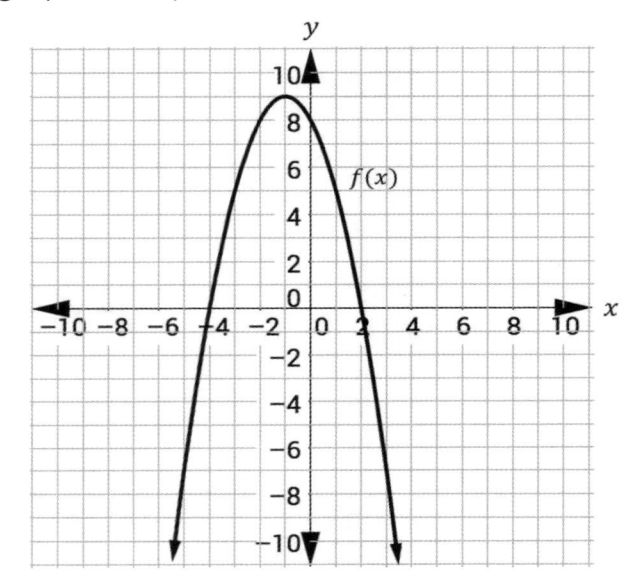

   Which statements about this graph are true? Select all that apply.

   ☐ The graph has a y-intercept at $(0, 8)$.
   ☐ The graph has a maximum point at $(-1, 9)$.
   ☐ The graph has an x-intercept at $(2, 0)$.
   ☐ The graph's line of symmetry is the y-axis.
   ☐ The graph has zeros of -4 and 2.
   ☐ The graph represents the function $f(x) = -(x - 1)^2 + 9$.

Section 6 – Topic 2
Nature of the Zeros of Quadratic Equations and Functions

Let's use the quadratic formula to discuss the nature of the zero(s) of a quadratic function.

Consider the graph of the function $f(x) = x^2 - 4x + 4$.

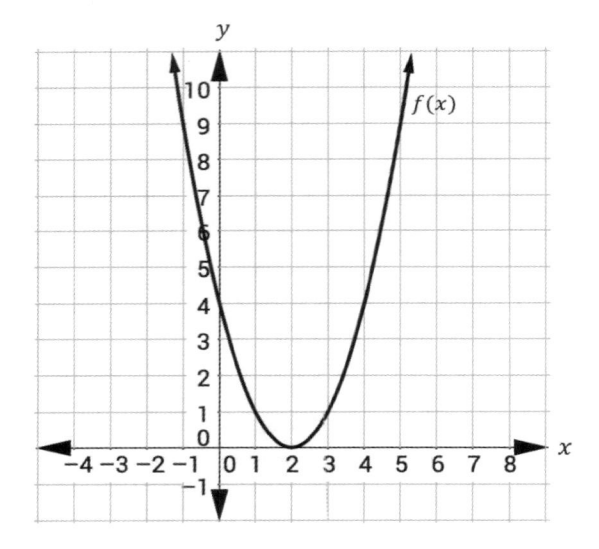

Where does the parabola intersect the x-axis?

Use the quadratic formula to find the zero(s) of the function.

Consider the graph of the function $f(x) = x^2 + 6x + 8$.

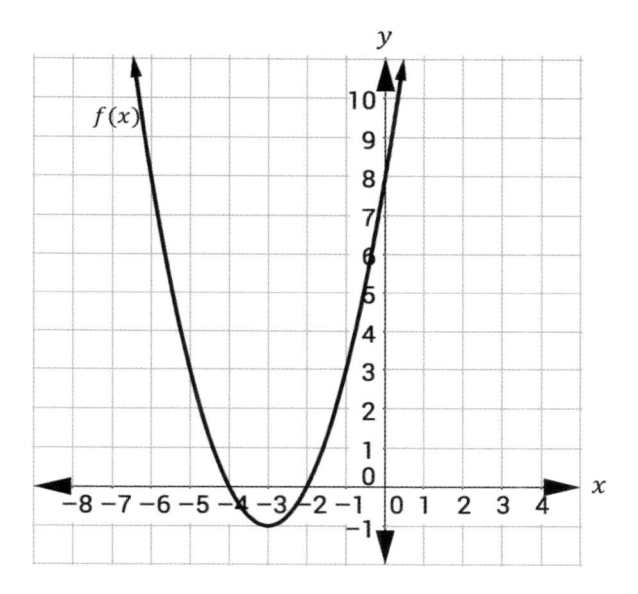

Where does the parabola intersect the x-axis?

Use the quadratic formula to find the zero(s) of the function.

Consider the graph of the function $f(x) = -x^2 + 6x - 11$.

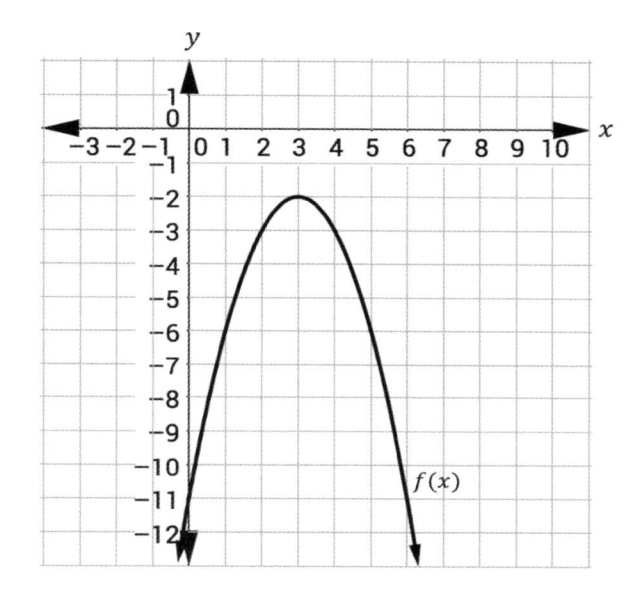

Where does the parabola intersect the x-axis?

Use the quadratic formula to find the zero(s) of the function.

Section 6: Quadratic Functions - Part 2

> **STUDY EDGE TIP:** When using the quadratic formula, if the discriminant of the quadratic function (the part under the radical) is a negative number, then the zeros are non-real, complex solutions.

Let's Practice!

1. Use the discriminant to determine if the following quadratic equations have complex or real zero(s).

   a. $2x^2 - 3x - 10 = 0$

   b. $x^2 - 6x + 9 = 0$

   c. $g(x) = x^2 - 8x + 20$

Try It!

2. Create a quadratic equation that has complex zeros. Justify your answer.

3. Create a quadratic equation that has one real zero. Justify your answer.

BEAT THE TEST!

1. Which of the following quadratic equations have real zeros? Select all that apply.

   ☐ $f(x) = -3x^2 + 5x - 11$
   ☐ $f(x) = -x^2 - 12x + 6$
   ☐ $f(x) = 2x^2 + x + 6$
   ☐ $f(x) = 5x^2 - 10x - 3$
   ☐ $f(x) = x^2 - 2x + 8$

Section 6 – Topic 3
Graphing Quadratic Functions Using a Table

Suppose you jump into a deep pool of water from a diving platform that is 25 feet above the ground. Your height with respect to time can be modeled by the function $H(t) = 25 - 16t^2$, where t is time in seconds.

Complete the table below.

Time (seconds)	0	0.25	0.5	0.75	1	1.25
Elevation (feet)						

Graph function $H(t)$ on the following coordinate grid.

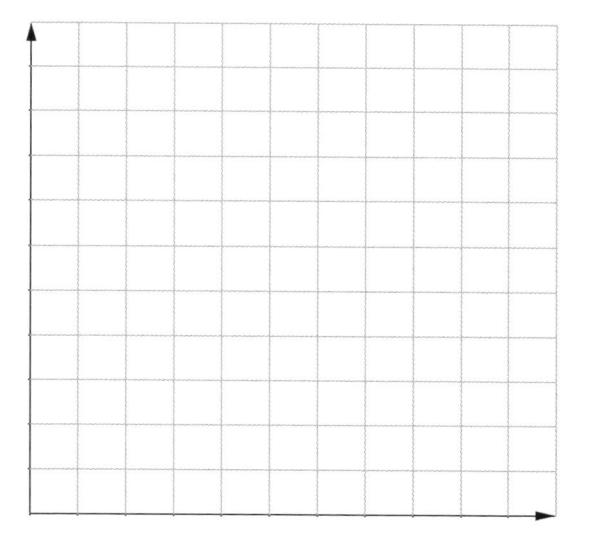

Want some help? You can always ask questions on the Algebra Wall and receive help from other students, teachers, and Study Experts. You can also help others on the Algebra Wall and earn Karma Points for doing so. Go to AlgebraNation.com to learn more and get started!

Section 6: Quadratic Functions - Part 2

Let's Practice!

1. A construction company builds houses on square-shaped lots of various sizes. The CEO of the company decided to diversify her lots and now has houses built on rectangular-shaped lots that are 6 feet longer and 4 feet narrower than her square-shaped lots.

   a. What is the function that models the size of the rectangular lots relative to the size of the square lots?

   b. Complete the table below and graph the function.

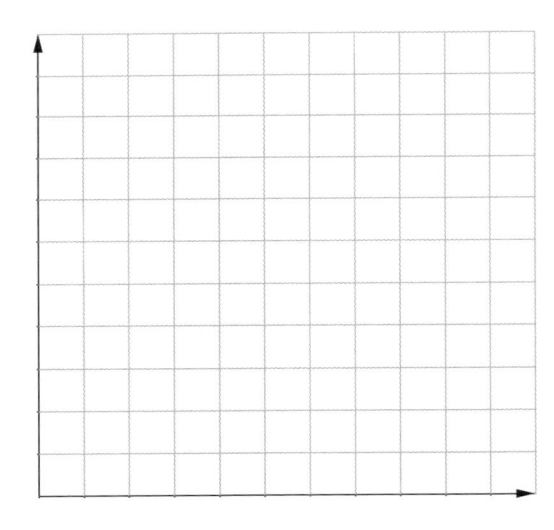

Try It!

2. A business owner recorded the following data for an entire year of sales.

Month	Sales (in thousands of dollars)
Jan	22
Feb	45
Mar	54
April	63
May	70
June	71
July	70
Aug	64
Sept	54
Oct	38
Nov	24
Dec	5

a. Plot the data on the graph below.

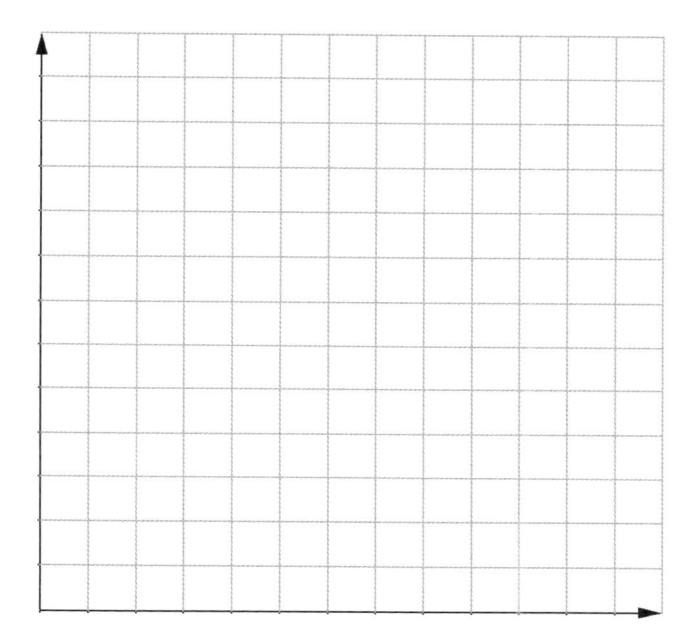

b. What type of business might be represented by this graph?

c. Would the quadratic model be an appropriate way to model data for this business going forward? Justify your answer.

BEAT THE TEST!

1. Consider the following table of values.

x	−5	−4	−3	−1	2	4
$f(x)$	−16	−6	0	0	−30	−70

   Which of the following graphs corresponds to the table of values?

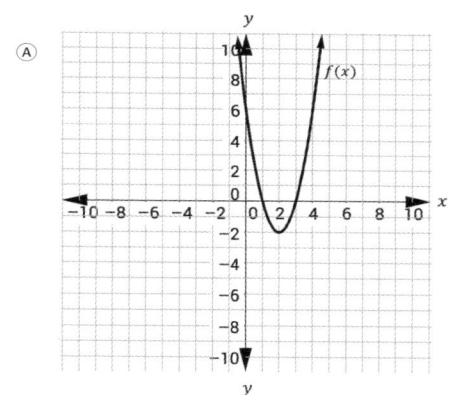

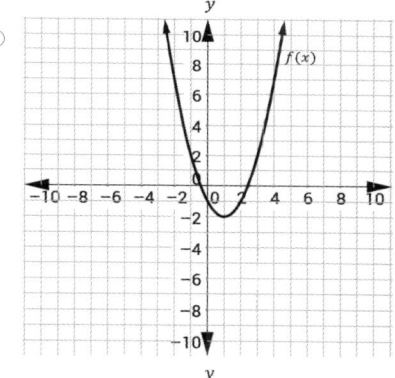

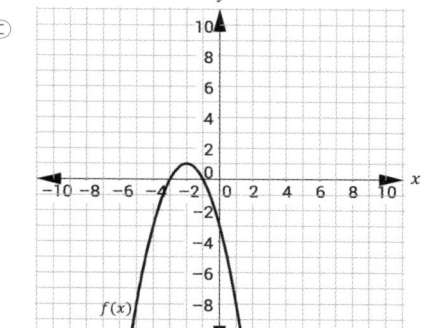

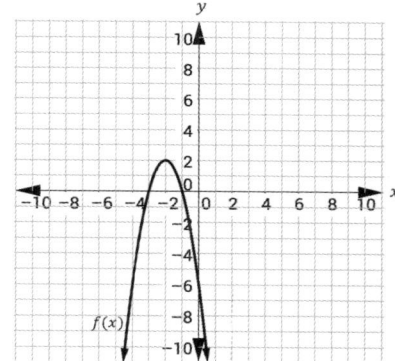

   Ⓐ   Ⓑ

   Ⓒ   Ⓓ

   > Want some help? You can always ask questions on the Algebra Wall and receive help from other students, teachers, and Study Experts. You can also help others on the Algebra Wall and earn Karma Points for doing so. Go to AlgebraNation.com to learn more and get started!
   >
   > Algebra Wall

Section 6: Quadratic Functions - Part 2

Section 6 – Topic 4
Graphing Quadratic Functions Using the Vertex and Intercepts

Given a quadratic equation in standard form, $f(x) = x^2 - 4x - 12$, use the following steps to graph $f(x)$ on the coordinate plane on the following page.

Step 1: Use the a-value to determine if the graph should open upward (positive a) or downward (negative a).

Step 2: Find and graph the axis of symmetry using the formula $x = -\frac{b}{2a}$. This is also the h-coordinate of the vertex.

Step 3: Find $f(h)$, the k-coordinate of the vertex, by substituting h into the equation. Plot the vertex, (h, k), on the graph.

Step 4: Find and plot the y-intercept, which is the constant c in $f(x) = ax^2 + bx + c$. If possible, use the axis of symmetry to find a reflection point.

Step 5: Find and plot the x-intercepts of the function. Factoring is one option, but you can always use the quadratic formula.

Graph of $f(x) = x^2 - 4x - 12$

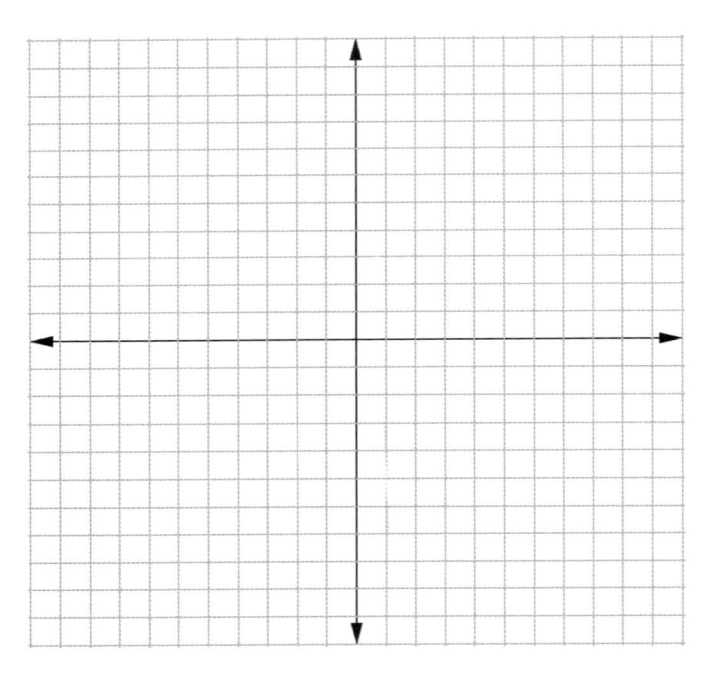

Section 6: Quadratic Functions - Part 2

Let's Practice!

1. Given the function $f(x) = -x^2 + 4x + 21$, use the following steps to graph $f(x)$ on the coordinate plane on the following page.

   a. Use the a-value to determine if the graph should open upward (positive a) or downward (negative a).

   b. Find and graph the axis of symmetry using the formula $x = \dfrac{-b}{2a}$. This is also the h-coordinate of the vertex.

   c. Find $f(h)$, the k-coordinate of the vertex, by substituting h into the equation. Plot the vertex, (h, k), on the graph.

   d. Find and plot the y-intercept, which is the constant c in $f(x) = ax^2 + bx + c$. If possible, use the axis of symmetry to find a reflection point.

   e. Find and plot the x-intercepts of the function. Factoring is one option, but you can always use the quadratic formula.

Graph of $f(x) = -x^2 + 4x + 21$

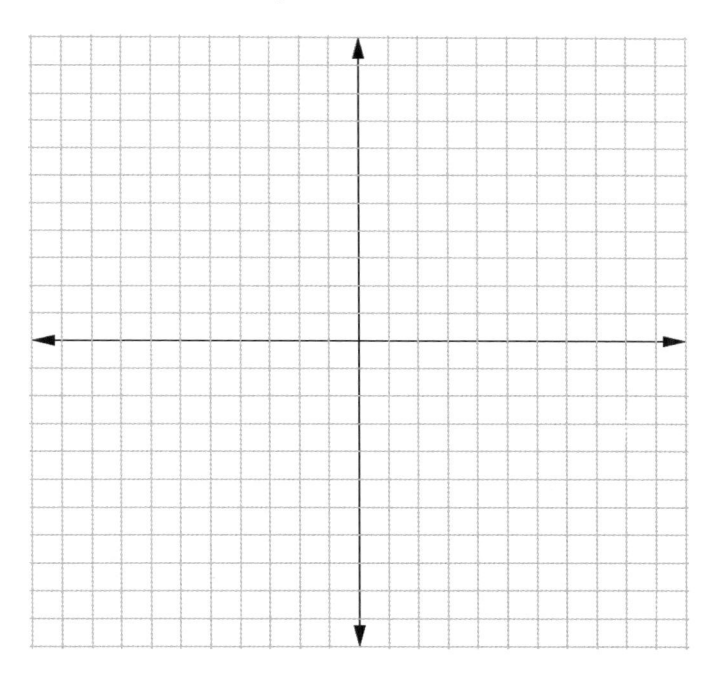

Section 6: Quadratic Functions - Part 2

Try It!

2. Jorah starts at the top of SlotZilla Zip Line in Las Vegas and rides down Fremont Street. The equation $h(t) = -2.3t^2 + 114$ models Jorah's height, in feet, above the ground over time, t seconds, while he rides the zip line.

   a. What is the vertex of the function $h(t)$?

   b. When will Jorah reach the ground?

   c. Sketch the graph that models Jorah's height over the time spent riding the zip line.

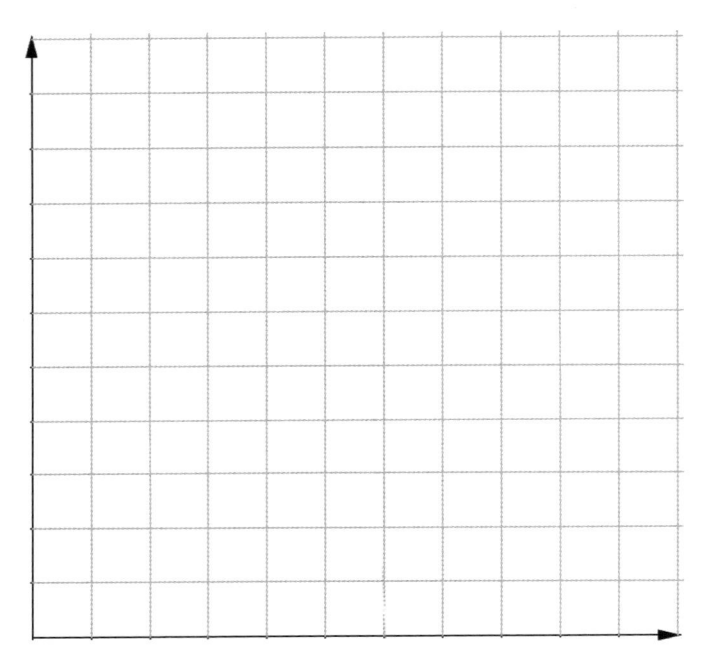

Section 6: Quadratic Functions - Part 2

BEAT THE TEST!

1. On a test, Mia graphed the quadratic function $f(x) = x^2 - 10x - 24$. The problem was marked as incorrect. Identify Mia's mistake.

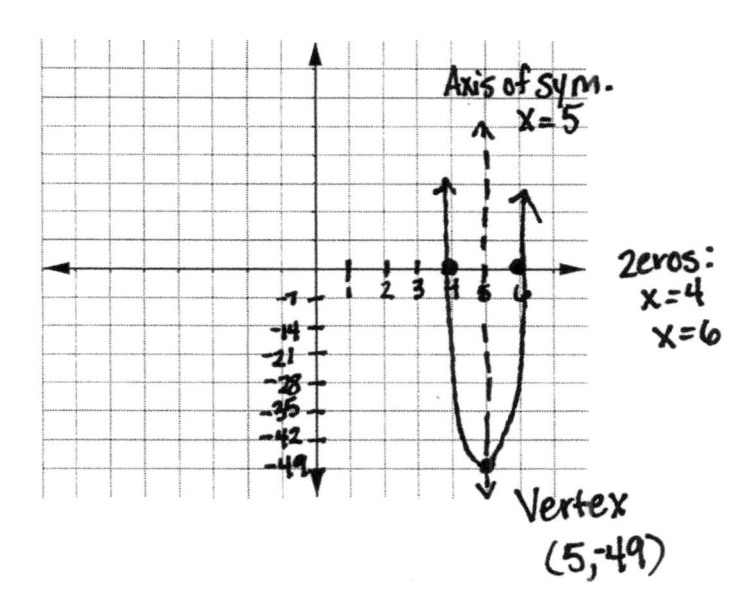

[Student's graph showing:
- *Axis of sym. x = 5*
- *Zeros: x = 4, x = 6*
- *Vertex (5, -49)]*

> Want some help? You can always ask questions on the Algebra Wall and receive help from other students, teachers, and Study Experts. You can also help others on the Algebra Wall and earn Karma Points for doing so. Go to AlgebraNation.com to learn more and get started!

Section 6 – Topic 5
Graphing Quadratic Functions Using Vertex Form – Part 1

Let's review vertex form.

Vertex Form: $f(x) = a(x - h)^2 + k$

> Point (h, k) is the vertex of the graph.

> Coefficient a determines if the graph opens up or down.

> Coefficient a also determines if the parabola is vertically stretched or compressed when compared to $f(x) = x^2$.

For example, function $s(t) = -16\left(t - \frac{3}{2}\right)^2 + 136$, where t is time in seconds, models the height of a ball (in feet) that is launched from a balcony of a residential building.

Determine and explain whether the graph of the function opens upward or downward.

Determine and interpret the coordinates for the vertex of the function.

Is the function vertically stretched or compressed in comparison to $s(t) = t^2$?

Section 6: Quadratic Functions - Part 2

Let's Practice!

1. Given the function $f(x) = (x-3)^2 + 4$, use the following steps to graph $f(x)$ on the coordinate plane on the following page.

    a. Use the a-value to determine if the graph should open upward (positive a) or downward (negative a).

    b. Find and graph the vertex, (h, k), and axis of symmetry, $x = h$.

    c. Find the y-intercept by substituting zero for x. Plot the y-intercept. If possible, use the axis of symmetry to plot a reflection point.

    d. Find the x-intercepts, or zeros, by substituting zero for $f(x)$ and solving for x using square roots. Plot the x-intercepts.

    e. Use the key features to sketch the graph.

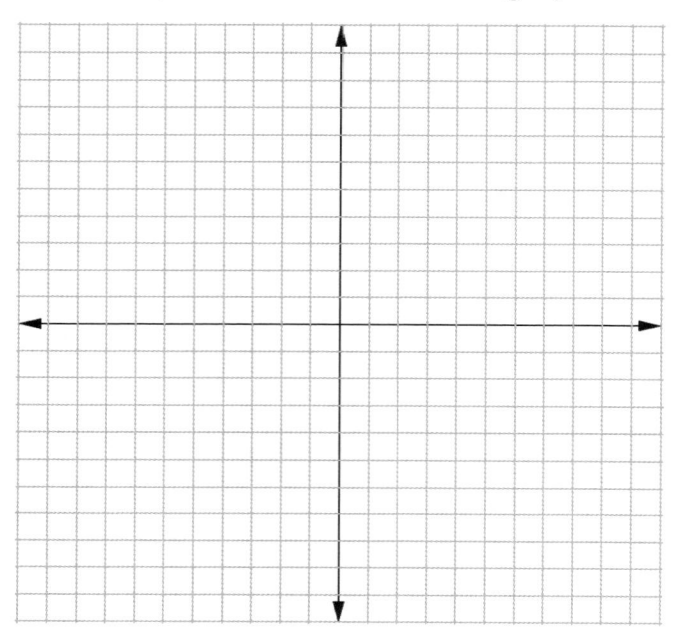

Try It!

2. The yearly profit made by a food truck selling tacos is represented by the following function, where x represents the number of tacos sold and $f(x)$ represents the profit.

$$f(x) = -\frac{1}{15750}(x - 28350)^2 + 44905$$

   a. The profit function was written in vertex form, $f(x) = a(x-h)^2 + k$. Examine the values of $a, h,$ and k in the profit function above and interpret their meaning(s).

b. Graph the profit function on the coordinate plane below.

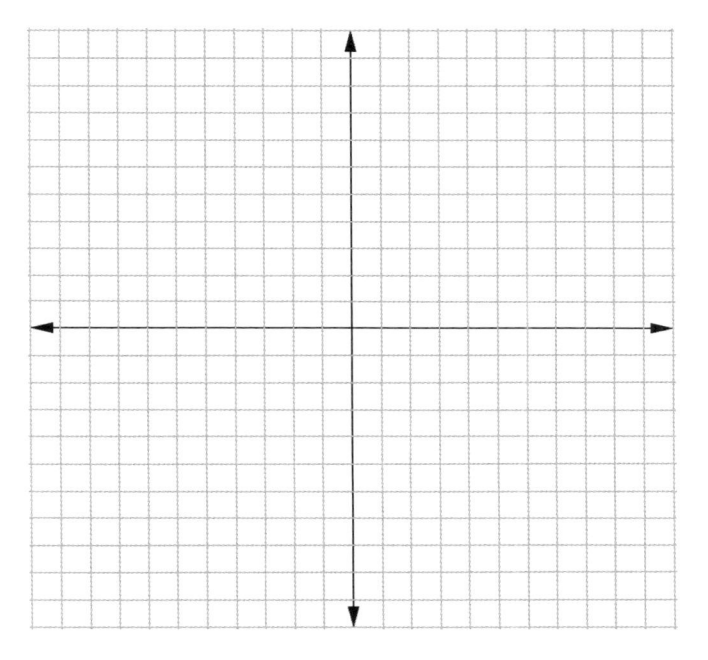

Section 6 – Topic 6
Graphing Quadratic Functions Using Vertex Form – Part 2

Oftentimes, quadratic equations are not written in vertex form. We can always use the process of completing the square to rewrite quadratic equations in vertex form.

Let's Practice!

1. Write the function, $f(x) = x^2 - 4x - 2$, in vertex form. Then, graph the function.

   a. Write the function in standard form.

   b. Group the quadratic and linear terms together.

   c. If a does not equal one, factor a out of the equation.

   d. Complete the square.

   e. Write the function in vertex form.

   f. Find the zeros, the maximum or minimum point, and the y-intercept.

Want some help? You can always ask questions on the Algebra Wall and receive help from other students, teachers, and Study Experts. You can also help others on the Algebra Wall and earn Karma Points for doing so. Go to AlgebraNation.com to learn more and get started!

g. Graph the quadratic, $f(x) = x^2 - 4x - 2$, on the coordinate plane below.

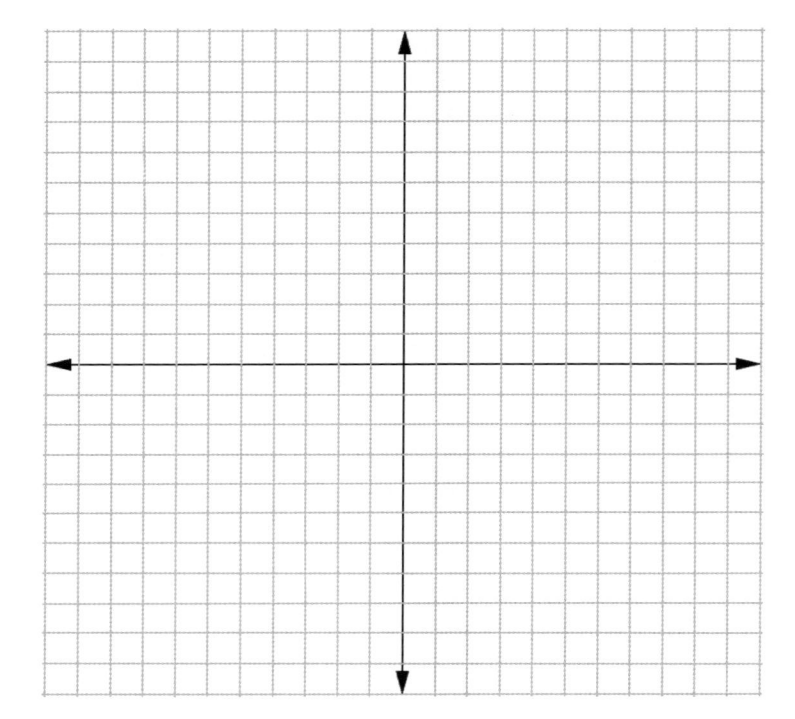

Try It!

2. Write the function, $g(x) = 2x^2 - 12x + 17$, in vertex form. Then, graph the function.

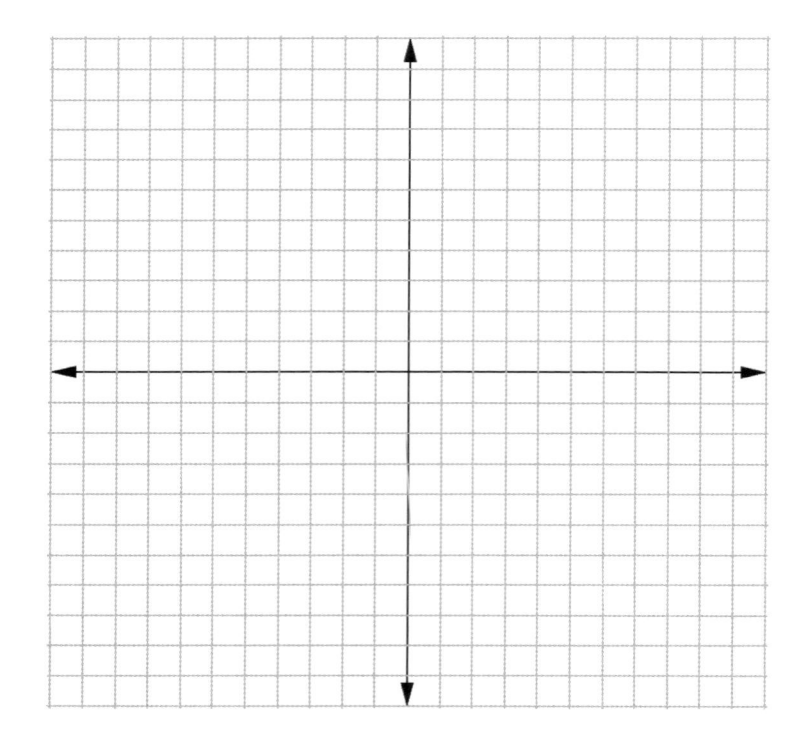

BEAT THE TEST!

1. The graph of $g(x)$ is shown below.

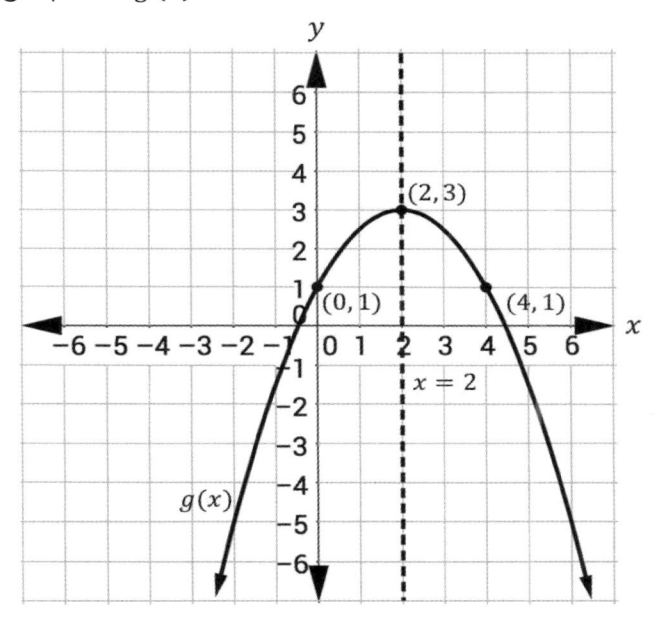

   Which function has a maximum that is greater than the maximum of the graph of $g(x)$?

   Ⓐ $y = (x - 2)^2 + 4$

   Ⓑ $y = (x + 3)^2 + 2$

   Ⓒ $y = -\frac{1}{2}(x - 2)^2 + 3$

   Ⓓ $y = -5(x + 3)^2 + 4$

2. Emma rewrote a quadratic function in vertex form.

   $$h(x) = 4x^2 + 16x + 5$$

   Step 1: $h(x) = 4(x^2 + 4x + \underline{}) + 5 + \underline{}$
   Step 2: $h(x) = 4(x^2 + 4x + 4) + 5 - 4$
   Step 3: $h(x) = 4(x + 2)^2 + 1$

   Part A: Emma said that the vertex is $(-2, 1)$. Identify the step where Emma made a mistake, then correct her work.

   Part B: Does the vertex of $h(x)$ represent a maximum or a minimum? Justify your answer.

Section 6: Quadratic Functions - Part 2

Section 6 – Topic 7
Transformations of the Dependent Variable of Quadratic Functions

Consider the graph and table for the function $f(x) = x^2$.

x	$f(x)$
-2	4
-1	1
0	0
1	1
2	4

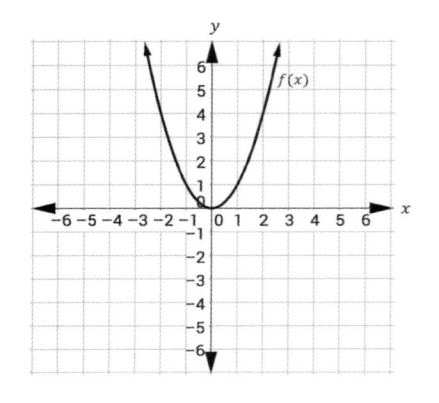

Consider the following transformations on the dependent variable $f(x)$.

$$g(x) = f(x) + 2$$
$$h(x) = f(x) - 2$$
$$m(x) = 2f(x)$$
$$n(x) = \frac{1}{2}f(x)$$
$$p(x) = -f(x)$$

Why do you think these are called transformations on the dependent variable?

Let's Practice!

1. Complete the table to explore what happens when we add a constant to $f(x)$.

x	$f(x)$	$g(x) = f(x) + 2$	$h(x) = f(x) - 2$
-2	4		
-1	1		
0	0		
1	1		
2	4		

2. Sketch the graphs of each function on the same coordinate plane with the graph of $f(x)$.

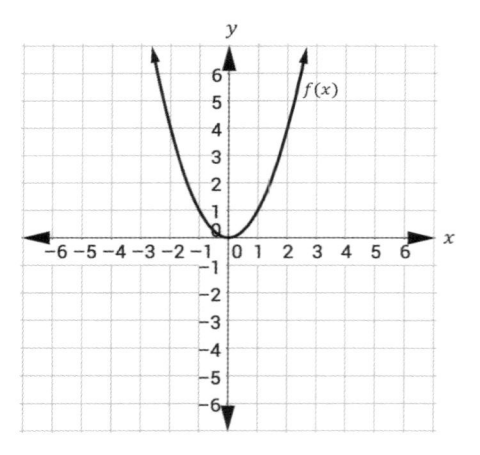

Section 6: Quadratic Functions - Part 2

Try It!

3. Complete the table to determine what happens when we multiply $f(x)$ by a constant.

x	$f(x)$	$m(x) = 2f(x)$	$n(x) = \frac{1}{2}f(x)$	$p(x) = -f(x)$
-2	4			
-1	1			
0	0			
1	1			
2	4			

4. Sketch the graphs of each function on the same coordinate plane with the graph of $f(x)$.

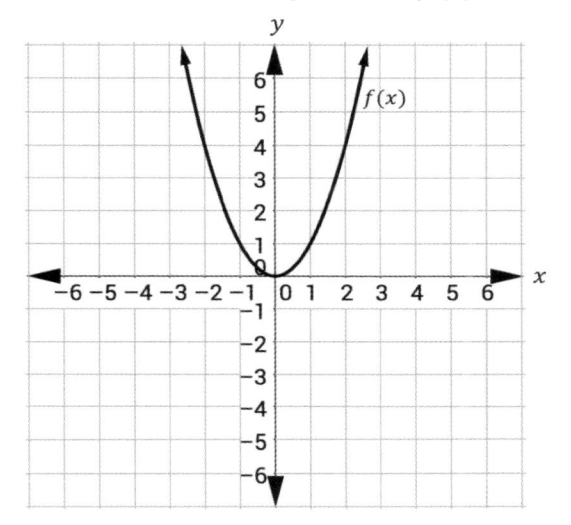

BEAT THE TEST!

1. Given the function $f(x) = x^2 + 3$, identify the effect on the graph of $f(x)$ by replacing $f(x)$ with:

$f(x) + k$, where $k > 0$.	**A.**	Vertically compressed $f(x)$ by a factor of k.
$f(x) + k$, where $k < 0$.	**B.**	Shifted $f(x)$ down k units.
$kf(x)$, where $k > 1$.	**C.**	Reflected $f(x)$ about the x-axis.
$kf(x)$, where $0 < k < 1$.	**D.**	Vertically stretched $f(x)$ by a factor of k.
$kf(x)$, where $k = -1$.	**E.**	Shifted $f(x)$ up k units.

Section 6: Quadratic Functions - Part 2

2. The graph of $g(x)$ is shown below.

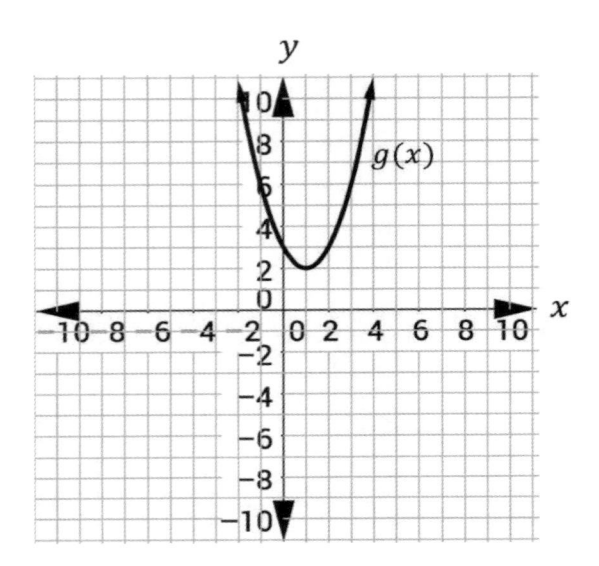

If $f(x) = 3g(x) + 2$, identify three ordered pairs that lie on $f(x)$.

Section 6 – Topic 8
Transformations of the Independent Variable of Quadratic Functions

Consider the graph and table for the function $f(x) = x^2$.

x	$f(x)$
-2	4
-1	1
0	0
1	1
2	4

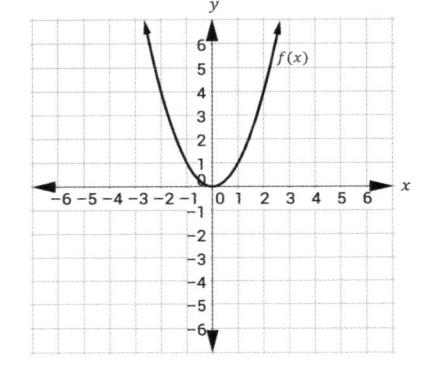

Consider the following transformations on the independent variable x.

$$g(x) = f(x + 2)$$
$$h(x) = f(x - 2)$$
$$m(x) = f(2x)$$
$$n(x) = f\left(\frac{1}{2}x\right)$$

Why do you think these are called transformations on the independent variable?

Want some help? You can always ask questions on the Algebra Wall and receive help from other students, teachers, and Study Experts. You can also help others on the Algebra Wall and earn Karma Points for doing so. Go to AlgebraNation.com to learn more and get started!

Let's Practice!

1. Complete the table to determine what happens when you add a positive constant to x.

x	$f(x)$
-2	4
-1	1
0	0
1	1
2	4

x	$g(x) = f(x+2)$	$g(x)$
-4	$g(-4) = f(-4+2) = f(-2)$	4
-3	$g(-3) = f(-3+2) = f(-1)$	1

2. Sketch the graph of $g(x)$ on the same coordinate plane with the graph of $f(x)$.

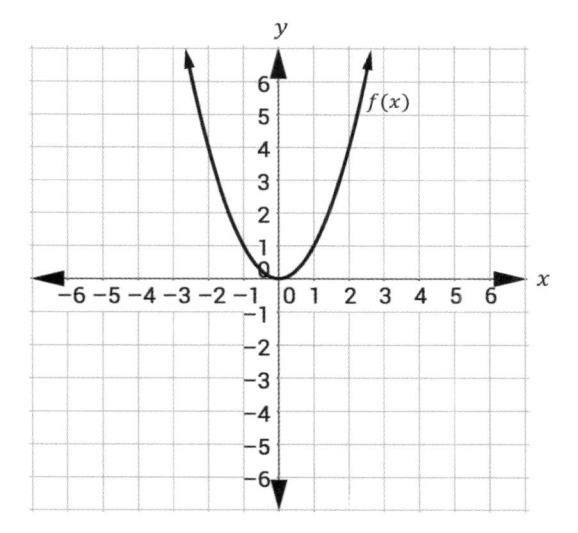

Try It!

3. Complete the table to determine what happens when you add a negative constant to x.

x	$f(x)$
-2	4
-1	1
0	0
1	1
2	4

x	$h(x) = f(x-2)$	$h(x)$
0	$h(0) = f(0-2) = f(-2)$	4
1	$h(1) = f(1-2) = f(-1)$	1

4. Sketch the graph of $h(x)$ on the same coordinate plane with the graph of $f(x)$.

Section 6: Quadratic Functions - Part 2

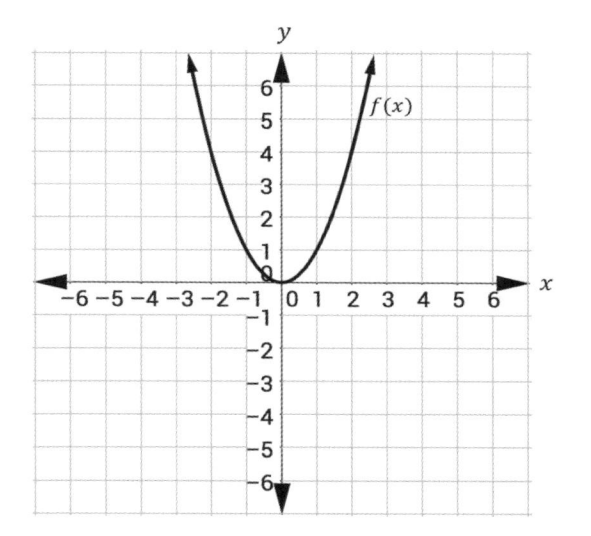

Let's Practice!

5. Complete the table to determine what happens when you multiply x by a number greater than 1.

x	$f(x)$
-2	4
-1	1
0	0
1	1
2	4

x	$m(x) = f(2x)$	$m(x)$
-1	$m(-1) = f(2 \cdot -1) = f(-2)$	4
$-\frac{1}{2}$	$m\left(-\frac{1}{2}\right) = f\left(2 \cdot -\frac{1}{2}\right) = f(-1)$	1

6. Sketch the graph of $m(x)$ on the same coordinate plane with the graph of $f(x)$.

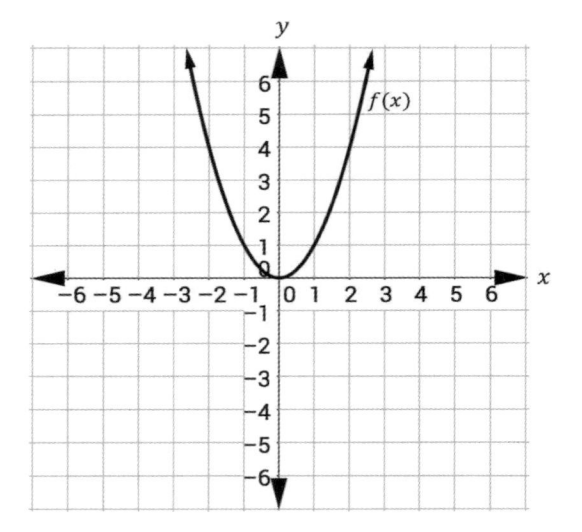

Try It!

7. Complete the table to determine what happens when you multiply x by a constant between 0 and 1.

x	$f(x)$
-2	4
-1	1
0	0
1	1
2	4

x	$n(x) = f\left(\frac{1}{2}x\right)$	$n(x)$
-4	$n(-4) = f\left(\frac{1}{2} \cdot -4\right) = f(-2)$	4
-2	$n(-2) = f\left(\frac{1}{2} \cdot -2\right) = f(-1)$	1

8. Sketch the graph of $n(x)$ on the same coordinate plane with the graph of $f(x)$.

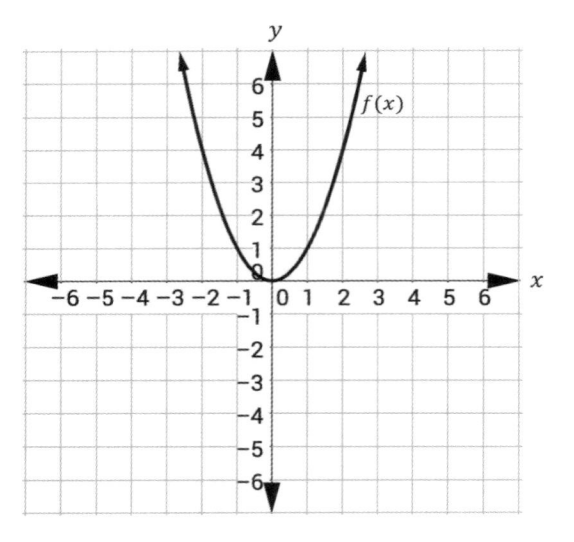

Section 6: Quadratic Functions - Part 2

BEAT THE TEST!

1. The table that represents the quadratic function $g(x)$ is shown below.

x	$g(x)$
−6	12
−4	2
1	12
7	90
11	182

   The function $f(x) = g\left(\frac{1}{3}x\right)$. Complete the following table for $f(x)$.

x	$f(x)$
−18	12
−12	2
3	12
21	90
33	182

Section 6 – Topic 9
Finding Solution Sets to Systems of Equations Using Tables of Values and Successive Approximations

We can find solutions to systems of linear and quadratic equations by looking at a graph or table.

Consider the following system of equations.

$$f(x) = x^2 + 5x + 6$$
$$g(x) = 2x + 6$$

The graph of the system is shown below.

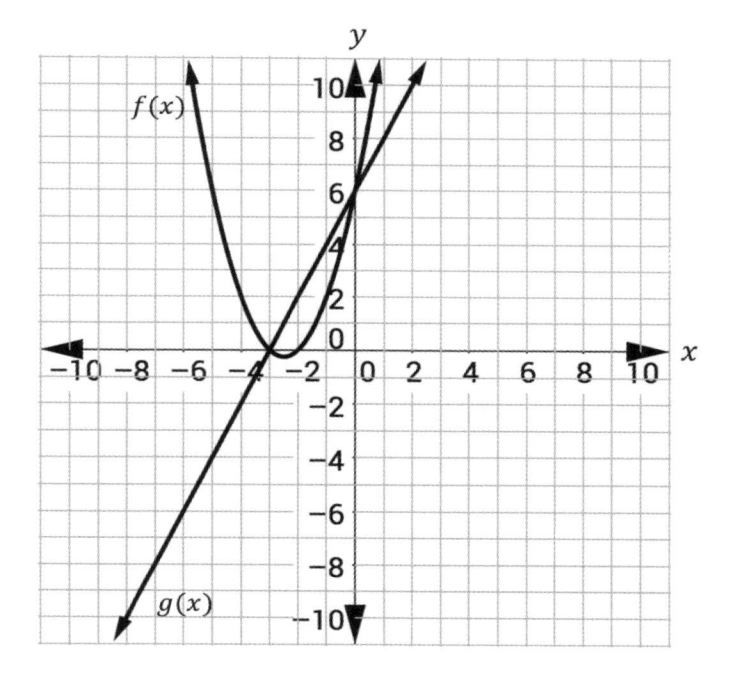

For which values of x does $f(x) = g(x)$?

We call these the **solutions** of $f(x) = g(x)$.

We can also identify the solutions by looking at tables. We can easily find the solutions by looking for the x-coordinate where $f(x) = g(x)$.

The table that represents the system is shown below.

x	$f(x)$	$g(x)$
−3	0	0
−2	0	2
−1	2	4
0	6	6
1	12	8
2	20	10
3	30	12

Use the table to identify the solutions of $f(x) = g(x)$.

We can also use a process called successive approximations. Consider the following system.

$$f(x) = x^2 + 2x + 1$$
$$g(x) = 2x + 3$$

The table that represents the system is shown below.

x	$f(x)$	$g(x)$
0	1	3
0.5	2.25	4
1	4	5
1.5	6.25	6
2	9	7
2.5	12.25	8
3	16	9

Since there are no x-coordinates where $f(x) = g(x)$, we must look for the x-coordinates that have the smallest absolute differences in $f(x)$ and $g(x)$.

➢ Find the absolute differences in $f(x)$ and $g(x)$ on the table above.

➢ Between which two x values must the positive solution lie?

➢ Which of the values does the solution lie closest to?

Let's Practice!

1. Using the same system, complete the table below.

$$f(x) = x^2 + 2x + 1$$
$$g(x) = 2x + 3$$

x	$f(x)$	$g(x)$
1	4	5
1.1	4.41	5.2
1.2		5.4
1.3	5.29	
1.4		
1.5	6.25	6

2. Find the absolute differences in $f(x)$ and $g(x)$ on the table above.

3. Use the table to find the positive solution (to the nearest tenth) for $f(x) = g(x)$.

Try It!

4. The graphs of $f(x)$ and $g(x)$ are shown below.

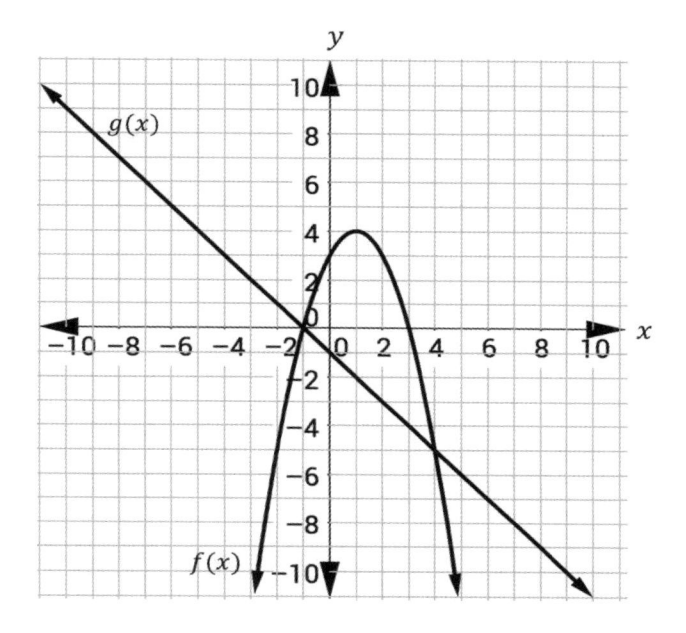

Use the graph to find the negative and positive solution of $f(x) = g(x)$.

BEAT THE TEST!

1. Consider the following system of equations.

$$g(x) = x^2 - 10$$
$$h(x) = x + 8$$

The table below represents the system.

x	$g(x)$	$h(x)$
-4	6	4
-3.5	2.25	4.5
-3	-1	5
-2.5	-3.75	5.5
-2	-6	6
-1.5	-7.75	6.5
-1	-9	7

Use successive approximations to find the negative solution for $g(x) = h(x)$.

Section 7: Exponential Functions

Topic 1: Geometric Sequences 181
Standards Covered: F-IF.3, F-BF.1.a, F-LE.2
- ☐ I can find a recursive formula and explicit formula for a geometric sequence.
- ☐ I can find the value of the "n^{th}" term in the sequence.
- ☐ I understand the connection between geometric sequences and exponential functions.

Topic 2: Comparing Arithmetic and Geometric Sequences 184
Standards Covered: F-IF.3, F-LE.1.a.b, F-LE.2, F-LE.3
- ☐ I can determine the type of sequence (arithmetic or geometric).

Topic 3: Exponential Functions 187
Standards Covered: F-LE.2
- ☐ I can represent exponential functions as graphs in the coordinate plane and ordered pairs in tables.
- ☐ I can write the equation of an exponential function.

Topic 4: Graphs of Exponential Functions - Part 1 192
Standards Covered: F-IF.7.e
- ☐ I can use the end behavior, y-intercept, and growth/decay rate to graph an exponential function.
- ☐ I can describe the end behavior of an exponential function.

Topic 5: Graphs of Exponential Functions - Part 2 195
Standards Covered: A-SSE.3.c, F-IF.7.e, F-IF.8.b
- ☐ I can use the end behavior, y-intercept, and growth/decay rate to graph an exponential function.
- ☐ I can describe the end behavior of an exponential function.

Topic 6: Growth and Decay Rates of Exponential Functions 197
Standards Covered: F-IF.8.b, F-LE.5
- ☐ I can determine whether a function represents exponential growth or decay.
- ☐ I can determine the exponential growth or decay factor of an exponential function in real-world context.

Visit MathNation.com or search "Math Nation" in your phone or tablet's app store to watch the videos that go along with this workbook!

Geometric Sequences

Consider the sequence 3, 6, 12, 24, ... What pattern do you notice in the sequence?

Each term is the product of the previous term and two

This is an example of a *geometric sequence*.

> Each term in the sequence is the __product__ of the previous term and some real number r.

Just like arithmetic sequences, we can represent this sequence in a table:

The following Michigan Mathematics Standards will be covered in this section:
F-IF.3 - Recognize that sequences are functions, sometimes defined recursively, whose domain is a subset of the integers.
F-BF.1.a - Write a function that describes a relationship between two quantities. a. Determine an explicit expression, a recursive process, or steps for calculation from a context.
F-LE.2 - Construct linear and exponential functions, including arithmetic and geometric sequences, given a graph, a description of a relationship, or two input/output pairs (including reading these from a table).
F-LE.1.a.b - Distinguish between situations that can be modeled with linear functions and with exponential functions. a. Prove that linear functions grow by equal differences over equal intervals, and that exponential functions grow by equal factors over equal intervals. b. Recognize situations in which one quantity changes at a constant rate per unit interval relative to another.
F-LE.3 - Observe using graphs and tables that a quantity increasing exponentially eventually exceeds a quantity increasing linearly, quadratically or (more generally) as a polynomial function.
F-IF.7.e - Graph functions expressed symbolically and show key features of the graph by hand in simple cases and using technology for more complicated cases. e. Graph exponential and logarithmic functions, showing intercepts and end behavior, and trigonometric functions, showing period, midline, and amplitude and using phase shift.
A-SSE.3.c - Choose and produce an equivalent form of an expression to reveal and explain properties of the quantity represented by the expression. c. Use the properties of exponents to transform expressions for exponential functions.
F-IF.8.b - Write a function defined by an expression in different but equivalent forms to reveal and explain different properties of the function. b. Use the properties of exponents to interpret expressions for exponential functions.
F-LE.5 - Interpret the parameters in a linear or exponential function in terms of a context. Construct linear and exponential functions, including arithmetic and geometric sequences, given a graph, a description of a relationship, or two input/output pairs (including reading these from a table).

Section 7: Exponential Functions

Section 7: Exponential Functions
Section 7 – Topic 1
Geometric Sequences

Consider the sequence $3, 6, 12, 24, \ldots$. What pattern do you notice in the sequence?

This is an example of a **geometric sequence**.

➤ Each term in the sequence is the _____ of the previous term and some real number r.

Just like arithmetic sequences, we can represent this sequence in a table.

Term Number	Sequence Term	Term
1	a_1	3
2	a_2	6
3	a_3	12
4	a_4	24
5	a_5	48
...	...	...
n	a_n	

Function Notation	
$f(1)$	a formula to find the 1st term
	a formula to find the 2nd term
$f(3)$	a formula to find the ___ term
$f(4)$	a formula to find the ___ term
	a formula to find the 5th term
...	...
$f(n)$	a formula to find the ___ term

How can we find the 10th term of this sequence?

➤ We can use the recursive process, where we use the previous term.

Term Number	Sequence Term	Term	Function Notation	
1	a_1	3	$A(1)$	a_1
2	a_2	$6 = 3 \cdot 2$	$A(2)$	$2a_1$
3	a_3	$12 = 6 \cdot 2$	$A(3)$	$2a_2$
4	a_4	$24 = 12 \cdot 2$	$A(4)$	$2a_3$
5	a_5	$48 = 24 \cdot 2$	$A(5)$	$2a_4$
6	a_6	$96 = 48 \cdot 2$	$A(6)$	$2a_5$
7	a_7	$192 = 96 \cdot 2$	$A(7)$	$2a_6$
8	a_8	$384 = 192 \cdot 2$	$A(8)$	$2a_7$
9	a_9		$A(9)$	$2a_8$
10	a_{10}		$A(10)$	$2a_9$

Write a recursive formula that we could use to find any term in the sequence.

➢ We can use the explicit process, where we relate back to the first term.

Term Number	Sequence Term	Term	Function Notation	
1	a_1	3	$A(1)$	a_1
2	a_2	$6 = 3 \cdot 2$	$A(2)$	$2a_1$
3	a_3	$12 = 3 \cdot 2 \cdot 2 = 3 \cdot 2^2$	$A(3)$	$2^2 a_1$
4	a_4	$24 = 3 \cdot 2 \cdot 2 \cdot 2 = 3 \cdot 2^3$	$A(4)$	$2^3 a_1$
5	a_5	$48 = 3 \cdot 2 \cdot 2 \cdot 2 \cdot 2 = 3 \cdot 2^4$	$A(5)$	$2^4 a_1$
6	a_6	$96 = 3 \cdot 2 \cdot 2 \cdot 2 \cdot 2 \cdot 2 = 3 \cdot 2^5$	$A(6)$	$2^5 a_1$
7	a_7	$192 = 3 \cdot 2 \cdot 2 \cdot 2 \cdot 2 \cdot 2 \cdot 2 = 3 \cdot 2^6$	$A(7)$	$2^6 a_1$
8	a_8	$384 = 3 \cdot 2 \cdot 2 \cdot 2 \cdot 2 \cdot 2 \cdot 2 \cdot 2 = 3 \cdot 2^7$	$A(8)$	$2^7 a_1$
9	a_9		$A(9)$	
10	a_{10}		$A(10)$	

Write an explicit formula that we could use to find any term in the sequence.

Sketch the graph of the geometric sequence found in the table.

Term Number	Term
1	3
2	6
3	12
4	24
5	48
6	96

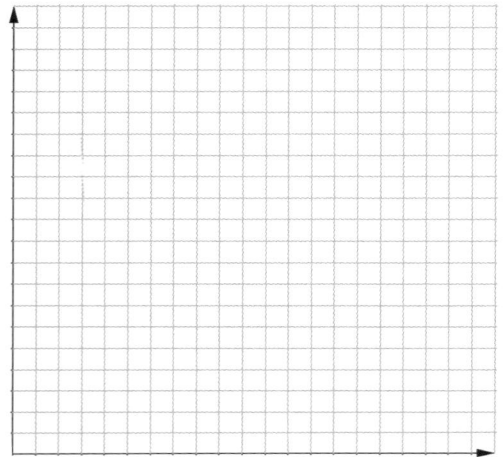

STUDY EDGE TIP

The recursive process uses the previous term while the explicit process uses the first term.

Section 7: Exponential Functions

Let's Practice!

1. Consider the sequence $-2, 4, -8, 16, \ldots$.

   a. Write a recursive formula for the sequence.

   b. Write an explicit formula for the sequence.

   c. Find the 12th term of the sequence.

Try It!

2. The first four terms of a geometric sequence are $7, 14, 28,$ and 56.

   a. Write a recursive formula for the sequence.

   b. Write an explicit formula for the sequence.

   c. Find the 20th term of the sequence.

BEAT THE TEST!

1. An art gallery was showcasing a 6-inch long photo of a geometric landscape. The picture was enlarged ten times, each time by 125% of the previous picture.

   Enter formulas that will give the length of each enlarged print.

   $a_1 = $ ▢

   Recursive formula:

   $a_n = $ ▢

   Explicit formula:

   $a_n = $ ▢

Section 7: Exponential Functions

Section 7 – Topic 2
Comparing Arithmetic and Geometric Sequences

The founder of a popular social media website is trying to inspire gifted algebra students to study computer programming. He is offering two different incentive programs for students.

Option 1: Students will earn one penny for completing their first math, science, or computer-related college course. The amount earned will double for each additional course they complete.

Option 2: Students will earn one penny for completing their first math, science, or computer-related college course. For each subsequent course they complete, they will earn $100.00 more than they did for the previous course.

Write an explicit formula for each option.

Compare the two scholarship options in the tables below.

Option 1	
Course	Amount
1	$0.01
2	$0.02
3	$0.04
4	$0.08
5	$0.16
6	$0.32
7	$0.64
8	$1.28
9	$2.56
10	$5.12
11	$10.24
12	$20.48
13	$40.96
14	$81.92
15	$163.84
16	$327.68
17	$655.36
18	$1,310.72
19	$2,621.44
20	$5,242.88
21	$10,485.76
22	$20,971.52
23	$41,943.04
24	$83,886.08
25	$167,772.16

Option 2	
Course	Amount
1	$0.01
2	$100.01
3	$200.01
4	$300.01
5	$400.01
6	$500.01
7	$600.01
8	$700.01
9	$800.01
10	$900.01
11	$1,000.01
12	$1,100.01
13	$1,200.01
14	$1,300.01
15	$1,400.01
16	$1,500.01
17	$1,600.01
18	$1,700.01
19	$1,800.01
20	$1,900.01
21	$2,000.01
22	$2,100.01
23	$2,200.01
24	$2,300.01
25	$2,400.01

Compare the two scholarship options in the graphs below.

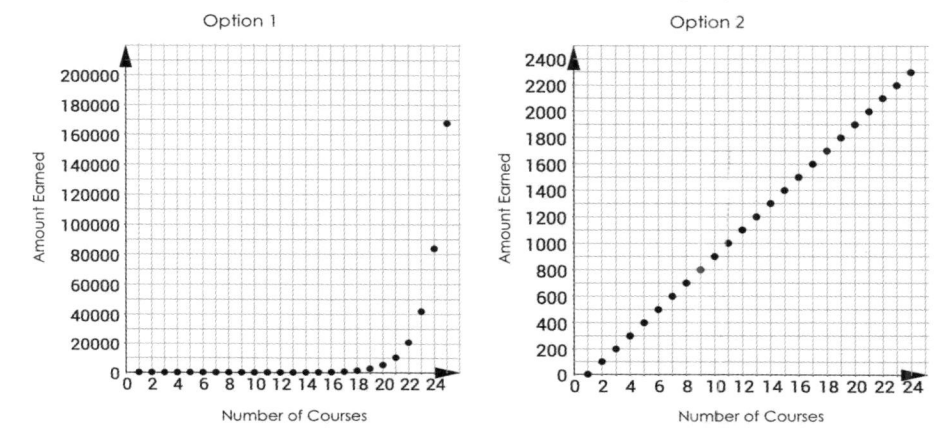

Option 1

Option 2

Option 1 is a geometric sequence.

➢ Each term is the product of the previous term and two.

➢ This geometric sequence follows a(n) _____ pattern.

➢ Evaluate the domain of this function.

Option 2 is an arithmetic sequence.

➢ Each term is the sum of the previous term and 100.

➢ Arithmetic sequences follow a(n) _____ pattern.

➢ Evaluate the domain of this function.

What can be said about the domain of arithmetic and geometric sequences?

Let's Practice!

1. Consider the two scholarship options for studying computer science.

    a. Which scholarship option is better if your college degree requires 10 math, engineering, or programming courses?

    b. What if your degree requires 25 math, engineering, or programming courses?

    c. Do you think that these graphs represent discrete or continuous functions? Justify your answer.

    d. Do you think Option 1 would ever be offered as a scholarship? Why or why not?

Section 7: Exponential Functions

Try It!

2. Pablo and Lily are saving money for their senior trip next month. Pablo's goal is to save one penny on the first day of the month and to triple the amount he saves each day for one month. Lily's goal is to save $10.00 on the first day of the month and increase the amount she saves by $5.00 each day.

   a. Pablo's savings plan is an example of a(n)
      - ○ arithmetic sequence.
      - ○ geometric sequence.

   b. Lily's savings plan is an example of a(n)
      - ○ arithmetic sequence.
      - ○ geometric sequence.

   c. Which person do you think will be able to meet his/her goal? Explain.

3. Circle the best answers to complete the following statement.

   Arithmetic sequences follow a(n) linear | exponential | quadratic pattern, whereas geometric sequences follow a(n) linear | exponential | quadratic pattern, and the domain of both sequences is a subset of the integers | radicals | exponents.

BEAT THE TEST!

1. On Sunday, Chris and Caroline will begin their final preparations for a piano recital the following Saturday. Caroline plans to practice 30 minutes on the Sunday prior to the recital and increase her practice time by 30 minutes every day leading up to the recital. Chris plans to practice half of Caroline's time on Sunday, but will double his practice time every day leading up to the recital.

   Part A: List Caroline's and Chris's practice times on the tables below.

Caroline's Practice Times	

Chris's Practice Times	

Section 7: Exponential Functions

Part B: Compare the graphs of Caroline's and Chris's practice times. Identify each graph as linear or exponential.

Caroline's Practice Time

Chris's Practice Time

_____   _____

Section 7 – Topic 3
Exponential Functions

Functions can be represented by:

➢ Verbal descriptions

➢ Algebraic equations

➢ Numeric tables

➢ Graphs

Let's review linear and quadratic functions.

Linear Functions

➢ Verbal description:

You are driving to visit your best friend in Gulfport. Since you have a long drive ahead, you turn on your cruise control. The cruise control keeps your car traveling at a constant rate of 60 mph.

➢ Algebraic equation:

The situation is represented by the function $f(h) = 60h$. Your distance, $f(h)$, in miles, depends on your time, h, in hours.

Want some help? You can always ask questions on the Algebra Wall and receive help from other students, teachers, and Study Experts. You can also help others on the Algebra Wall and earn Karma Points for doing so. Go to AlgebraNation.com to learn more and get started!

- Numeric table:

h	$f(h)$
1	60
2	120
3	180
4	240
5	300
6	360
7	420

- Graph:

Total Distance

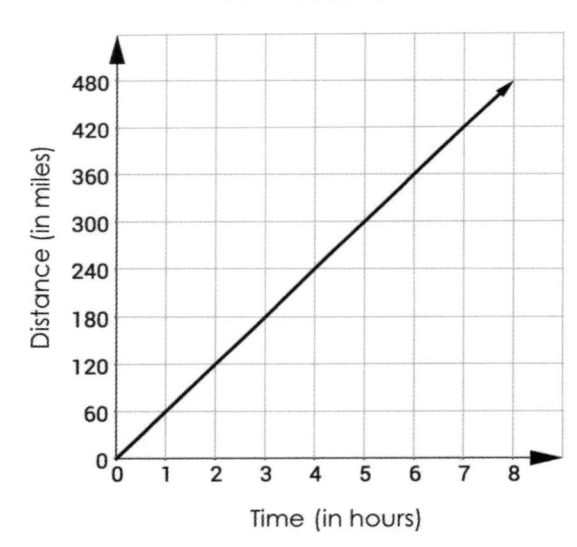

[Graph showing a straight line through the origin with Distance (in miles) on the y-axis (0 to 480) and Time (in hours) on the x-axis (0 to 8)]

Quadratic Functions

- Verbal description:

You are observing the height of a ball as it's dropped from a 150 ft tall building. Because of the force of gravity, the more time that passes, the faster the ball travels. The ball does not travel at a constant speed, like your car on cruise control.

- Algebraic equation:

The height of the ball (h), in feet, is a function of, or depends on, the time (t), in seconds. The quadratic function can be represented by the equation $h(t) = -16t^2 + 150$.

- Numeric table:

t	$h(t)$
1	134
2	86
3	6

Section 7: Exponential Functions

➢ Graph:

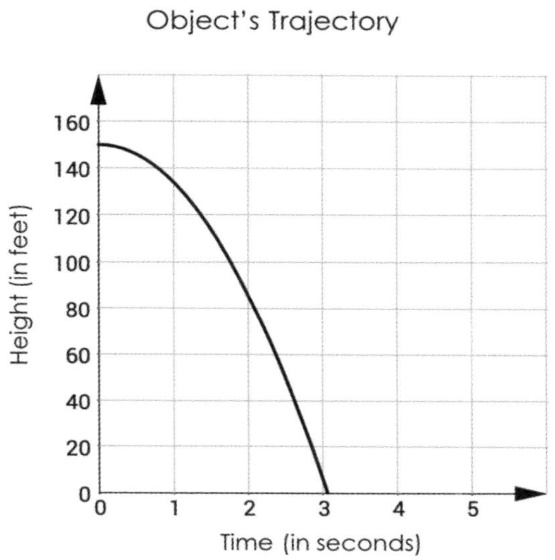
Object's Trajectory
Height (in feet)
160
140
120
100
80
60
40
20
0
0
1
2
3
4
5
Time (in seconds)

Exponential Functions

➢ Verbal description:

You are performing an experiment in science class in which you start with 100 bacteria and the amount of bacteria doubles every hour.

➢ Numeric table:

t	$b(t)$
0	100
1	200
2	400
3	800
4	1,600
5	3,200
6	6,400

➢ Graph:

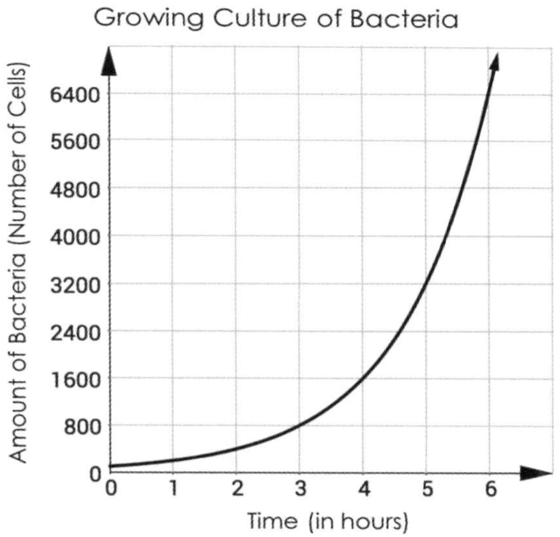
Growing Culture of Bacteria
Amount of Bacteria (Number of Cells)
6400
5600
4800
4000
3200
2400
1600
800
0
0
1
2
3
4
5
6
Time (in hours)

➤ Algebraic equation:

Use the following steps to write the equation for the exponential function.

- Pick two points. It's helpful to use the y-intercept and the coordinate where $x = 1$.

- Substitute the coordinates into the exponential equation $y = ab^x$. Solve for a and b.

- Substitute a and b into the equation $y = ab^x$.

Let's Practice!

1. The table and graph below represent an exponential function:

x	y
-1	$\dfrac{4}{3}$
0	4
1	12
2	36
3	108

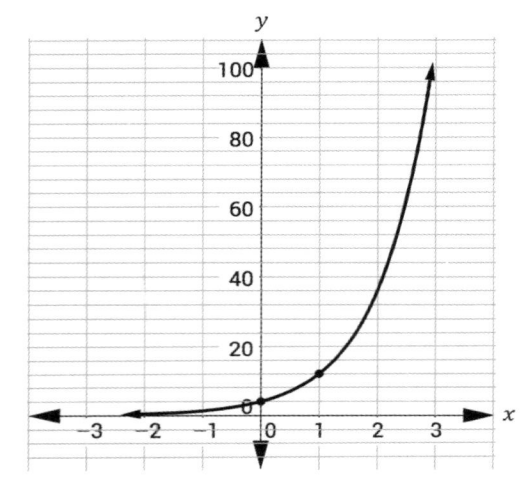

a. Write an equation for the exponential function.

b. Form a hypothesis relating the a term to one of the key features of the graph.

c. Form a hypothesis relating the b term to one of the key features of the graph.

Section 7: Exponential Functions

Try It!

2. The table and graph below represent an exponential function.

x	y
-1	4
0	2
1	1
2	$\frac{1}{2}$
3	$\frac{1}{4}$

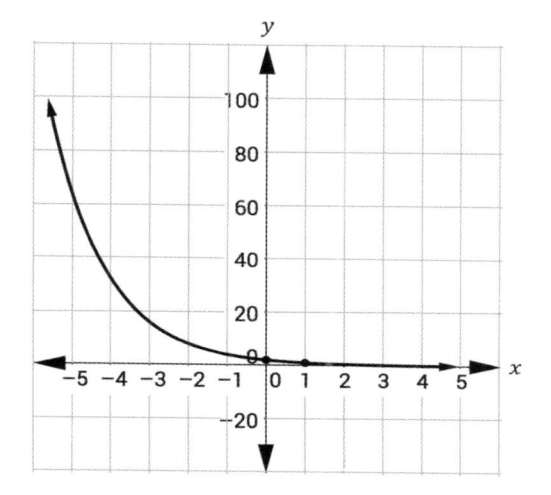

a. Write an equation to represent the exponential function.

b. Did your earlier hypothesis hold true for this equation?

BEAT THE TEST!

1. Match the graphs below with the following functions.

$$f(x) = 3^x \quad f(x) = 2 \cdot 3^x \quad f(x) = -3^x \quad f(x) = -2 \cdot 3^x$$

Want some help? You can always ask questions on the Algebra Wall and receive help from other students, teachers, and Study Experts. You can also help others on the Algebra Wall and earn Karma Points for doing so. Go to AlgebraNation.com to learn more and get started!

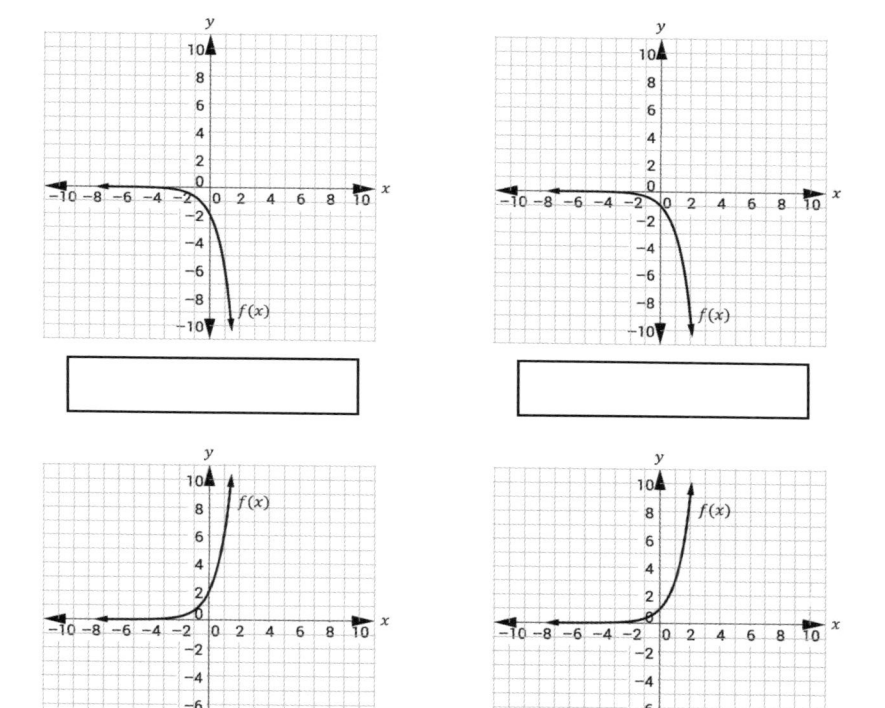

Algebra Wall

Section 7: Exponential Functions

Section 7 – Topic 4
Graphs of Exponential Functions – Part 1

Let's review what we learned in the previous video about exponential functions.

Consider an exponential function written in the form $f(x) = a \cdot b^x$.

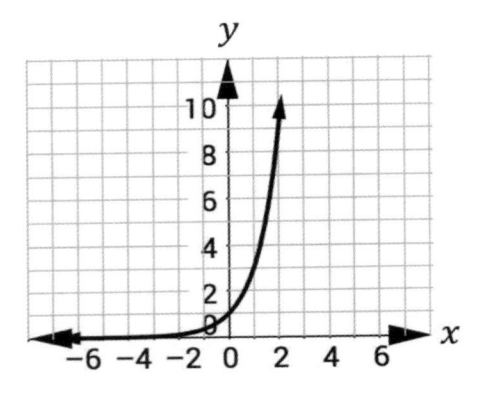

Which key feature of the exponential function does the a term represent?

- o x-intercept
- o y-intercept
- o common ratio

Which key feature of the exponential function does the b term represent?

- o x-intercept
- o y-intercept
- o common ratio

Let's Practice!

1. Consider the exponential equation $y = 2^x$.

    a. Sketch the graph of the exponential equation.

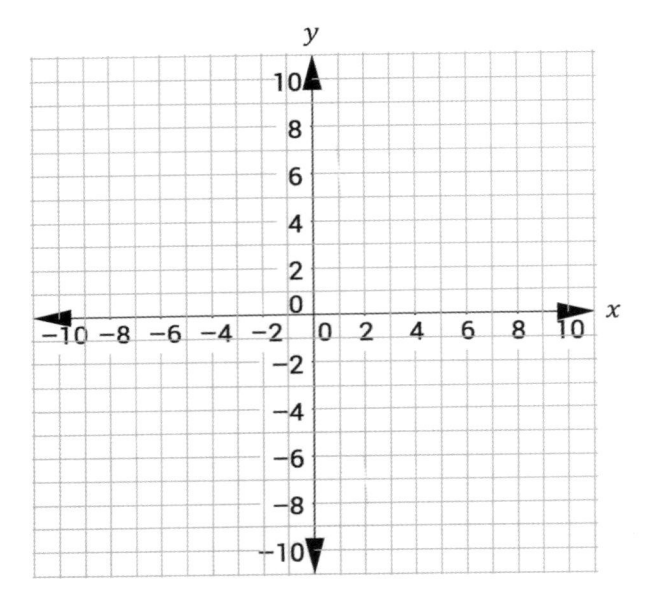

    b. Is the graph increasing or decreasing?

    c. Describe the end behavior of the graph.

    As x increases, y _____.

    As x decreases, y _____.

2. Consider the exponential equation $y = \left(\frac{1}{2}\right)^x$.

   a. Sketch the graph of the exponential equation.

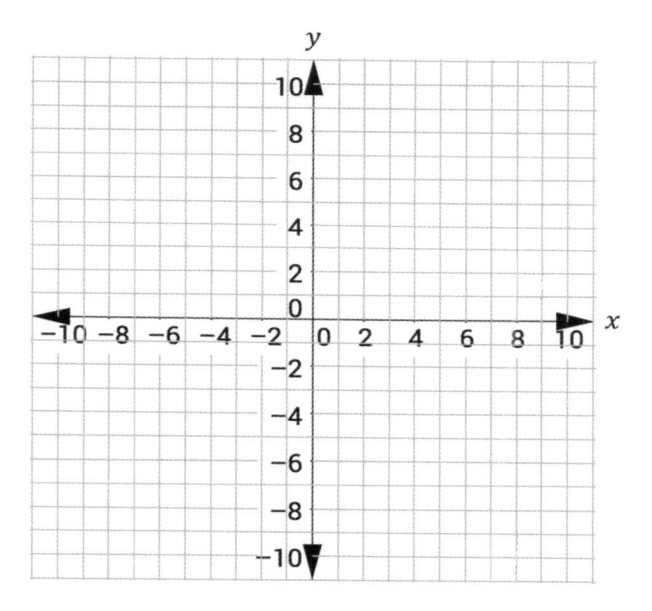

   b. Is the graph increasing or decreasing?

   c. Describe the end behavior of the graph.

   As x increases, y _____.

   As x decreases, y _____.

   STUDY EDGE TIP: Remember, you can always write an exponential function such as $g(x) = 3^x$ in the form $g(x) = a \cdot b^x$ by writing the understood 1 in the front.

3. Consider the exponential equation $y = -2^x$.

   a. Sketch the graph of the exponential equation.

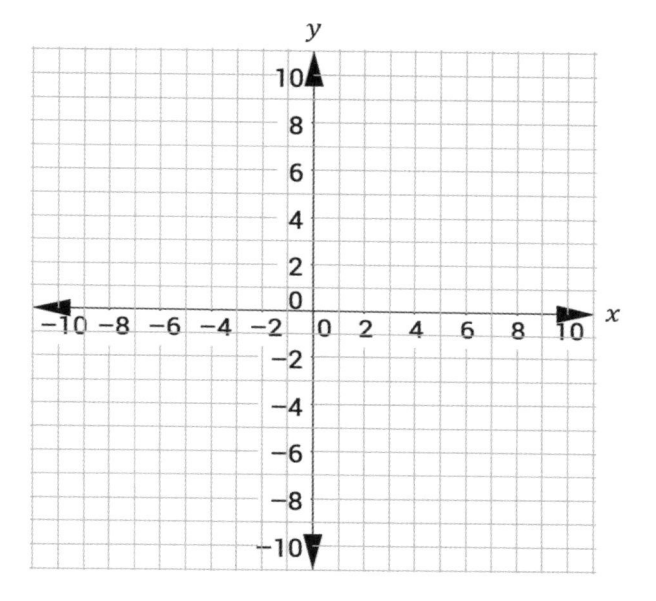

   b. Is the graph increasing or decreasing?

   c. Describe the end behavior of the graph.

   As x increases, y _____.

   As x decreases, y _____.

Section 7: Exponential Functions

Try It!

4. Consider the exponential equation $y = -\left(\frac{1}{2}\right)^x$.

   a. Sketch the graph of the exponential equation.

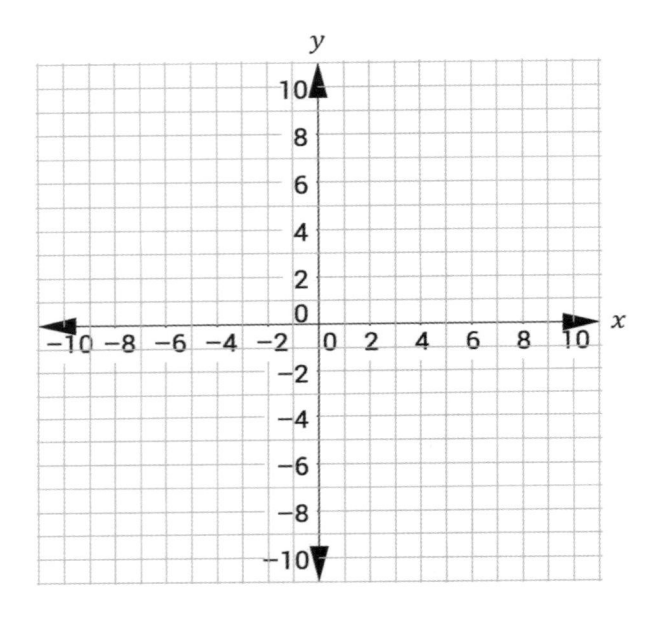

   b. Is the graph increasing or decreasing?

   c. Describe the end behavior of the graph.

   As x increases, y _____.

   As x decreases, y _____.

5. Make a hypothesis about the relationship between the y-intercept, common ratio, and end behavior of a graph. Use your hypothesis to complete the table below.

y-intercept	Common Ratio, r	Increasing or Decreasing	End Behavior: As x Increases	End Behavior: As x Decreases
positive	$r > 1$			
positive	$0 < r < 1$			
negative	$r > 1$			
negative	$0 < r < 1$			

STUDY EDGE TIP

If you get confused about end behavior, you can sketch the graph of $y = a \cdot b^x$ and its key features to see the end behavior.

Algebra Wall

Want some help? You can always ask questions on the Algebra Wall and receive help from other students, teachers, and Study Experts. You can also help others on the Algebra Wall and earn Karma Points for doing so. Go to AlgebraNation.com to learn more and get started!

Section 7 – Topic 5
Graphs of Exponential Functions – Part 2

Sometimes we can use the properties of exponents to easily sketch exponential functions.

How can we use the properties of exponents to sketch the graph of $y = 2^{x+2}$?

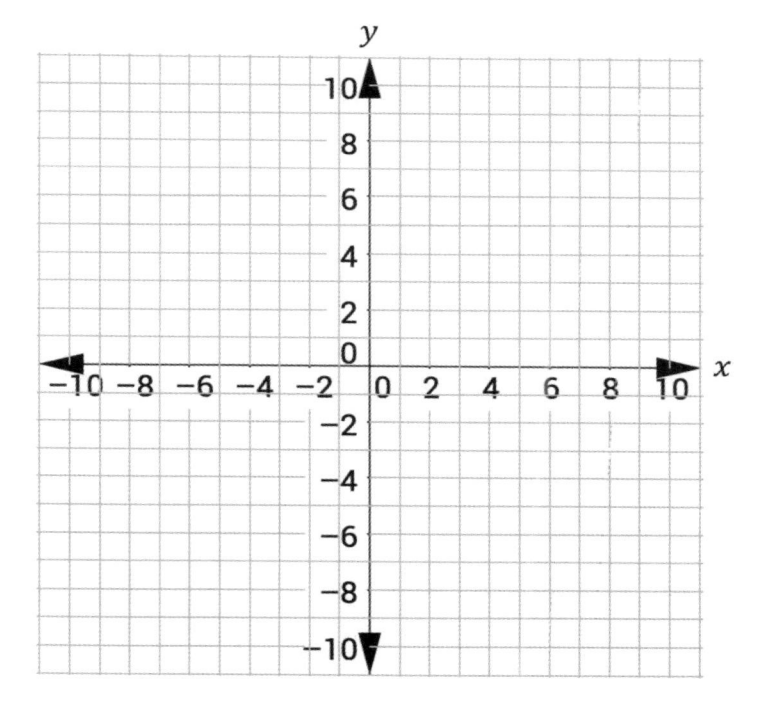

Let's Practice!

1. Use the properties of exponents to sketch the graph of $y = 3^{-x}$.

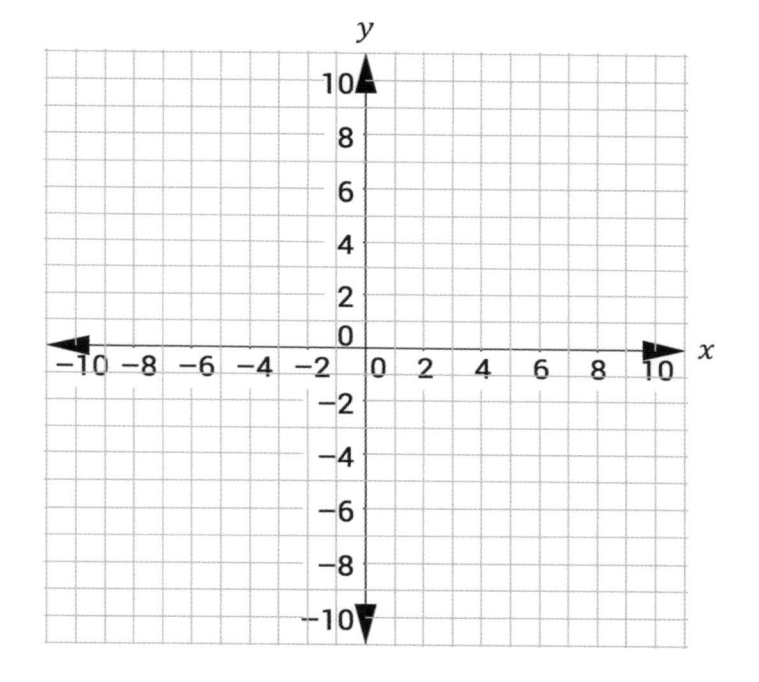

Section 7: Exponential Functions

Try It!

2. Use the properties of exponents to sketch the graph of $y = 2^{x-3}$.

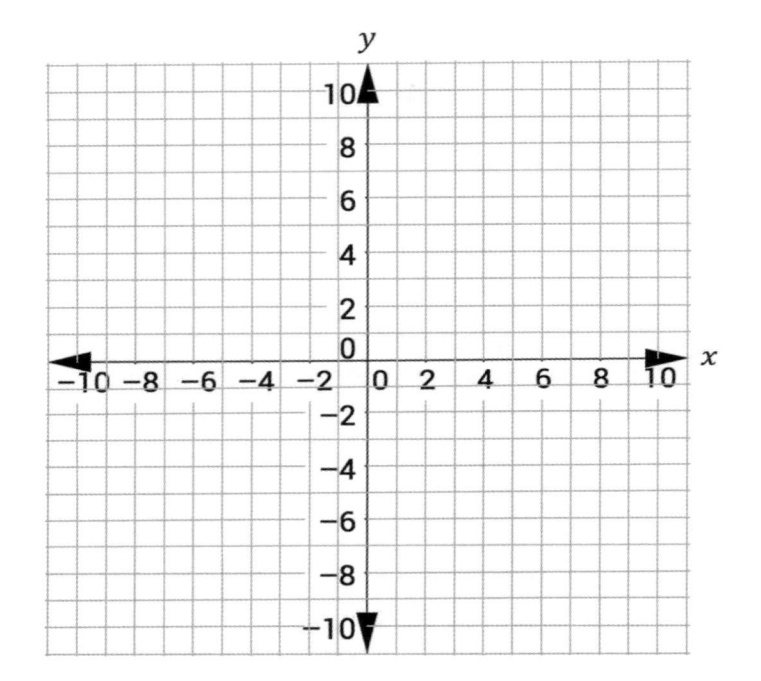

BEAT THE TEST!

1. The graph that represents the function $f(x) = -3 \cdot 2^x$ has a y-intercept of
   - ○ $(0, -3)$.
   - ○ $(0, 2)$.

   The graph is
   - ○ increasing
   - ○ decreasing

   by a common ratio of 2, is decreasing as
   - ○ x increases,
   - ○ x decreases,

   and approaches 0 as
   - ○ x increases.
   - ○ x decreases.

2. Which of the following have the same graphic representation as the function $f(x) = 8 \cdot 2^x$? Select all that apply.

   - ☐ $y = (2^x)^3$
   - ☐ $y = 2^{4x}$
   - ☐ $y = 2^{x+3}$
   - ☐ $y = 2 \cdot 2^{2x}$
   - ☐ $y = 4 \cdot 2^{x+1}$

Want some help? You can always ask questions on the Algebra Wall and receive help from other students, teachers, and Study Experts. You can also help others on the Algebra Wall and earn Karma Points for doing so. Go to AlgebraNation.com to learn more and get started!

Section 7 – Topic 6
Growth and Decay Rates of Exponential Functions

Consider an exponential function in the form $f(x) = a \cdot b^x$.
Assume that a (the _____) is positive.

➤ If b (the _____) is greater than 1, the function is _____.

➤ If b is between 0 and 1, the function is _____.

What are some examples of exponential growth?

What are some examples of exponential decay?

Let's Practice!

1. Consider the exponential function $f(x) = 500 \cdot 1.05^x$, which models the amount of money in Tyler's savings account, where x represents the number of years since Tyler invested the money.

   a. Is the money in the account growing or decaying?

   b. What is the rate of growth or decay?

   c. What does 500 represent?

   d. Consider $f(8) = 738.727721895$. While this is correct, is it an appropriate answer in this context?

STUDY EDGE TIP: You will see the rate of growth/decay expressed as a decimal or a percentage.

2. Consider the exponential function $f(x) = 21{,}000 \cdot 0.91^x$, which models the value of Robert's car, where x represents the number of years since he purchased the car.

   a. Is the value of Robert's car growing or decaying?

   b. What is the rate of growth or decay?

   c. What does 21,000 represent?

Try It!

3. Consider the exponential function $f(x) = 1{,}250 \cdot 1.08^x$, which models the amount of money invested in a bond fund, where x represents the number of years since the money was invested.

   a. What is the rate of growth or decay?

   b. What does 1,250 represent?

STUDY EDGE TIP

To find the decay rate, you must subtract b from 1. To find the growth rate, you subtract 1 from b.

4. Consider the exponential function $f(x) = 25{,}000 \cdot 0.88^x$, which models the amount of money remaining in Lola's retirement fund, where x represents the number of years since Lola began withdrawing the money.

   a. What is the rate of growth or decay?

   b. What does 25,000 represent?

BEAT THE TEST!

1. The equation $y = 250 \cdot 1.04^x$ models
   - ○ exponential growth.
   - ○ exponential decay.

   The rate of growth/decay is
   - ○ 4%.
   - ○ 96%.
   - ○ 104%.

2. The function $f(x) = 350 \cdot 0.75^x$ models the amount of money remaining in Alicia's summer budget, where x represents the number of weeks since summer began. Which of the following are true statements? Select all that apply.

   - ☐ The function models exponential decay.
   - ☐ 350 represents the amount of money Alicia had in the budget at the beginning of summer.
   - ☐ The rate of decay is 25%.
   - ☐ Alicia spent $262.50 during the first week of summer.
   - ☐ At the end of the second week, Alicia will have less than $200.00 in the budget.

Great job! You have reached the end of this section. Now it's time to try the "Test Yourself! Practice Tool," where you can practice all the skills and concepts you learned in this section. Log in to Algebra Nation and try out the "Test Yourself! Practice Tool" so you can see how well you know these topics!

Section 8: Summary of Functions

Topic 1: Comparing Linear, Quadratic, and Exponential Functions - Part 1 202
Standards Covered: F-IF.4, F-LE.1a.b.c, F-LE.3
- ☐ I can compare and contrast the key features of linear, quadratic, and exponential functions.

Topic 2: Comparing Linear, Quadratic, and Exponential Functions - Part 2 204
Standards Covered: F-IF.4, F-IF.6, F-LE.1.a.b.c
- ☐ I can compare and contrast the key features of linear, quadratic, and exponential functions.

Topic 3: Modeling with Functions 206
Standards Covered: A-CED.2, F-IF.5, F-IF.7.a
- ☐ I can model situations given in verbal, tabular, or graphical representation.

Topic 4: Understanding Piecewise-Defined Functions 210
Standards Covered: F-IF.7.b, F-BF.2
- ☐ I can graph piecewise-defined functions within real-world context.

Topic 5: Writing Piecewise-Defined Functions 214
Standards Covered: F-BF.1
- ☐ I can write a piece-wise defined function given the graph.

Topic 6: Absolute Value Functions 216
Standards Covered: F-IF.7.b, A-REI.10
- ☐ I can graph an absolute value function.
- ☐ I can write an absolute value function as a piecewise-defined function.

Topic 7: Graphing Power Functions - Part 1 218
Standards Covered: F-IF.7.b, A-REI.10
- ☐ I can graph square root, cube root, and cubic functions.

Topic 8: Graphing Power Functions - Part 2 220
Standards Covered: F-IF.7.b, A-REI.10
- ☐ I can graph square root, cube root, and cubic functions.

Visit MathNation.com or search "Math Nation" in your phone or tablet's app store to watch the videos that go along with this workbook!

Comparing Linear, Quadratic, and Exponential Functions – Part 1

Complete the table below to describe the characteristics of linear functions.

Linear Functions	
Equation	$y = mx + b$
Shape	linear
Rate of Change	constant
Number of x-intercepts	0, 1, infinitely many
Number of y-intercepts	1
Number of vertices	0
Domain	$\{x \mid x \in \mathbb{R}\}$

The following Michigan Mathematics Standards will be covered in this section:
F-IF.4 - For a function that models a relationship between two quantities, interpret key features of graphs and tables in terms of the quantities, and sketch graphs showing key features given a verbal description of the relationship. Key features include: intercepts; intervals where the function is increasing, decreasing, positive, or negative; relative maximums and minimums; symmetries; end behavior; and periodicity.
F-LE.1.a.b.c - Distinguish between situations that can be modeled with linear functions and with exponential functions. a. Prove that linear functions grow by equal differences over equal intervals, and that exponential functions grow by equal factors over equal intervals. b. Recognize situations in which one quantity changes at a constant rate per unit interval relative to another. c. Recognize situations in which a quantity grows or decays by a constant percent rate per unit interval relative to another.
F-LE.3 - Observe using graphs and tables that a quantity increasing exponentially eventually exceeds a quantity increasing linearly, quadratically, or (more generally) as a polynomial function.
F-IF.6 - Calculate and interpret the average rate of change of a function (presented symbolically or as a table) over a specified interval. Estimate the rate of change from a graph.
A-CED.2 - Create equations in two or more variables to represent relationships between quantities; graph equations on coordinate axes with labels and scales.
F-IF.5 - Relate the domain of a function to its graph and, where applicable, to the quantitative relationship it describes. For example, if the function h(n) gives the number of person-hours it takes to assemble n engines in a factory, then the positive integers would be an appropriate domain for the function.
F-IF.7.a.b - Graph functions expressed symbolically and show key features of the graph, by hand in simple cases and using technology for more complicated cases. a. Graph functions (linear and quadratic) and show intercepts, maxima, and minima. b. Graph square root, cube root, and piecewise-defined functions, including step functions and absolute value functions.
F-BF.2 - Use function notation, evaluate functions for inputs in their domains, and interpret statements that use function notation in terms of a context.
F-BF.1 - Write a function that describes a relationship between two quantities.
A-REI.10 - Understand that the graph of an equation in two variables is the set of all its solutions plotted in the coordinate plane, often forming a curve (which could be a line).

Section 8: Summary of Functions

Section 8: Summary of Functions
Section 8 – Topic 1
Comparing Linear, Quadratic, and Exponential Functions – Part 1

Complete the table below to describe the characteristics of linear functions.

Linear Functions	
Equation	
Shape	
Rate of Change	
Number of x-intercepts	
Number of y-intercepts	
Number of vertices	
Domain	
Range	

Sketch the graphs of three linear functions that show all the possible combinations above.

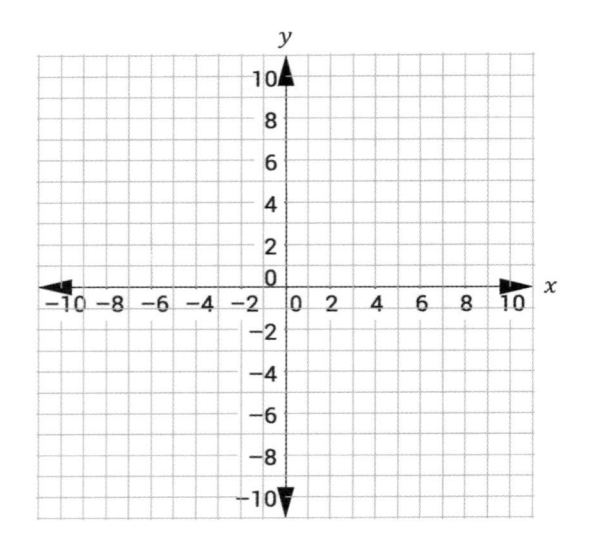

Complete the table below to describe the characteristics of quadratic functions.

Quadratic Functions	
Equation	
Shape	
Rate of Change	
Number of x-intercepts	
Number of y-intercepts	
Number of vertices	
Domain	
Range	

Sketch the graphs of three quadratic functions that show all the possible combinations above.

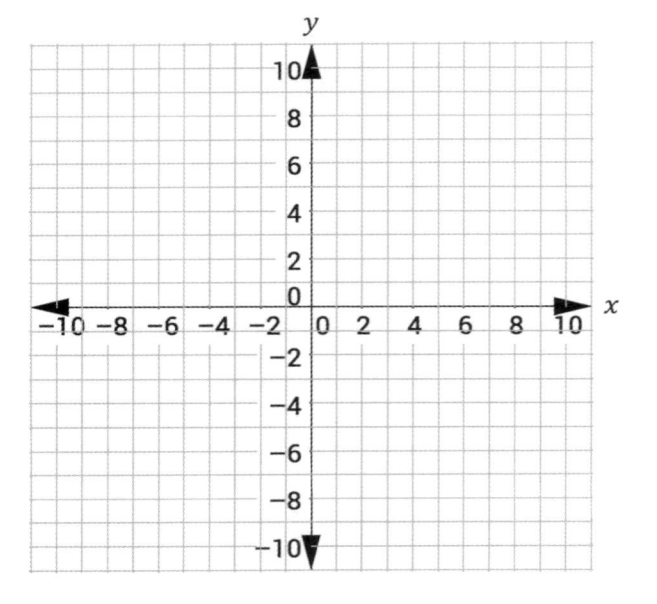

Complete the table below to describe the characteristics of exponential functions.

Exponential Functions	
Equation	
Shape	
Rate of Change	
Number of x-intercepts	
Number of y-intercepts	
Number of vertices	
Domain	
Range	

Sketch the graphs of two exponential functions that show all the possible combinations above.

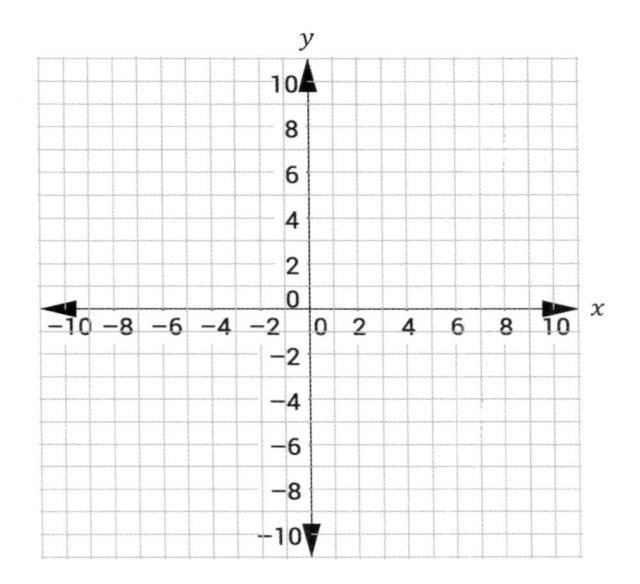

Consider the following tables that represent a linear and a quadratic function and find the differences.

Linear Function	
x	$f(x)$
0	5
1	7
2	9
3	11
4	13

Quadratic Function	
x	$f(x)$
0	3
1	4
2	7
3	12
4	19

How can you distinguish a linear function from a quadratic function?

Consider the following table that represents an exponential function.

Exponential Function	
x	$f(x)$
0	1
1	3
2	9
3	27
4	81
5	243

_____

_____

_____

_____

_____

How can you determine if a function is exponential by looking at a table?

Section 8 – Topic 2
Comparing Linear, Quadratic, and Exponential Functions – Part 2

Let's Practice!

1. Identify whether the following key features indicate a model could be linear, quadratic, or exponential.

Key Feature	Linear	Quadratic	Exponential
Rate of change is constant.	○	○	○
2nd differences, but not 1st, are constant.	○	○	○
Graph has a vertex.	○	○	○
Graph has no x-intercept.	○	○	○
Graph has two x-intercepts.	○	○	○
Graph has one y-intercept.	○	○	○
Domain is all real numbers.	○	○	○
Range is $\{y|y > 0\}$.	○	○	○
Range is $\{y|y \leq 0\}$.	○	○	○
Range is all real numbers.	○	○	○

Want some help? You can always ask questions on the Algebra Wall and receive help from other students, teachers, and Study Experts. You can also help others on the Algebra Wall and earn Karma Points for doing so. Go to AlgebraNation.com to learn more and get started!

Try It!

2. Determine whether each table represents a linear, quadratic, or exponential function.

x	y
0	1
1	2
2	5
3	10
4	17

- Linear
- Quadratic
- Exponential

x	y
0	7
3	13
6	19
9	25
15	37

- Linear
- Quadratic
- Exponential

x	y
0	2
1	6
2	18
3	54
4	162

- Linear
- Quadratic
- Exponential

BEAT THE TEST!

1. Identify whether the following real-world examples should be modeled by a linear, quadratic, or exponential function.

Real-World Example	Linear	Quadratic	Exponential
Growing a culture of bacteria	○	○	○
The distance a Boeing 737 MAX can travel at a certain speed over a given period of time	○	○	○
Kicking a ball into the air	○	○	○
Running a race at a constant speed	○	○	○
A pumpkin decaying	○	○	○
Jumping from a high dive	○	○	○

Section 8: Summary of Functions

2. Complete the following table so that $f(x)$ represents a linear function and $g(x)$ represents an exponential function.

x	$f(x)$	$g(x)$
−5		
−4		
−3		
−2		
−1		

Section 8 – Topic 3
Modeling with Functions

Let's discuss the modeling cycle process.

Consider and complete the following diagram that displays the modeling cycle process.

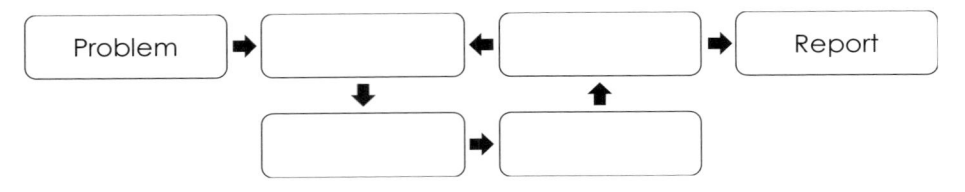

Problem → ☐ ← ☐ → Report
          ↓   ↑
          ☐   →   ☐

Let's Practice!

1. The table below represents the population estimates (in thousands) of the Cape Coral-Fort Myers metro area in years since 2010. Employ the modeling cycle to create a graph and a function to model the population growth. Use the function to predict the population in 2020.

x	0	1	2	3	4	5	6
$f(x)$	619	631	645	661	679	699	721

Problem – Identify the variables in the situation and select those that represent essential features.

a. What are the variables in this situation and what do they represent?

Formulate a model by creating and selecting geometric, graphical, tabular, algebraic, or statistical representations that describe relationships between the variables.

b. Determine what type of function models the context.

Compute – Analyze and perform operations on these relationships to draw conclusions.

c. Sketch the graph and find the function that models the table.

Population of Cape Coral-Fort Myers Metro Area

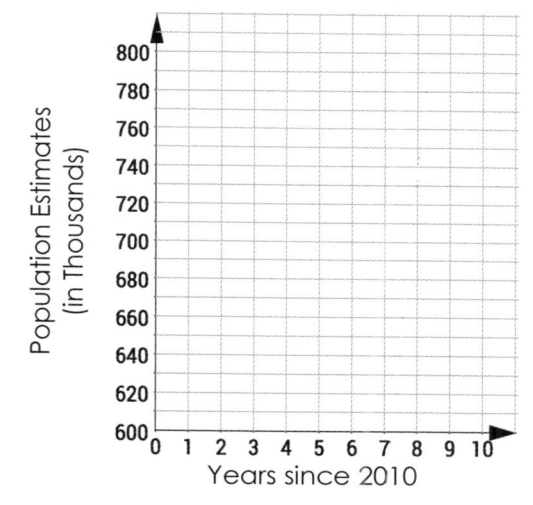

(Graph: Population Estimates (in Thousands) vs. Years since 2010; y-axis from 600 to 800, x-axis from 0 to 10)

d. Use the model to predict the population in the year 2020.

Interpret the results of the mathematics in terms of the original situation.

e. What do the results tell you about the population growth in Cape Coral-Fort Myers metro area as it relates to the original table?

Validate the conclusions by comparing them with the situation, and then either improve the model, or, if it is acceptable, move to the reporting phase.

f. What methods can we use to validate the conclusions?

Report on the conclusions and the reasoning behind them.

g. What key elements should be included in your report?

Try It!

2. According to Florida's Child Labor Law, minors who are 14 or 15 years old may work a maximum of 15 hours per week, and minors that are 16 or 17 years old may work a maximum of 30 hours per week. The relationship between the number of hours that a 15-year old minor in Florida works and his total pay is modeled by the graph below. What is the maximum amount that he can earn in a week?

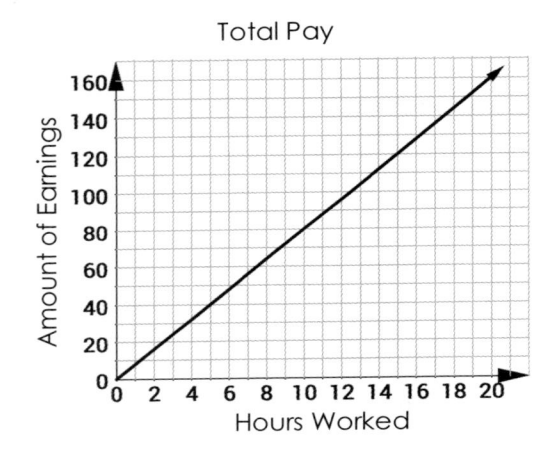

Total Pay

[Graph showing Amount of Earnings (y-axis, 0 to 160) vs. Hours Worked (x-axis, 0 to 20), with a straight line from the origin.]

Phase 1: _____

a. Identify the variables in the situation and what they represent.

Phase 2: _____

b. What type of function can be represented by this graph?

c. Describe the end behavior of the graph.

d. What does the end behavior tell you about the function?

Phase 3: _____

e. What strategy will you use to create the model for this situation?

f. Find the function of the graph.

Phase 4: _____

g. Complete the following statement.

The domain that best describes this situation is

$\{x | x \in$
- o rational numbers}.
- o natural numbers}.
- o whole numbers}.

h. What constraints on the domain would exist for a 14-year old? A 17-year old?

i. How much does the student make per hour? Justify your answer algebraically.

Phase 5: _____

    j. Verify that your function accurately models the graph.

    k. Are there other ways to validate your function?

Phase 6: _____

    l. What would you report?

BEAT THE TEST!

1. Dariel employed the modeling cycle to solve the following problem.

   > Hannah's uncle works at the BMW plant in Spartanburg, South Carolina. He purchased a 2017 BMW M2 for Hannah at the manufacturer's suggested retail price (MSRP) of $52,500. Suppose over the next ten years, the car will depreciate an average of 9% per year. Hannah wishes to sell the car when it is valued at $22,000. When should she sell the car?

   When Dariel got to the compute phase, he knew something was wrong. His work is shown below.

   Problem: The variables in the situation are the number of years Hannah has owned the car and the value of the car after a given number of years.

   Let x = number of years Hannah has owned the car.

   Let $f(x)$ = current value of the car when Hannah has owned it x years.

   Formulate: An exponential function should be used to model the context because the car is depreciating at a common ratio.

   Compute: The function $f(x) = 52,500(.09)^x$ models the context where x is the years since 2017 and $f(x)$ is the value of the car. I am going to use a table of values starting at year 2 to try to determine when the car is worth 15,000.

x	$f(x)$
2	$425.25

   Ugh! This cannot be correct. A 2017 BMW M2 can't be worth just $425.25   HELP!!

Section 8: Summary of Functions

Part A: Critique his reasoning and give feedback on where he went wrong.

Part B: Complete the modeling cycle.

Section 8 – Topic 4
Understanding Piecewise-Defined Functions

What is a **piecewise function**?

➢ A function made up of distinct "_____" based on different rules for the _____.

➢ The "pieces" of a piecewise function are graphed together on the same coordinate plane.

➢ The **domain** is the _____, or the x-values.

➢ The **range** is the ___-values, or output.

➢ Since it is a function, all "pieces" pass the vertical line test.

Describe an example of a piecewise function used in our daily lives.

Consider the following piecewise-defined function.

$$f(x) = \begin{cases} x^2 - 2, \text{when } x \leq 0 \\ 2x + 1, \text{when } x > 0 \end{cases}$$

➢ Each function has a defined _____ value, or rule.

  ○ x is less than or equal to zero for the first function.
  ○ x is greater than zero for the second function.

➢ Both of these functions will be on the same graph. They are the "pieces" of this completed piecewise-defined function.

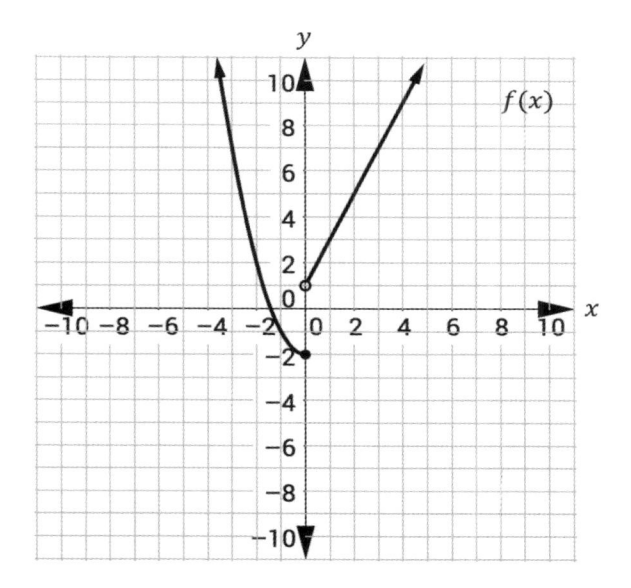

Label the "pieces" of $f(x)$ above.

Let's note some of the features of the graph.

➢ The domain of the piecewise graph can be represented with intervals. If we define the first interval as $x \leq 0$, the second interval would be _____.

➢ The graph is nonlinear (curved) when the domain is _____.

➢ The graph is linear when the domain is _____.

➢ There is one closed endpoint on the graph, which means that the particular domain value, zero, is _____ in that piece of the function. This illustrates the inclusion of zero in the function _____.

➢ There is one open circle on the graph, which means that the particular value, zero, is _____ _____ in that piece of the function. This illustrates the constraint that $x > 0$ for the function _____.

Section 8: Summary of Functions

Let's Practice!

1. Airheadz, a trampoline gym, is open seven days a week for ten hours a day. Their prices are listed below:

   Two hours or less: $15.00
   Between two and five hours: $25.00
   Five or more hours: $30.00

   The following piecewise function represents their prices:

   $$f(x) = \begin{cases} 15, \text{when } 0 < x \leq 2 \\ 25, \text{when } 2 < x < 5 \\ 30, \text{when } 5 \leq x \leq 10 \end{cases}$$

   Graph the above function on the following grid.

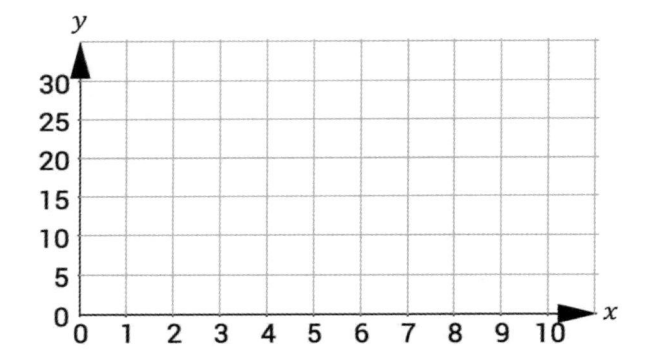

- $f(x)$ is a special type of piecewise function known as a _____ function, which resembles a series of steps.

- Step functions pair every x-value in a given interval (particular section of the _____) with a single value in the range (_____-value).

Try It!

2. Consider the previous graph in exercise 1.

   a. How many pieces are in the step function? Are the pieces linear or nonlinear?

   b. How many intervals make up the step function? What are the interval values?

   c. Why are open circles used in some situations and closed circles in others?

   d. How do you know this is a function?

   e. What is the range of this piecewise function?

Section 8: Summary of Functions

BEAT THE TEST!

1. Evaluate the piecewise-defined function for the given values of x by matching the domain values with the range values.

$$f(x) = \begin{cases} x - 1, & x \leq -2 \\ 2x - 1, & -2 < x \leq 4 \\ -3x + 8, & x > 4 \end{cases}$$

x	$f(x)$
8	7
−2	3
4	−3
2	−16
−5	−6
0	−1

2. Complete the following sentences by choosing the correct answer from each box.

   Part A: Piecewise-defined functions are represented by
   - o one function
   - o at least one function
   - o at least two functions

   that must correspond to
   - o different domain values.
   - o different range values.
   - o real numbers.

   Part B: When evaluating piecewise-defined functions, choose which equation to use based on the
   - o constant,
   - o x-value,
   - o slope,

   then substitute and evaluate using
   - o exponent rules.
   - o order of operations.
   - o your instincts.

Section 8: Summary of Functions

Section 8 – Topic 5
Writing Piecewise-Defined Functions

We write piecewise-defined functions by first defining the individual pieces or the _____.

Let's Practice!

1. Consider the piecewise-defined function.

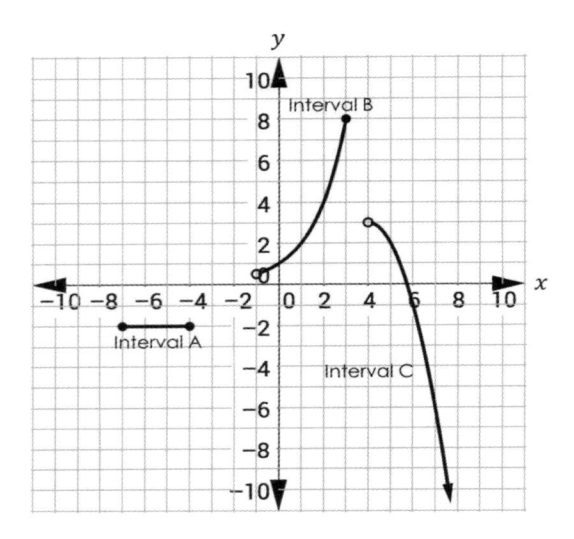

Use the table below to describe each interval.

	Type of Function	Algebraic Representation	Domain
Interval A			
Interval B			
Interval C			

2. Write the piecewise-defined function for the graph in exercise 1.

Try It!

3. Consider the following piecewise-defined function.

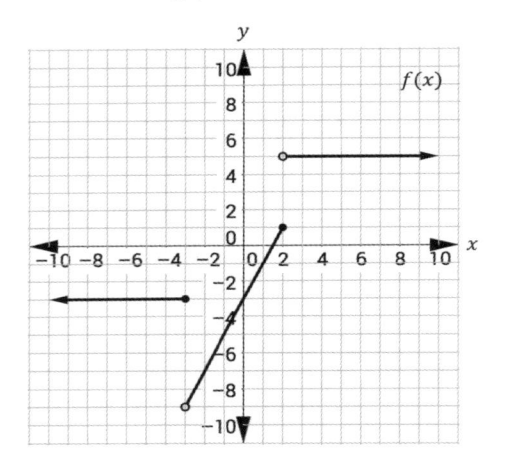

Choose the correct expressions below to represent the piecewise-defined function.

$$f(x) \begin{cases} \boxed{\begin{array}{c} -8 \\ -3 \\ 3 \end{array}} & \text{when } x \leq -3 \\ \\ \boxed{\begin{array}{c} x-2 \\ x-3 \\ 2x-3 \end{array}} & \text{when } -3 < x \leq 2 \\ \\ \boxed{\begin{array}{c} 2 \\ 5 \\ 7 \end{array}} & \text{when } x > 2 \end{cases}$$

4. Define each of the intervals and write a piecewise-defined function for the graph below.

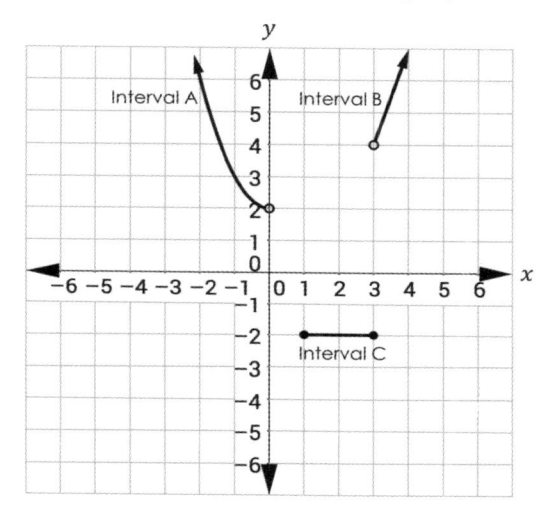

Interval A:

Interval B:

Interval C:

Piecewise-defined function:

BEAT THE TEST!

1. In a math contest, the contestants were given a piecewise function graph. For the final question, they were asked to write the function rule that describes the graph.

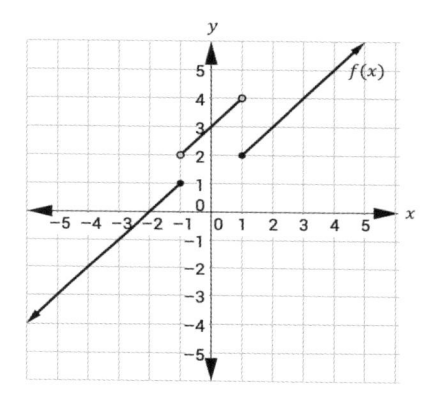

Students' answers are shown below.

Student 1:
$$f(x) = \begin{cases} 1 & 0 \le x < 2 \\ 3 & 2 \le x < 4 \\ 5 & 4 \le x < 6 \end{cases}$$

Student 2:
$$f(x) = \begin{cases} x+2, & x < -1 \\ x+3, & -1 \le x \le 1 \\ x-1, & x > 1 \end{cases}$$

Student 3:
$$f(x) = \begin{cases} x+2, & x \le -1 \\ x+3, & -1 < x < 1 \\ x+1, & x \ge 1 \end{cases}$$

Student 4:
$$f(x) = \begin{cases} x+2, & x \le -1 \\ x+3, & -1 \le x \le 1 \\ x+1, & x \ge 1 \end{cases}$$

Which of the following competitors answered correctly?

Ⓐ Student 1
Ⓑ Student 2
Ⓒ Student 3
Ⓓ Student 4

Section 8: Summary of Functions

Section 8 – Topic 6
Absolute Value Functions

Consider the absolute value function: $f(x) = |x|$.

Sketch the graph of $f(x)$ by completing the table of values.

x	$f(x)$
-2	
-1	
0	
1	
2	

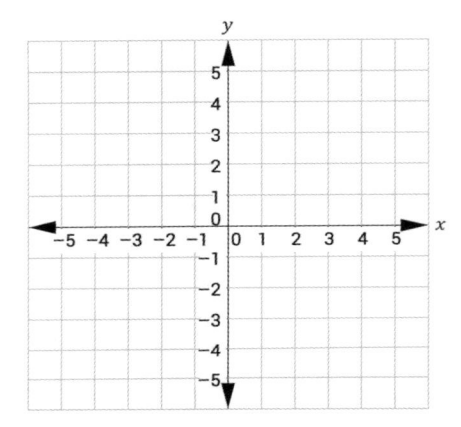

Absolute value functions are a special case of a _____ function.

Write a different function that represents $f(x)$.

Let's Practice!

1. Sketch the graph of $g(x) = |x| + 1$.

x	$g(x)$
-2	
-1	
0	
1	
2	

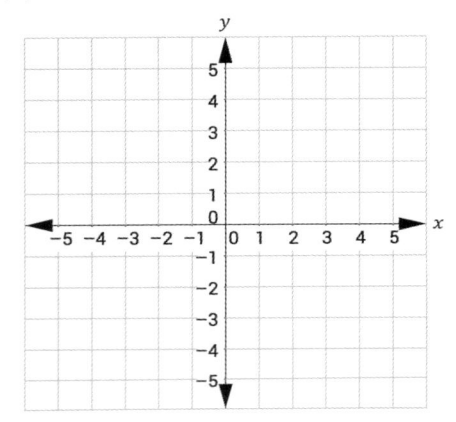

Write $g(x)$ as a piecewise-defined function.

2. Consider the function below.

$$t(x) = \begin{cases} x + 2, \text{ when } x < -2 \\ -x - 2, \text{ when } x \geq -2 \end{cases}$$

Write the absolute value function that represents $t(x)$.

Try It!

3. Sketch the graph $f(x) = |x - 2| + 3$.

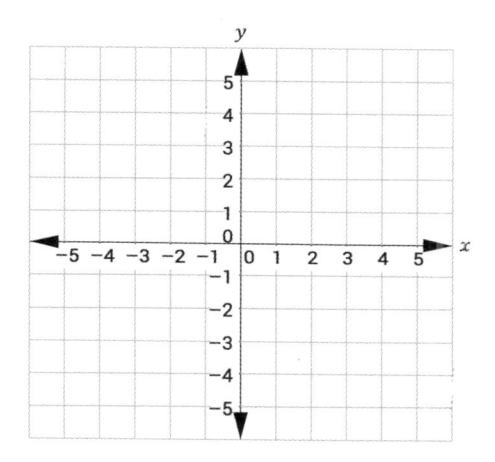

Write $f(x)$ as a piecewise-defined function.

4. Compare and contrast $h(x)$ and $m(x)$.

$$h(x) = |x - 1| \qquad m(x) = \begin{cases} x - 1, \text{when } x < 0 \\ -x - 1, \text{when } x \geq 0 \end{cases}$$

BEAT THE TEST!

1. Consider the following piecewise-defined function.

$$f(x) = \begin{cases} -x - 3, \text{when } x < 0 \\ x - 3, \text{when } x \geq 0 \end{cases}$$

Which of the following functions also represent $f(x)$?

Ⓐ $g(x) = |x - 3|$
Ⓑ $h(x) = |x + 3|$
Ⓒ $m(x) = |x| - 3$
Ⓓ $n(x) = |x| + 3$

Section 8: Summary of Functions

Section 8 – Topic 7
Graphing Power Functions – Part 1

A **power function** is a function in the form of $f(x) = kx^n$, where k and n represent the set of all real numbers.

A **square root function** is an example of a _____ function.

Sketch the graph of $f(x) = \sqrt{x}$ on the set of axes below.

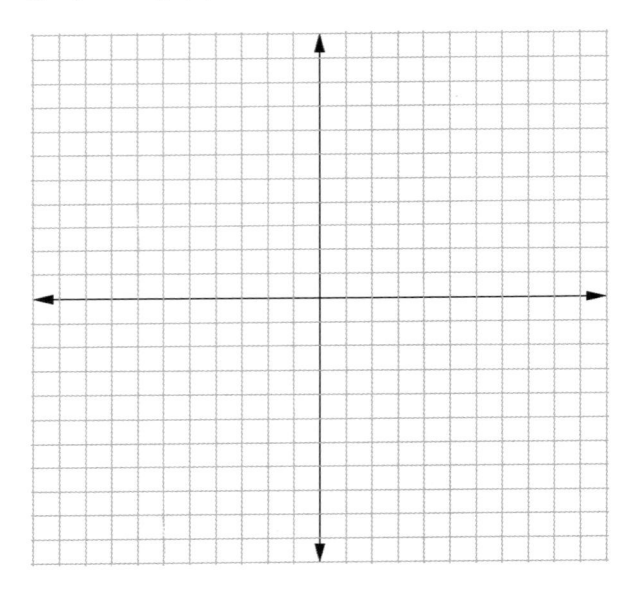

Describe the domain and range.

A _____ _____ is a number that multiplies by itself three times in order to create a cubic value. A function is called a **cube root function** if _____.

Sketch the graph of $f(x) = \sqrt[3]{x}$ on the set of axes below.

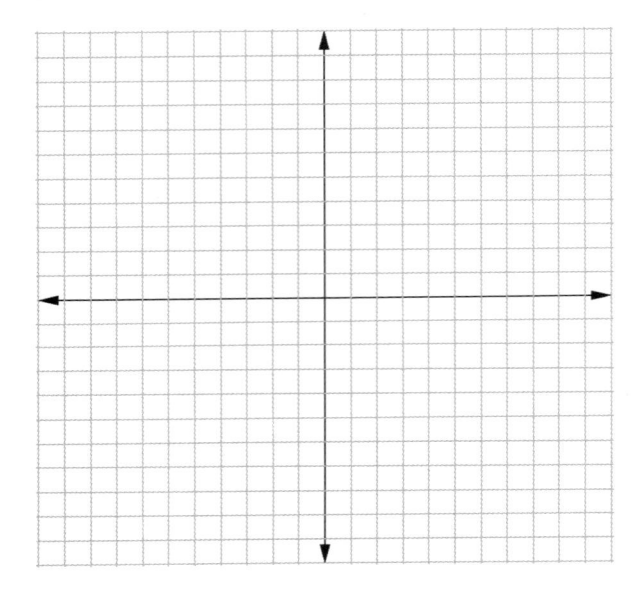

Describe the domain and range.

Let's Practice!

1. Consider the following function.

$$f(x) = \sqrt{x} + 2$$

   a. Sketch the graph of $f(x)$ on the set of axes below.

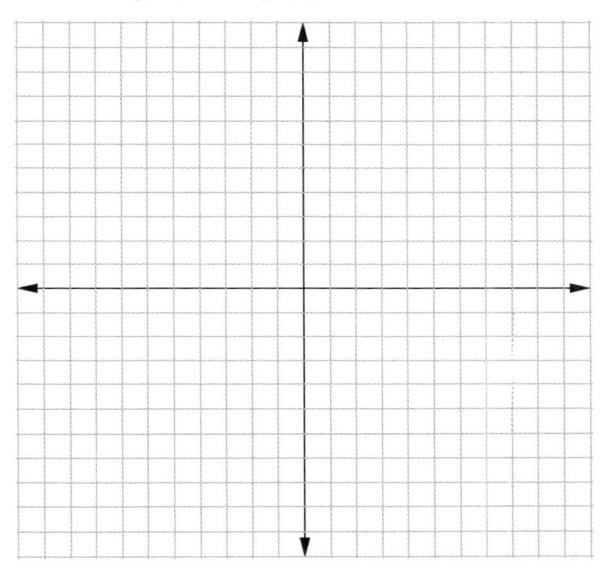

   b. Describe the domain and range.

2. Consider the following function.

$$g(x) = \sqrt[3]{x} - 2$$

   a. Sketch the graph of $g(x)$ on the set of axes below.

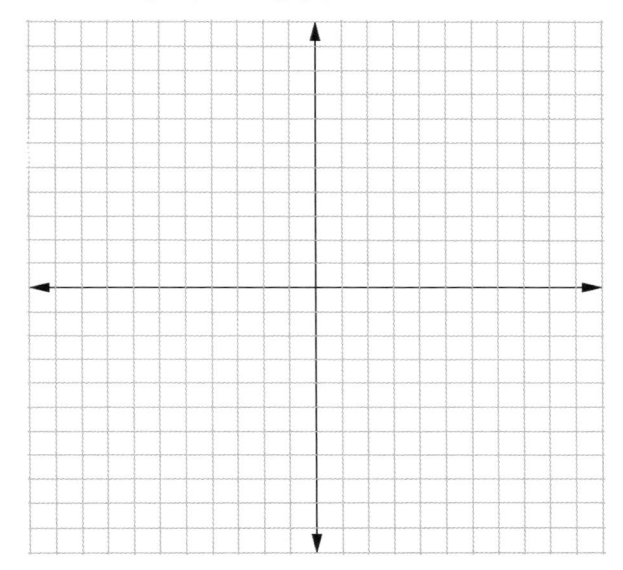

   b. Describe the domain and range.

Section 8: Summary of Functions

Try It!

3. Consider the following functions.

$$h(x) = \sqrt{x} - 1$$
$$m(x) = \sqrt[3]{x} - 1$$

a. Sketch the graphs of $h(x)$ and $m(x)$ on the set of axes below.

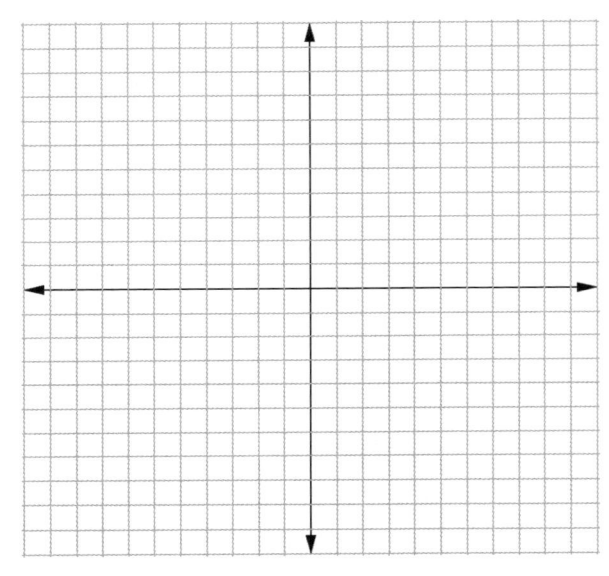

b. Compare and contrast the graphs of $h(x)$ and $m(x)$.

Section 8 – Topic 8
Graphing Power Functions – Part 2

A **cubic function** is any function of the form _____.

Sketch the graph of $f(x) = x^3$ on the set of axes below.

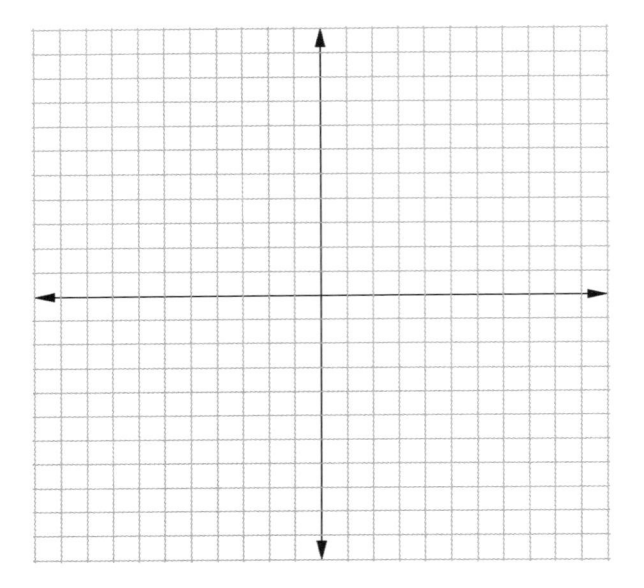

Describe the domain and range.

Let's Practice!

1. Consider the following function.

$$f(x) = x^3 + 1$$

   a. Sketch the graph of $f(x)$ on the set of axes below.

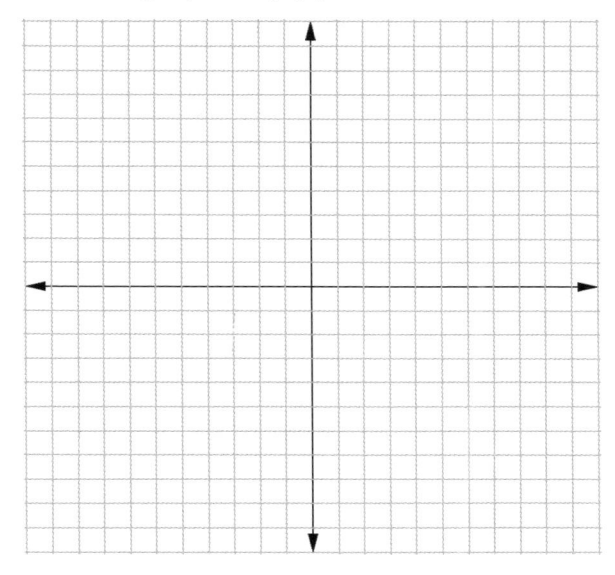

   b. Describe the domain and range.

Try It!

2. Consider the following functions.

$$g(x) = x^3$$
$$h(x) = \sqrt[3]{x}$$

   a. Sketch the graphs of $g(x)$ and $h(x)$ on the set of axes below.

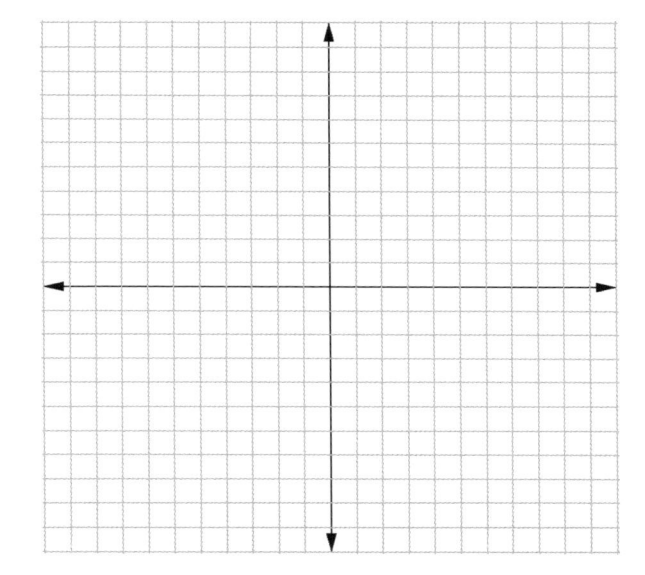

   b. What observations can you make about the relationship between $g(x)$ and $h(x)$?

Section 8: Summary of Functions

BEAT THE TEST!

1. Consider the following functions.

$$m(x) = \sqrt{x}$$
$$p(x) = \sqrt[3]{x}$$
$$t(x) = x^3$$

Which of the following statements is correct about the graph of $m(x)$, $p(x)$, and $t(x)$?

Ⓐ The domain of $m(x)$, $p(x)$, and $t(x)$ is all real numbers.
Ⓑ The range of $p(x)$ and $t(x)$ is $[3, \infty)$.
Ⓒ The range of $m(x)$ is $[0, \infty)$.
Ⓓ $m(x)$, $p(x)$, and $t(x)$ share the points $(0,0)$, $(1,1)$, and $(-1,-1)$.

2. A cube's volume, $V(s)$, is given by the equation $V(s) = s^3$, where s is the length of each side.

Part A: Sketch the graph that models the relationship between the volume and length of each side of a cube.

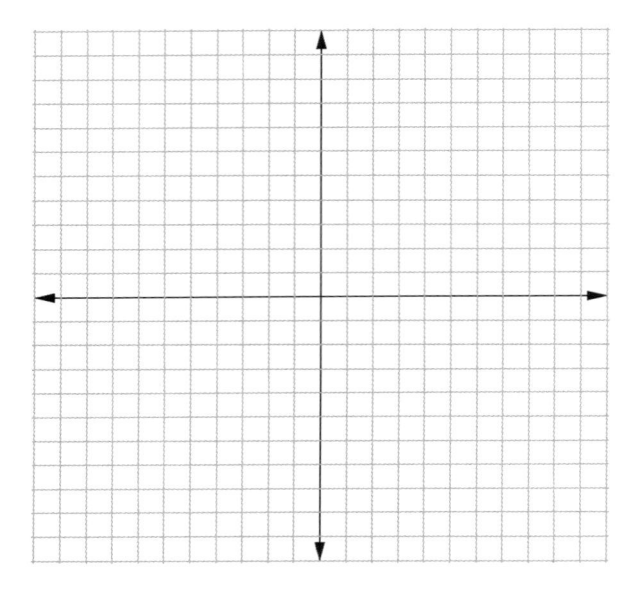

Part B: What are the domain and range of this relation?

Part C: If we know the volume of a cube, write a function $s(V)$ that we can use to find the length of the sides of the cube.

Part D: How would the graph of $s(V)$ compare to the graph of $V(s)$?

Test Yourself! Practice Tool Great job! You have reached the end of this section. Now it's time to try the "Test Yourself! Practice Tool," where you can practice all the skills and concepts you learned in this section. Log in to Algebra Nation and try out the "Test Yourself! Practice Tool" so you can see how well you know these topics!

Section 9: One-Variable Statistics

Topic 1: Dot Plots 226
Standards Covered: S-ID.1
☐ I can represent and interpret data with a dot plot.

Topic 2: Histograms 229
Standards Covered: S-ID.1
☐ I can represent and interpret data with a histogram.

Topic 3: Box Plots - Part 1 231
Standards Covered: S-ID.1
☐ I can represent and interpret data with a box plot.
☐ I can calculate and interpret the five-number summary of a data set.

Topic 4: Box Plots - Part 2 233
Standards Covered: S-ID.1
☐ I can interpret data in a real-world context using box plots.

Topic 5: Measures of Center and Shapes of Distributions 236
Standards Covered: S-ID.2
☐ I can calculate and compare measures of center.

Topic 6: Measures of Spread - Part 1 238
Standards Covered: S-ID.2
☐ I can calculate and compare measures of spread.

Topic 7: Measures of Spread - Part 2 240
Standards Covered: S-ID.2
☐ I can interpret similarities and differences in shape, center, and spread when given two or more data sets in real-world situations.

Topic 8: Outliers in Data Sets 242
Standards Covered: S-ID.3
☐ I can predict the effect an outlier will have on the shape, center, and spread of a data set.

Visit MathNation.com or search "Math Nation" in your phone or tablet's app store to watch the videos that go along with this workbook!

Visit MathNation.com or search "Math Nation" in your phone or tablet's app store to watch the videos that go along with this workbook!

Dot Plots

Statistics is the science of collecting, organizing, and analyzing data.

Two major classifications of data:

- **Categorical** (_categories_)
  - based on "qualities" such as color, taste, or texture, rather than measurements

- **Quantitative** (_numerical_)
  - based on measurements

The following Michigan Mathematics Standards will be covered in this section:
S-ID.1 - Represent data with plots on the real number line (dot plots, histograms, and box plots).
S-ID.2 - Use statistics appropriate to the shape of the data distribution to compare center (median, mean) and spread (interquartile range, standard deviation) of two or more different data sets.
S-ID.3 - Interpret differences in shape, center, and spread in the context of the data sets, accounting for possible effects of extreme data points (outliers).

Section 9: One-Variable Statistics

Section 9: One-Variable Statistics
Section 9 – Topic 1
Dot Plots

Statistics is the science of collecting, organizing, and analyzing data.

There are two major classifications of data.

- **Categorical** (_____)
  - Based on "qualities" such as color, taste, or texture, rather than measurements

- **Quantitative** (_____)
  - Based on measurements

There are two types of quantitative data.

- **Discrete**
  - There is a finite number of possible data values.

- **Continuous**
  - There are too many possible data values so data needs to be measured over intervals.

Classify the following variables.

Height
- o Categorical
- o Discrete quantitative
- o Continuous quantitative

Favorite subject
- o Categorical
- o Discrete quantitative
- o Continuous quantitative

Number of televisions in a household
- o Categorical
- o Discrete quantitative
- o Continuous quantitative

Area code
- o Categorical
- o Discrete quantitative
- o Continuous quantitative

Distance a football is thrown
- o Categorical
- o Discrete quantitative
- o Continuous quantitative

Number of siblings
- o Categorical
- o Discrete quantitative
- o Continuous quantitative

STUDY EDGE TIP: To differentiate between quantitative and categorical data ask yourself: Can I take the average of this data, and is it meaningful? If the average is meaningful, then the data is quantitative.

A group of college students were surveyed about the number of books they read each month. The data set is listed below.

$$1, 2, 2, 2, 3, 3, 3, 3, 4, 4, 4, 4, 4, 5, 5, 5, 5, 6, 6, 7$$

➢ Let's display the above data in a **dot plot**.

Reading Frequency Survey

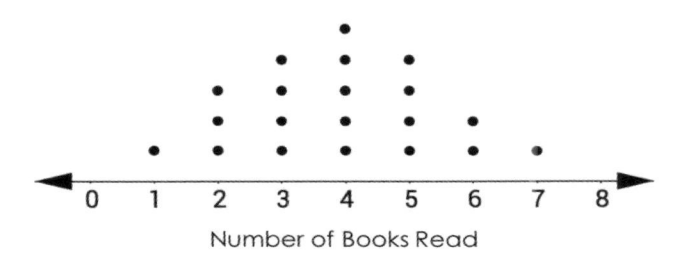

[Dot plot showing frequencies above numbers 0-8 on "Number of Books Read" axis]

➢ Each data value is represented with a _____ above the number line.
➢ The dot plot shows the _____ of data values.
➢ Always include the title and an appropriate scale on the number line for the dot plot.
➢ Dot plots are often used for:
   o smaller sets of data
   o discrete data

What is **frequency**?

Let's Practice!

1. The amount of time 26 students spent on their phones on a given day (rounded to the nearest hour) is recorded as follows.

$$0, 3, 4, 4, 5, 5, 6, 6, 6, 7, 7, 7, 7, 8, 8, 8, 8, 9, 9, 9, 10, 10, 10, 11, 11, 12$$

Create a dot plot of the data above.

Section 9: One-Variable Statistics

Try It!

2. Mrs. Ferrante surveyed her class and asked each student, "How many siblings do you have?" The results are displayed below.

   0, 4, 2, 2, 3, 4, 8, 1, 0, 1, 2, 2, 3, 0, 3, 1, 1, 2

   a. Construct a dot plot of the data.

   b. What observations can you make about the shape of the distribution?

   c. Are there any values that don't seem to fit? Justify your answer.

BEAT THE TEST!

1. The cafeteria at Just Dance Academy offers items at seven different prices. The manager recorded the price each time an item was sold in a two-hour period and created a dot plot to display the data.

   Items Sold at Just Dance Academy

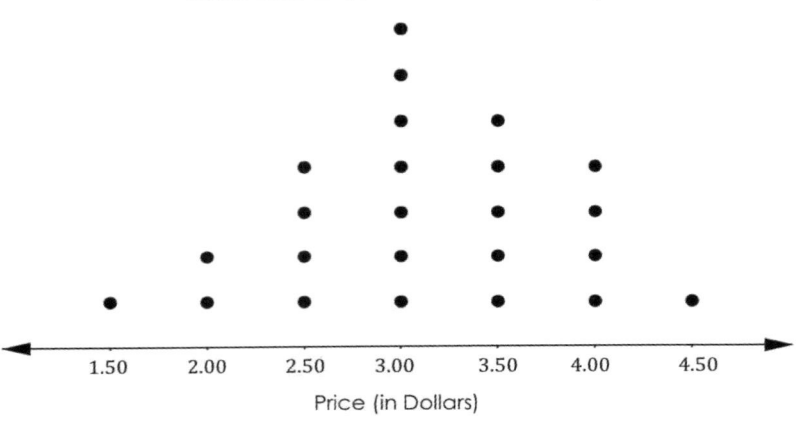

   Price (in Dollars)

   Describe the data from the dot plot.

Section 9: One-Variable Statistics

Section 9 – Topic 2
Histograms

College students were asked how well they did on their first statistics exam. Their scores are shown below.

$$100, 98, 77, 76, 85, 62, 73, 88, 85, 92, 93, 72, 66, 70, 90, 100$$

We can use a histogram to represent the data.

➢ A **histogram** is a bar-style data display showing frequency of data measured over _____, rather than displaying each individual data value.

➢ Each interval width must be the _____.

➢ Always _____ the graph and _____ both axes.

➢ Choose the appropriate scale on the y-axis and the appropriate intervals on the x-axis.

➢ Histograms are often used for:
  o larger sets of data
  o continuous data

Describe an interval.

Represent the following students' scores on a histogram.

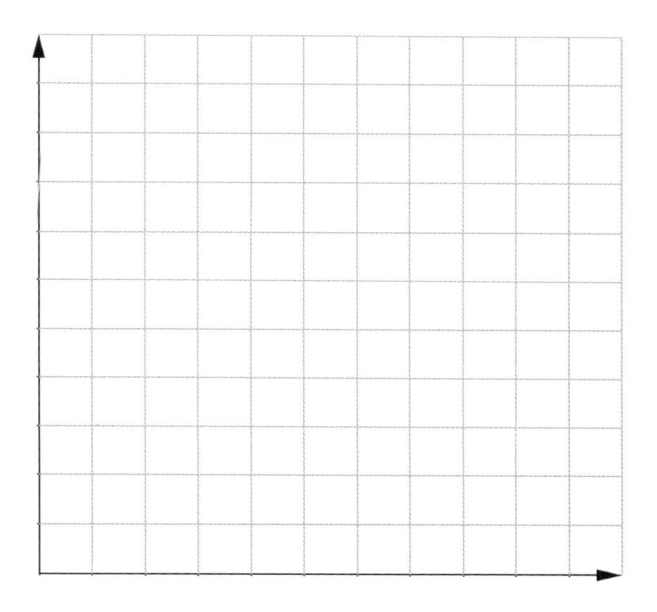

$$100, 98, 77, 76, 85, 62, 73, 88, 85, 92, 93, 72, 66, 70, 90, 100$$

Section 9: One-Variable Statistics

Let's Practice!

1. Those same students from our first example were also asked how long in minutes it took them to complete the exam. The data is shown below.

   40.3, 42.4, 43.2, 44.1, 45.0, 55.7, 64.3, 70.3, 72.1, 32.3, 44.4, 54.5, 71.3, 66.1, 35.8, 67.2

   Construct a histogram to represent the data.

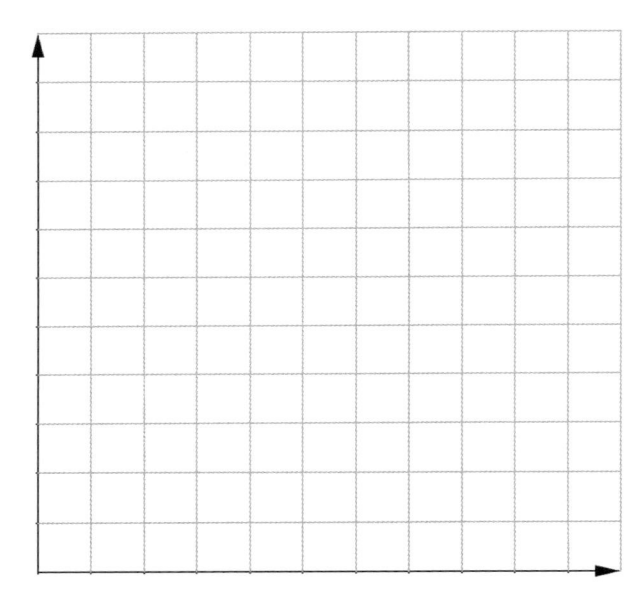

Try It!

2. Determine the sets of data where it would be better to use a histogram instead of a dot plot. Select all that apply.

   ☐ Average daily temperatures for Albany, NY over a year
   ☐ Daily temperatures for Albany, NY over a month
   ☐ The results of rolling two dice over and over
   ☐ Height of high school football players statewide
   ☐ Finishing times of 125 randomly selected athletes for a 100-meter race

Section 9: One-Variable Statistics

BEAT THE TEST!

1. Last year, the local men's basketball team had a great season. The total points scored by the team for each of the 20 games are listed below:

   45, 46, 46, 52, 53, 53, 55, 56, 57, 58, 62, 62, 64, 64, 65, 67, 67, 76, 76, 89

   Create a frequency table, and construct a histogram of the data.

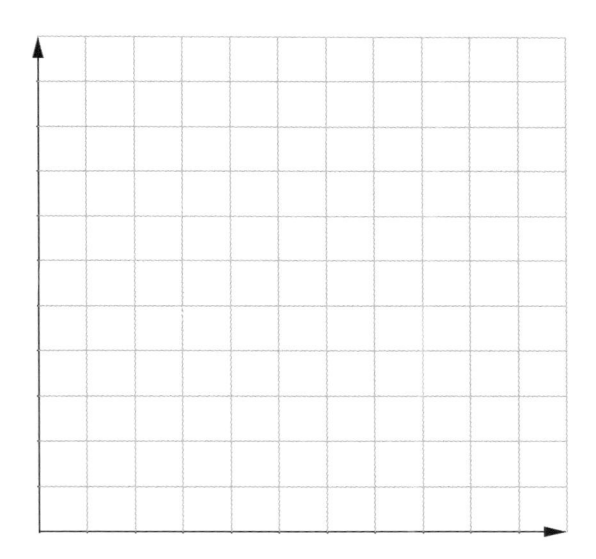

Section 9 – Topic 3
Box Plots – Part 1

The following **box plot** graphically displays a summary of the data set {1, 2, 2, 2, 3, 3, 3, 3, 4, 4, 4, 4, 4, 5, 5, 5, 5, 6, 6, 7}.

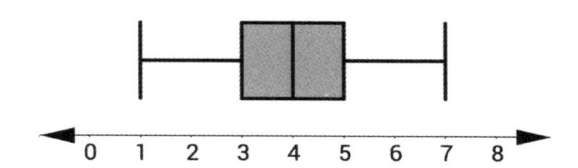

A box plot displays the **five-number summary** for a data set.

> The five-number summary of a data set consists of the minimum, first quartile, median, third quartile, and maximum values.

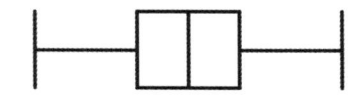

What is a quartile?

Section 9: One-Variable Statistics

Even data set:

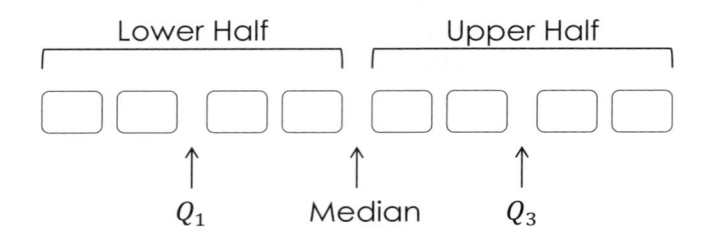

Lower Half | Upper Half

↑ Q_1 ↑ Median   ↑ Q_3

Odd data set:

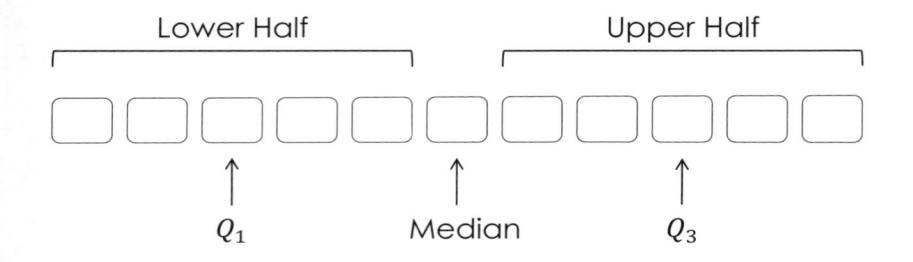

Lower Half | Upper Half

↑ Q_1 ↑ Median   ↑ Q_3

Consider the following data set with an even number of data values.

$$6, 2, 1, 4, 7, 3, 8, 5$$

The minimum value of the data set is _____.

The maximum value of the data set is _____.

The median is the number in the middle when the data is ordered from least to greatest. The median of the data set is _____.

The first quartile of the data set is _____.

The third quartile of the data set is _____.

Use the five-number summary to represent the data with a box plot.

Section 9: One-Variable Statistics

Some observations from our box plot:

> The lowest 50% of data values are from ____ to ____.

> The highest 50% of data values are from ____ to ____.

> The middle 50% (the box area) represents the values from _____ to _____.
>   ○ The middle 50% is also known as the IQR (interquartile range).

> The first quartile represents the lower 25% of the data (_____ percentile).

> The third quartile represents the first 75% of the data (_____ percentile).

> 75% of the values are above _____.

> 25% of the values are above _____.

> The median of the lower half of the data is _____.

> The median of the upper half of the data is _____.

Section 9 – Topic 4
Box Plots – Part 2

Consider the following data sets.

Data set #1: 1, 3, 5, 7, 9, 11, 13, 23

Data set #2: 1, 3, 5, 7, 9, 11, 13, 15

Complete the following table.

	Minimum	Maximum	Median	First Quartile	Third Quartile
Data Set #1					
Data Set #2					

Construct the box plots for both data sets, one above the other.

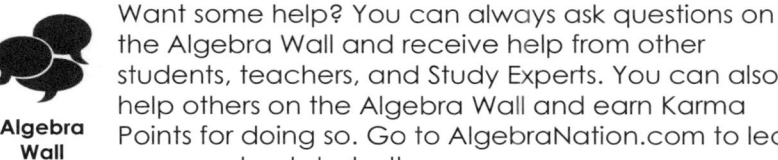

Want some help? You can always ask questions on the Algebra Wall and receive help from other students, teachers, and Study Experts. You can also help others on the Algebra Wall and earn Karma Points for doing so. Go to AlgebraNation.com to learn more and get started!

Section 9: One-Variable Statistics

Compare and contrast both box plots.

Explain which box plot is not symmetrical. Justify your answer.

Let's Practice!

1. Consider the following data set with an odd number of data values.

   $$3, 7, 10, 11, 15, 18, 21$$

   a. The minimum value of the data set is _____.
   b. The maximum value of the data set is _____.
   c. The median of the data set is _____.
   d. The first quartile of the data set is _____.
   e. The third quartile of the data set is _____.
   f. Use the five-number summary to construct a box plot.

Try It!

2. The time, rounded to the nearest hour, that 26 tourists spent on excursions in Cat Island, Mississippi on a given day was recorded as follows. (Cat Island is not actually an island for cats.)

   $$0, 3, 4, 4, 5, 5, 6, 6, 6, 7, 7, 7, 7, 8, 8, 8, 8, 9, 9, 9, 10, 10, 10, 11, 11, 12$$

   a. Construct a box plot to represent the data. Label the minimum, maximum, first quartile, third quartile, and median.

   b. The bottom 25% of tourists spent, at most, _____ hours on excursions.

Section 9: One-Variable Statistics

BEAT THE TEST!

1. Mrs. Bridgewater recorded the number of Snapchats 10 different students sent in one day and constructed the box plot below for the data.

   Part A: Use the following vocabulary to label the box plot.
   Hint: You will not use all of the words on the list.

   > **A.** Average
   > **B.** First Quartile
   > **C.** Maximum
   > **D.** Mean
   > **E.** Median
   > **F.** Minimum
   > **G.** Third Quartile

   Snapchats Sent In One Day

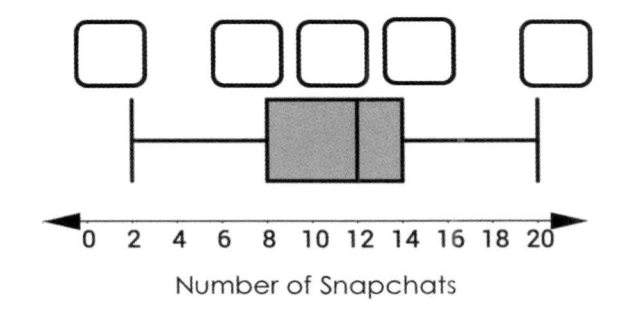

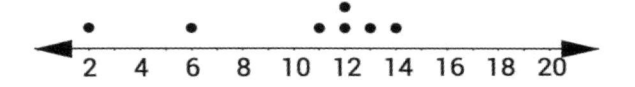

   Number of Snapchats

   Part B: The 50th percentile of the data set is _____.

   Part C: Half of the data values are between
   > 2 and 20.
   > 8 and 12.
   > 8 and 14.
   > 10 and 12.

   Part D: 75% of students send
   > 12
   > 13
   > 14
   > 15

   or fewer Snapchats per day.

   Part E: Add dots to the number line below to complete the dot plot so that it could also represent the data.

   Snapchats Sent In One Day

   Number of Snapchats

Algebra Wall

Want some help? You can always ask questions on the Algebra Wall and receive help from other students, teachers, and Study Experts. You can also help others on the Algebra Wall and earn Karma Points for doing so. Go to AlgebraNation.com to learn more and get started!

Section 9: One-Variable Statistics

Section 9 – Topic 5
Measures of Center and Shapes of Distributions

Data displays can be used to describe the following elements of a data set's distribution:

- Center
- Shape
- Spread

There are three common **measures of center**.

- **Mean:** The _____ of the data values.

- **Median:** The _____ value of the ordered data set.

- **Mode:** The _____ _____ occurring value(s).

Mr. Gray gave a test on a regular school day with no special activities. The scores are listed below.

$$60, 60, 70, 70, 70, 80, 80, 80, 80, 90, 90, 90, 100, 100$$

The dot plot for the data is as follows:

Mr. Gray's Class Score Distribution

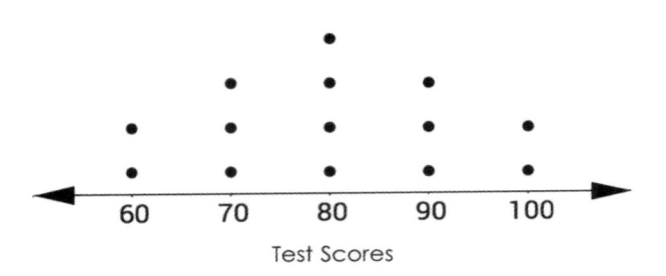

Test Scores

Looking at the dot plot, what do you think is the value of the median?

What is the value of the mean?

Why is it important to know where the center is?

The shape of a dot plot also gives important information about a data set's distribution. The data in the previous dot plot is symmetrical and follows a **normal distribution**. What do you notice about the shape of a normal distribution?

Let's Practice!

1. Mr. Gray then gave a test the day after a basketball game against the school's rival. The scores were as follows.

   65, 65, 65, 65, 65, 70, 70, 70, 70, 70, 70, 75, 75, 75, 75, 80, 80, 80, 80, 85, 90, 90, 95, 100

   Mr. Gray's Class Score Distribution

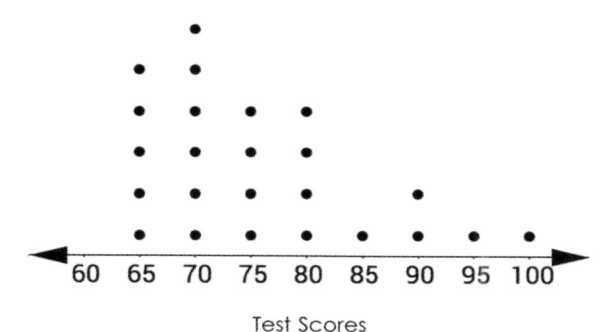

   Test Scores

   a. What are the mean and the median of this data set?

   b. Which measure is a more appropriate measure of center, the mean or the median?

   c. Does this data set have a normal distribution? Why or why not?

   d. The shape of this distribution is _____ _____.

Try It!

2. Mr. Gray then gave a test the day after a mid-week early release day. The scores were as follows.

   50, 60, 70, 70, 80, 80, 80, 90, 90, 90, 90, 90, 100, 100, 100

   a. Which value do you think will be smaller: the mean or the median?

   b. Consider the dot plot for the data.

   Mr. Gray's Class Score Distribution

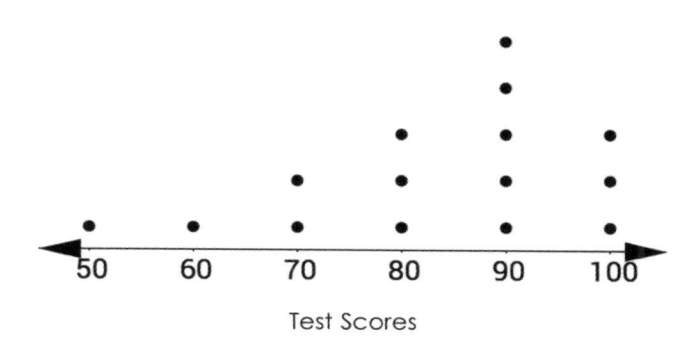

   Test Scores

   Which measure is a more appropriate measure of center, the mean or the median?

   c. The shape of this distribution is _____ _____.

   d. For a normal-shaped data set the best measure of center is the _____, whereas for a skewed-shaped data set, the _____ is better.

Section 9: One-Variable Statistics

BEAT THE TEST!

1. Mr. Logan surveyed his junior and senior students about the time they spent studying math in one day. He then tabulated the results and created a dot plot displaying the data for both groups.

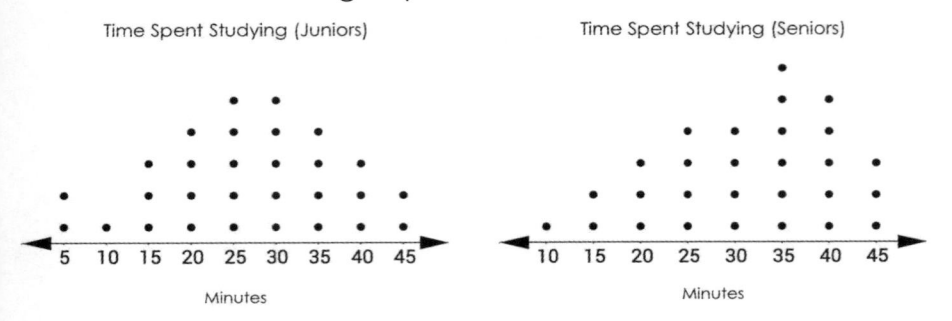

   Time Spent Studying (Juniors) — dot plot on axis labeled Minutes from 5 to 45.

   Time Spent Studying (Seniors) — dot plot on axis labeled Minutes from 10 to 45.

   Part A: The value of the larger median for the two groups is _____.

   Part B: The value of the larger mean for the two groups is _____.

   Part C: Using one to two sentences, describe the difference between the number of minutes the juniors and seniors studied by comparing the center and shapes for the groups.

Algebra Wall — Want some help? You can always ask questions on the Algebra Wall and receive help from other students, teachers, and Study Experts. You can also help others on the Algebra Wall and earn Karma Points for doing so. Go to AlgebraNation.com to learn more and get started!

Section 9 – Topic 6
Measures of Spread – Part 1

A meteorologist recorded the average weekly temperatures over a 13-week period and displayed the data below.

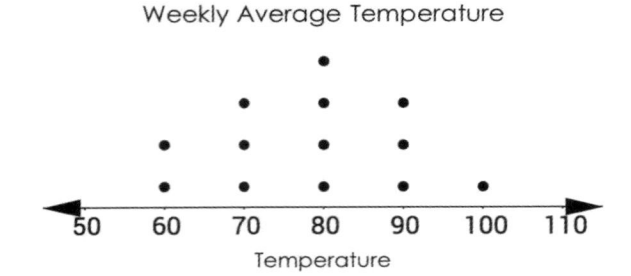

Weekly Average Temperature — dot plot on axis labeled Temperature from 50 to 110.

A meteorologist in a different state also recorded the average weekly temperatures over a 13-week period and displayed the data below.

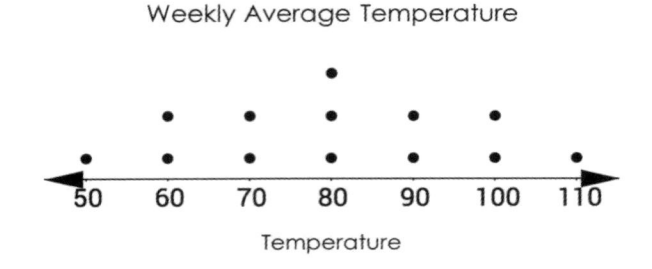

Weekly Average Temperature — dot plot on axis labeled Temperature from 50 to 110.

Measures of spread tell us how much a data sample is spread out or scattered.

What are the differences between the spreads of the two data sets?

There are two primary ways to measure the spread of data.

> **Interquartile Range (IQR)** = represents the middle 50% of the data and is typically used to describe the spread of _____ data.

Consider the following data set.

$$5, 5, 6, 7, 8, 8, 8, 9, 10, 12, 12$$

What are the first and third quartiles of the data?

Calculate the interquartile range (IQR) of the data.

Why do you think IQR is used to measure spread in skewed data?

> **Standard deviation** is the typical distance of the data values from the mean. The larger the standard deviation, the _____ the individual values are from the mean. It is typically used for _____ _____.

Consider the dot plots below.

A.

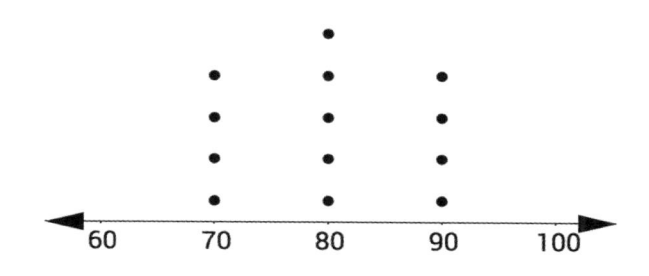

B.

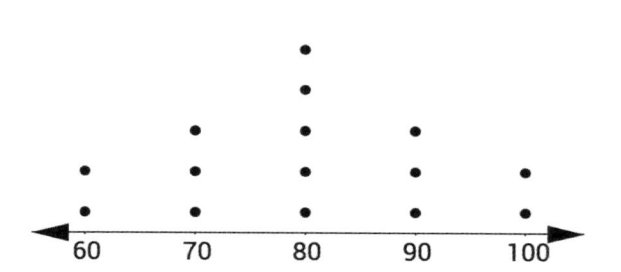

Which has a larger standard deviation? Explain your answer.

Want some help? You can always ask questions on the Algebra Wall and receive help from other students, teachers, and Study Experts. You can also help others on the Algebra Wall and earn Karma Points for doing so. Go to AlgebraNation.com to learn more and get started!

Algebra Wall

Section 9: One-Variable Statistics

Section 9 – Topic 7
Measures of Spread – Part 2

Let's Practice!

1. The Bozeman Bucks and Tate Aggies cross-country teams ran an obstacle course. The times for each team are summarized below.

   Bozeman Bucks' Obstacle Course Times

4:25	4:43	4:49	5:02	5:12
5:21	5:31	5:32	5:37	5:52
5:54	6:08	6:20	6:26	6:33
6:48	6:53	7:16	7:23	8:05

   Tate Aggies' Obstacle Course Times

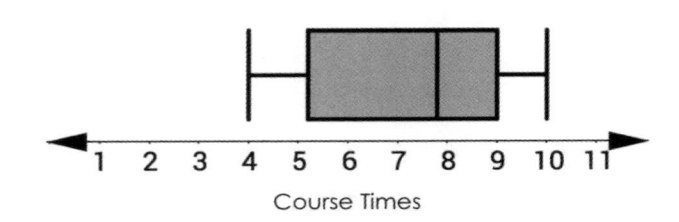

   Which statements are true about the data for the Bozeman Bucks and the Tate Aggies? Select all that apply.

   ☐ The median time of the Bozeman Bucks is less than the median time of the Tate Aggies.
   ☐ The fastest 25% of athletes on both teams complete the obstacle course in about the same amount of time.
   ☐ The interquartile range of the Bozeman Bucks is less than the interquartile range of the Tate Aggies.
   ☐ Approximately 50% of Tate Aggies have times between 5 and 6 minutes.
   ☐ The data for the Bozeman Bucks is skewed to the left.

Try It!

2. The following box plots represent the starting salaries (in thousands of dollars) of 12 recent business graduates, 12 recent engineering graduates, and 12 recent psychology graduates.

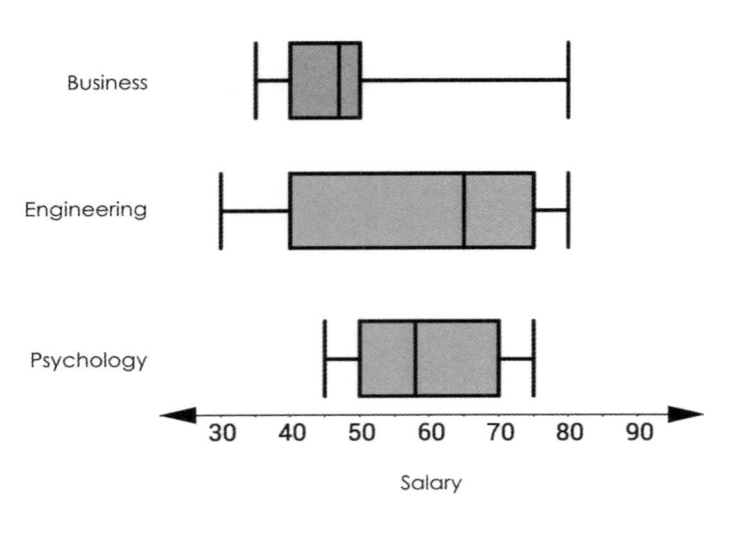

   a. Describe the shape of each major's data distribution.

      Business:

      Engineering:

      Psychology:

   b. Which major has the largest median salary? The largest IQR?

BEAT THE TEST!

1. Data on the time that Mrs. Lannister's students spend studying math and science on a given night are summarized below.

   Math

   Mean: 75 minutes
   Minimum: 0 minutes
   First Quartile: 65 minutes
   Median: 78 minutes
   Third Quartile: 100 minutes
   Maximum: 145 minutes
   Standard deviation: 8 minutes

   Science

   Mean: 25 minutes
   Minimum: 0 minutes
   First Quartile: 15 minutes
   Median: 30 minutes
   Third Quartile: 35 minutes
   Maximum: 50 minutes
   Standard deviation: 12 minutes

   Tyrion spent 10 minutes studying math and 50 minutes studying science. If Tyrion spent all 60 minutes studying math, which of the following would be affected?

	Increases	Decreases	Stays the Same
Interquartile Range of Math Time	o	o	o
Standard Deviation of Math Time	o	o	o

2. The data from a survey of the ages of people in a CrossFit class were skewed to the right.

   Part A: The appropriate measure of center to describe the data distribution is the
   - o mean.
   - o median.

   The
   - o interquartile range
   - o standard deviation

   is the appropriate measure to describe the spread.

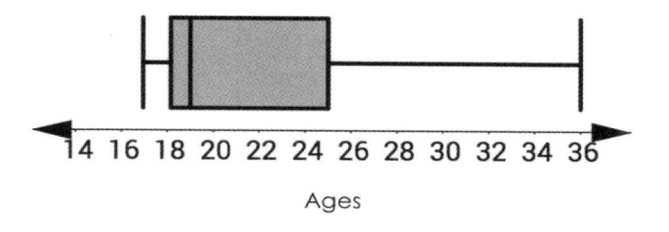

   Part B: The box plot below represents the data. Calculate the appropriate measure of spread.

   Age Distribution in a CrossFit Class

   14 16 18 20 22 24 26 28 30 32 34 36
   Ages

Section 9: One-Variable Statistics

Section 9 – Topic 8
Outliers in Data Sets

A survey about the average number of text messages sent per day was conducted at a retirement home.

$$5, 5, 5, 5, 5, 5, 5, 10, 10, 10, 10, 10, 15, 15, 15$$

The mean for this data set is 8.7 and the median is 10.

Grandma Gadget is up-to-date on the latest technology and loves to text her 25 grandchildren. She sends an average of 85 texts per day. Her data point is substituted for one of the original data points of 15.

The new data set is:

$$5, 5, 5, 5, 5, 5, 5, 10, 10, 10, 10, 10, 15, 15, 85$$

Which measure of center will be most affected by substituting Grandma Gadget – the mean or the median? Justify your answer.

Does Grandma Gadget's data point have a greater effect on standard deviation or interquartile range? Justify your answer.

Grandma Gadget's data point is called an **outlier**.

An **outlier** is an _____ value in a data set that is very distant from the others.

Let's Practice!

1. The table below lists the number of customers who visited a car dealership during 30 randomly selected days.

26	29	27	33	29	28
31	36	26	31	35	32
34	34	28	11	35	35
33	37	31	26	37	33
29	35	37	29	27	33

Identify the outlier and describe how it affects the mean and the standard deviation.

The outlier is _____. The outlier in the data set causes the mean to _____ and the standard deviation to _____.

242

Section 9: One-Variable Statistics

Try It!

2. The students in Mrs. Gomez's class were surveyed about the number of text messages they send per day. The data set is as follows.

    0, 24, 26, 28, 28, 30, 33, 35, 35, 36, 38, 39, 42, 42, 45, 50

    a. What value would you predict to be an outlier?

    b. How does the outlier affect the mean?

    c. How does the outlier affect the median?

    d. Which measure of center would best describe the data, the mean or the median?

    e. How does the outlier affect the standard deviation?

    f. How does the outlier affect the interquartile range?

    g. Which measure of spread would best describe the data, the standard deviation or the interquartile range?

BEAT THE TEST!

1. The dot plot below compares the arrival times of 30 flights for two different airlines.

    Arrival Times for Airlines P and Q

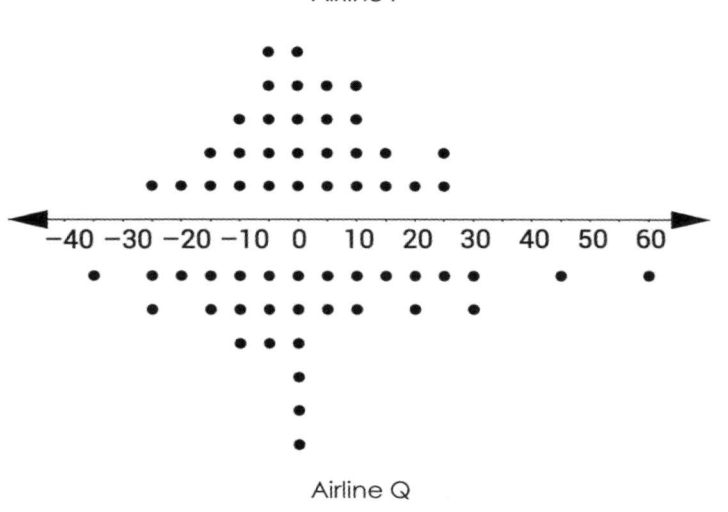

    Airline P

    Airline Q

    A negative number represents the number of minutes the flight arrived before its scheduled time.

    A positive number represents the number of minutes the flight arrived after its scheduled time.

    A zero indicates that the flight arrived at its scheduled time.

    Based on these data, from which airline would you choose to buy your ticket? Use your knowledge of shape, center, outliers, and spread to justify your choice.

Section 9: One-Variable Statistics

2. After a long day at Disney World, a group of students were asked how many times they each rode Space Mountain. The values are as follows.

$$4, 3, 19, 1, 2, 2, 4, 3, 5, 3, 4, 5, 4, 5$$

Part A: Are there any outliers in the data set above? Explain.

Part B: The outlier causes the
- ○ mean
- ○ median

to be greater than the
- ○ mean.
- ○ median.

Part C: If the outlier were changed to 5, the interquartile range would
- ○ increase
- ○ decrease
- ○ stay the same

and the standard deviation would
- ○ increase.
- ○ decrease.
- ○ stay the same.

Test Yourself! Practice Tool

Great job! You have reached the end of this section. Now it's time to try the "Test Yourself! Practice Tool," where you can practice all the skills and concepts you learned in this section. Log in to Algebra Nation and try out the "Test Yourself! Practice Tool" so you can see how well you know these topics!

THIS PAGE WAS INTENTIONALLY LEFT BLANK

Section 10: Two-Variable Statistics

Topic 1: Relationship between Two Categorical Variables – Marginal and Joint Relative Frequency - Part 1 247
Standards Covered: S-ID.5
- ☐ I can create a two-way frequency table to summarize data.
- ☐ I can interpret data displayed in a two-way frequency table.
- ☐ I can calculate joint and marginal relative frequencies in the context of data.

Topic 2: Relationship between Two Categorical Variables – Marginal and Joint Relative Frequency - Part 2 248
Standards Covered: S-ID.5
- ☐ I can use a two-way frequency table to interpret data.
- ☐ I can calculate and interpret joint and marginal relative frequencies.

Topic 3: Relationship between Two Categorical Variables – Conditional Relative Frequency 250
Standards Covered: S-ID.5
- ☐ I can calculate conditional relative frequencies.
- ☐ I can use conditional relative frequencies to determine if there is an association between two categorical variables.

Topic 4: Scatter Plots and Function Models 252
Standards Covered: S-ID.6.a.c
- ☐ I can classify and interpret scatterplots.
- ☐ I can find the line of best fit for a data set.

Topic 5: Scatter Plots and Lines of Best Fit 255
Standards Covered: S-ID.6.a.c, S-ID.7
- ☐ I can fit a linear function for a scatter plot that suggests a linear association.
- ☐ I can use the function fitted to data to solve problems in the context of the data.

Topic 6: Residuals and Residual Plots - Part 1 258
Standards Covered: S-ID.6.b
- ☐ I can calculate and graph residuals.
- ☐ I can use residual plot to determine if a model is appropriate for a dataset.

Topic 7: Residuals and Residual Plots - Part 2 261
Standards Covered: S-ID.6.b
- ☐ I can use residual plot to determine if a model is appropriate for a dataset.

Topic 8: Examining Correlation 263
Standards Covered: S-ID.8, S-ID.9
- ☐ I can calculate and interpret the correlation coefficient for linear data.
- ☐ I can distinguish between correlation and causation.

Visit MathNation.com or search "Math Nation" in your phone or tablet's app store to watch the videos that go along with this workbook!

Relationship between Two Categorical Variables – Marginal and Joint Relative Frequency – Part 1

Two categorical variables can be represented with a **two-way frequency table.**

Consider the following survey.

149 elementary students were asked to choose whether they prefer math or English class. The data were broken down by gender.

42 males prefer math class.
47 males prefer English class.
35 females prefer math cla...

The following Michigan Mathematics Standards will be covered in this section:
S-ID.5 - Summarize categorical data for two categories in two-way frequency tables. Interpret relative frequencies in the context of the data (including joint, marginal, and conditional relative frequencies). Recognize possible associations and trends in the data.
S-ID.6.a.b.c - Represent data on two quantitative variables on a scatter plot, and describe how the variables are related. a. Fit the function to the data; use functions fitted to data to solve problems in the context of the data. Use given functions or choose a function suggested by the context. Emphasize linear, quadratic, and exponential models. b. Informally assess the fit of a function by plotting and analyzing residuals. c. Fit a linear function for a scatter plot that suggests a linear association.
S-ID.7 - Interpret the slope (rate of change) and the intercept (constant term) of a linear model in the context of the data.
S-ID.8 - Compute (using technology) and interpret the correlation coefficient of a linear fit.
S-ID.9 - Distinguish between correlation and causation.

Section 10: Two-Variable Statistics
Section 10 – Topic 1
Relationship between Two Categorical Variables – Marginal and Joint Relative Frequency – Part 1

Two categorical variables can be represented with a **two-way frequency table**.

Consider the following survey.

149 elementary students were asked to choose whether they prefer math or English class. The data were broken down by gender.

> 42 males prefer math class.
> 47 males prefer English class.
> 35 females prefer math class.
> 25 females prefer English class.

A two-way frequency table is a visual representation of the frequency counts for each categorical variable. The table can also be called a **contingency table**.

Elementary Students' Subject Preferences

	Math	English	Total
Males			
Females			
Total			

The total frequency for any row or column is called a **marginal frequency**.

> ➤ Why do you think these total frequencies are called marginal frequencies?

Joint frequencies are the counts in the body of the table that join one variable from a row and one variable from a column.

> ➤ Why do you think these frequencies are called joint frequencies?

Draw a box around the marginal frequencies. Circle the joint frequencies in the "Elementary Students' Subject Preferences" contingency table.

Frequency tables can be easily changed to show **relative frequencies**.

> To calculate relative frequency, divide each count in the frequency table by the overall total.

Complete the following relative frequency table.

Elementary Students' Subject Preferences

	Math	English	Total
Males			
Females			
Total			

Why do you think these ratios are called relative frequencies?

Draw a box around the **marginal relative frequencies** and circle the **joint relative frequencies** in the table.

Interpret the marginal relative frequency for male students.

Interpret the joint relative frequency for females who prefer math.

Want some help? You can always ask questions on the Algebra Wall and receive help from other students, teachers, and Study Experts. You can also help others on the Algebra Wall and earn Karma Points for doing so. Go to AlgebraNation.com to learn more and get started!

Section 10 – Topic 2
Relationship between Two Categorical Variables – Marginal and Joint Relative Frequency – Part 2

Let's Practice!

1. A survey of high school students asked if they play video games. The following frequency table was created based on their responses.

Student Video Game Activity

	Play Video Games	Do Not Play Video Games	Total
Males	69	60	
Females	65	85	
Total			

a. Compute the joint and marginal relative frequencies in the table.

b. How many female students do not play video games?

c. What percentage of students interviewed were females who do not play video games?

248

Section 10: Two-Variable Statistics

Try It!

2. Consider the frequency table "Student Video Game Activity."

    a. How many male students were interviewed?

    b. One of the interviewed students is selected at random. What is the probability that a student interviewed is male?

    c. Which numbers represent joint frequencies?

    d. Which numbers represent joint relative frequencies?

    e. What percentage of the subjects interviewed play video games?

BEAT THE TEST!

1. A survey conducted at Ambidextrous High School asked all 1,700 students to indicate their grade level and if they are left-handed or right-handed. Only 59 of the 491 freshmen are left-handed. Out of the 382 students in the sophomore class, 289 of them are right-handed. There are 433 students in the junior class and 120 of them are left-handed. There are 307 right-handed seniors.

    Part A: Complete the frequency table to display the results of the survey.

    Dominant Hand Survey

					Total
Right-handed					
Left-handed					
Total					

    Part B: What is the joint relative frequency for right-handed freshmen?

    Part C: What does the relative frequency $\frac{491}{1,700}$ represent?

    Part D: Circle the smallest marginal frequency.

Section 10: Two-Variable Statistics

Section 10 – Topic 3
Relationship between Two Categorical Variables – Conditional Relative Frequency

Recall the students' class subject preference data.

Elementary Students' Subject Preferences

	Math	English	Total
Males	42	47	89
Females	35	25	60
Total	77	72	149

The principal says that males in the interview have a stronger preference for math than females. Why might the principal say this?

We can determine the answer to questions like this by comparing **conditional relative frequencies**.

Complete the conditional relative frequency table on the following page to determine whether males or females showed stronger math preference in the survey.

Conditional Relative Frequency Table

	Math	English	Total
Males			
Females			
Total			

What percentage of male students prefer math?

What percentage of female students prefer math?

These percentages are called **conditional relative frequencies**.

➢ Make a conjecture as to why they are called conditional relative frequencies.

When trying to predict a person's class preference, does it help to know his/her gender?

Section 10: Two-Variable Statistics

To evaluate whether there is a relationship between two categorical variables, look at the conditional relative frequencies.

> - If there is a significant difference between the conditional relative frequencies, then there is evidence of an association between two categorical variables.

Is there an association between gender and class preference?

Let's Practice!

Consider the high school students who were asked if they play video games.

Video Games Survey

	Play Video Games	Do Not Play Video Games	Total
Males	69	60	129
Females	65	85	150
Total	134	145	279

1. What percentage of the students who do not play video games are female?

2. Given that a student is female, what is the probability that the student does not play video games?

Try It!

3. Of the students who are male, what is the probability that the student plays video games?

4. What percentage of the students who play video games are male?

Section 10: Two-Variable Statistics

BEAT THE TEST!

1. Freshmen and sophomores were asked about their preferences for an end-of-year field trip for students who pass their final examinations. Students were given the choice to visit an amusement park, a water park, or a mystery destination. A random sample of 100 freshmen and sophomores was selected. The activities coordinator constructed a frequency table to analyze the data.

Students' Field Trip Preferences

	Amusement Park	Water Park	Mystery Destination	Total
Freshmen	25	10	20	55
Sophomores	35	5	5	45
Total	60	15	25	100

Part A: What does the relative frequency $\frac{10}{55}$ represent?

Part B: What percentage of students who want to go to an amusement park are sophomores?

Part C: What activity should the coordinator schedule for sophomores? Justify your answer.

Want some help? You can always ask questions on the Algebra Wall and receive help from other students, teachers, and Study Experts. You can also help others on the Algebra Wall and earn Karma Points for doing so. Go to AlgebraNation.com to learn more and get started!

Section 10 – Topic 4
Scatter Plots and Function Models

Let's consider quantitative data involving two variables.

Consider the data below showing the performance intelligence quotient (IQ) scores and height (in inches) of 38 college students.

Person's Height and IQ Score

Height (in Inches)	Performance IQ Score	Height (in inches)	Performance IQ Score
64.5	124	66	90
73.3	150	68	96
68.8	128	68.5	120
65	134	73.5	102
69	110	66.3	84
64.5	131	70	86
66	98	76.5	84
66.3	84	62	134
68.8	147	68	128
64.5	124	63	102
70	128	72	131
69	124	68	84
70.5	147	77	110
63	72	66.5	81
66.5	124	66.5	128
62.5	132	70.5	124
67	137	64.5	94
75.5	110	74	74
69	86	75.5	89

Source: Willerman, L., Schultz, R., Rutledge, J. N., and Bigler, E. (1991), In Vivo Brain Size and Intelligence, Intelligence, 15, 223-228.

A **scatterplot** of the data is also shown on the following page.

A scatterplot is a graphical representation of the relationship between two quantitative variables.

Person's Height and IQ Score

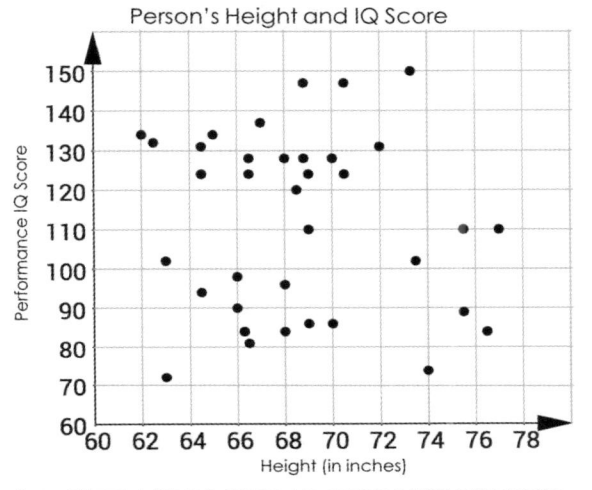

Source: Willerman, L., Schultz, R., Rutledge, J. N., and Bigler, E. (1991), In Vivo Brain Size and Intelligence, Intelligence, 15, 223-228.

What do the values on the *x*-axis represent?

What do the values on the *y*-axis represent?

What does the ordered pair $(66, 90)$ represent?

Describe the relationship between height and Performance IQ Score.

Let's Practice!

1. Classify the relationship represented in each of the scatterplots below as linear, quadratic, or exponential.

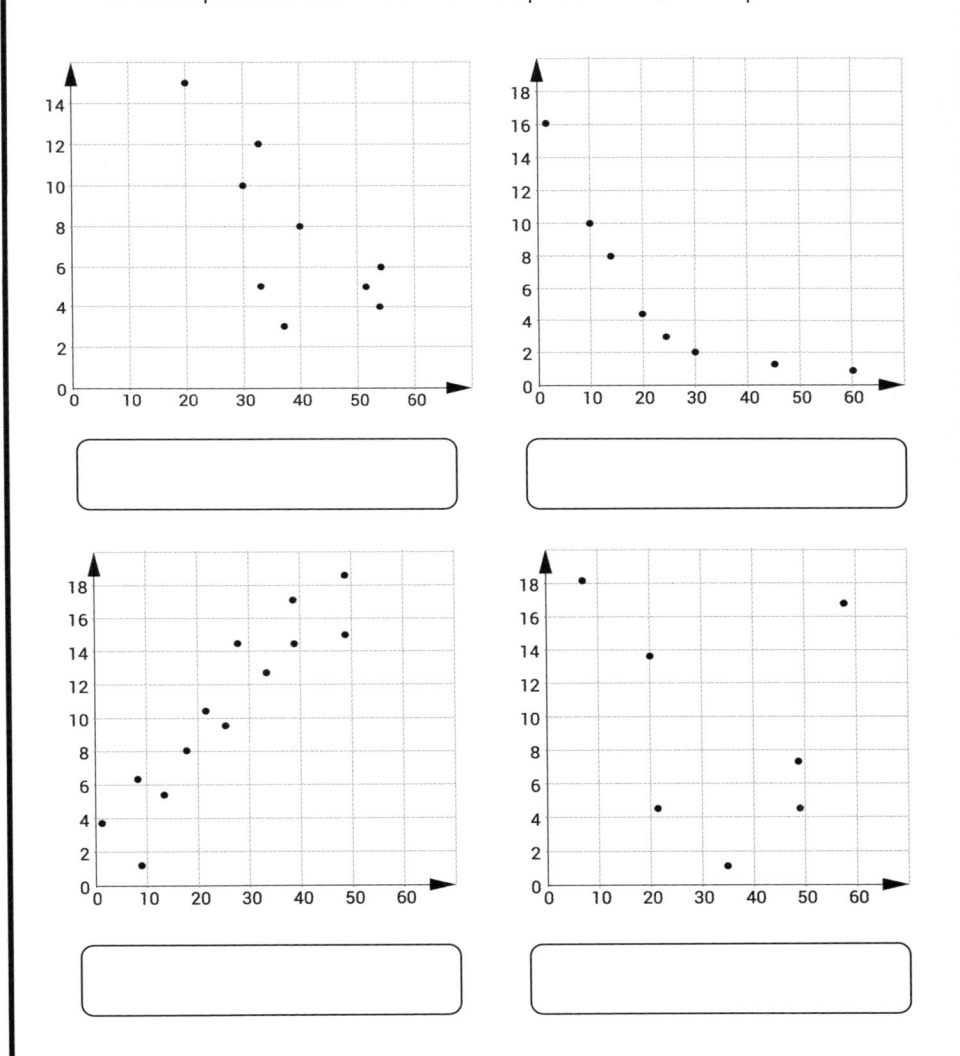

Section 10: Two-Variable Statistics

Try It!

2. Over a nine-month period, students at Oak Grove High School collected data on their total number of Instagram posts each month. The results are summarized below.

Month	1	2	3	4	5	6	7	8	9
# Posts	36	52	108	146	340	515	742	1,042	1,529

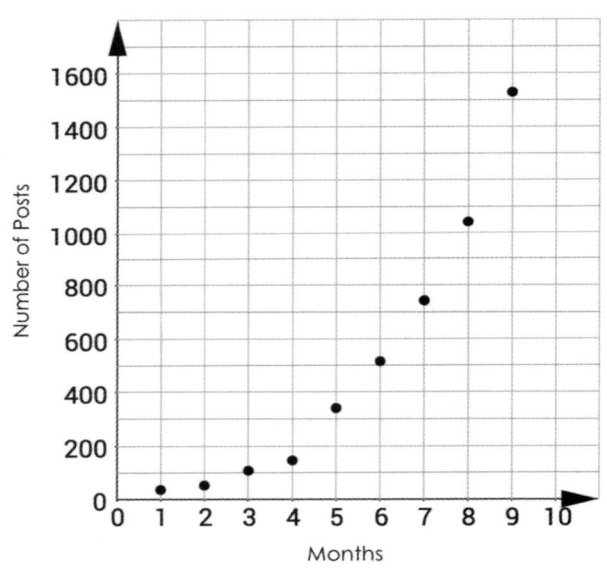

Instagram Posts

The linear regression equation fit to this data is $f(x) = 176.32x - 380.47$, and the exponential regression equation fit to this data is $g(x) = 23.30 \cdot 1.62^x$.

a. What is the predicted number of posts for month 11 using the linear function?

b. What is the predicted number of posts for month 11 using the exponential function?

c. Is the linear equation or the exponential equation the best model for this data?

BEAT THE TEST!

1. The scatterplot below shows the number of violent crimes committed in the United States for the years 1993-2012.

   Violent Crimes in the United States, 1993-2012

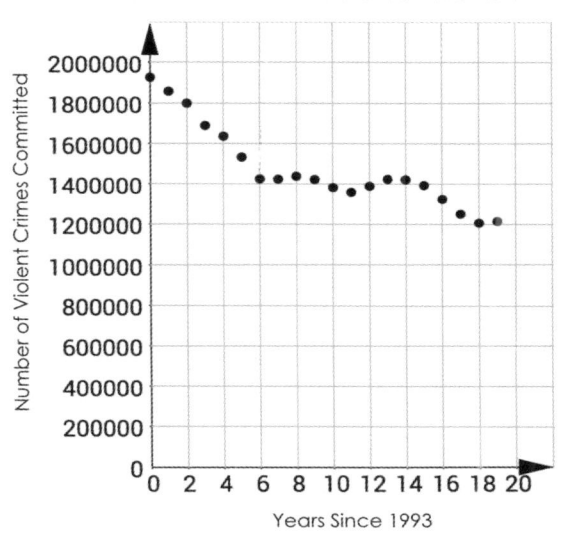

   [Scatterplot: x-axis "Years Since 1993" from 0 to 20; y-axis "Number of Violent Crimes Committed" from 0 to 2000000]

   Source: United States Department of Justice, https://ucr.fbi.gov/

   The linear equation that best models this relationship is $y = -31{,}256x + 1{,}773{,}900$, where x represents the number of years since 1993 and y represents the number of violent crimes.

   If the trend continues, predict the number of violent crimes in the year 2020.

Section 10 – Topic 5
Scatter Plots and Lines of Best Fit

Consider the data below showing the life expectancy (in years) for newborns in India since 1881.

Infant Life Expectancy, 1881-2009

Year (1881-2009)	Average Life Expectancy	Year (1881-2009) continued	Average Life Expectancy continued
1881	25.442	1966	47.058
1891	24.266	1971	50.566
1901	23.486	1976	54.154
1905	23.980	1981	56.261
1911	23.146	1986	57.831
1915	24.020	1991	59.252
1921	24.858	1993	59.252
1925	27.610	1996	61.153
1931	29.314	2001	63.095
1941	32.593	2003	63.095
1951	36.185	2006	64.925
1956	39.630	2007	64.925
1961	43.213	2009	64.925

Source: Our World In Data, https://ourworldindata.org/life-expectancy/

Algebra Wall — Want some help? You can always ask questions on the Algebra Wall and receive help from other students, teachers, and Study Experts. You can also help others on the Algebra Wall and earn Karma Points for doing so. Go to AlgebraNation.com to learn more and get started!

Section 10: Two-Variable Statistics

Infant Life Expectancy, 1881 to 2009

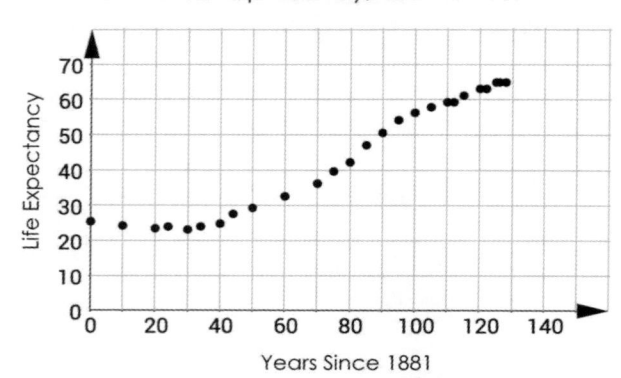

Source: Our World In Data, https://ourworldindata.org/life-expectancy/

When data is displayed on a scatter plot, it is often helpful to represent the data with a _____ _____ in order to predict unknown values that are not on the data set.

A trend line or **line of best fit** is a straight line that _____ represents the data on a scatter plot.

The line may pass through _____, _____, or _____ of the points of the data set.

Steps to approximate a line of best fit:

Step 1: Create a scatter plot of the data.

Step 2: Choose a line as close as possible to the plotted points.

Step 3: Find two points on the line.

Step 4: Calculate the slope of the line through the two points.

Step 5: Use one point and the slope to find the y-intercept.

Step 6: Write the equation of the line.

This equation can be used to predict information that is _____ plotted on the scatter plot.

Section 10: Two-Variable Statistics

Let's Practice!

1. The scatterplot shows life expectancy (in years) for newborns in India since 1881.

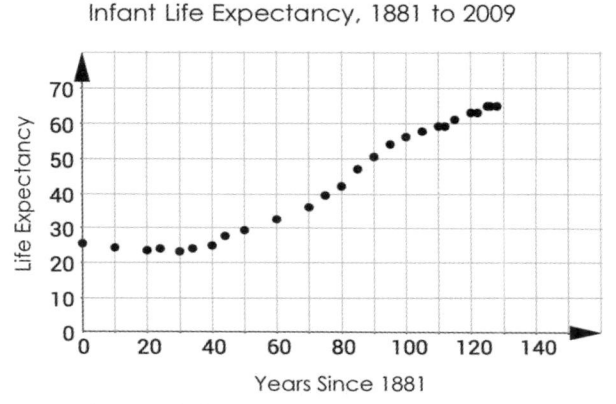

   Infant Life Expectancy, 1881 to 2009

   Source: Our World In Data, https://ourworldindata.org/life-expectancy/

   a. Approximate a line of best fit for the average life expectancy (in years) since 1881.

   b. Use the line to predict the average life expectancy in the year 2020.

   c. Using a calculator, we find the line of best fit to be $y = 0.395x + 14.047$. Use this to predict the average life expectancy in the year 2020. How does this compare to your answer in part b?

Predicting values that fall outside the range of the given data is known as _____. Predicting values that are inside the range of the given data is known as _____.

Try It!

2. The scatterplot below represents total fat of various sandwiches at Zingerman's Deli in Ann Arbor and their total calories.

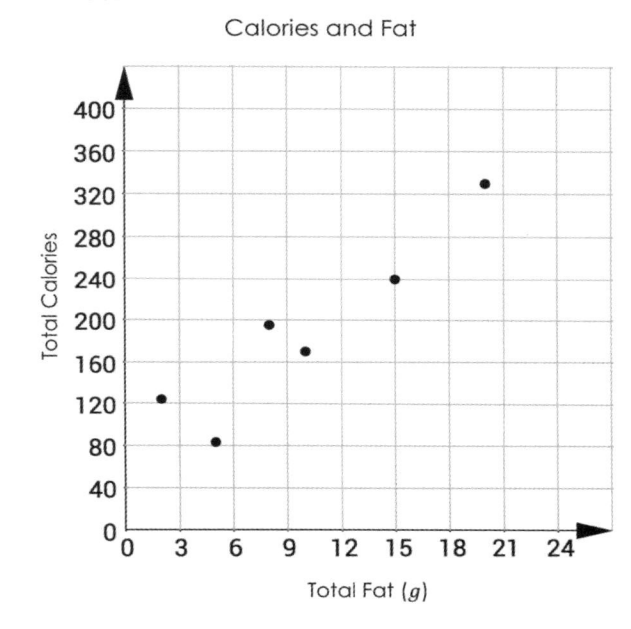

   Calories and Fat

   a. Approximate a line of best fit for the data.

   b. Estimate the total calories in a sandwich with 12 grams of fat.

Section 10: Two-Variable Statistics

BEAT THE TEST!

1. The scatterplot below shows the relationship between a person's age and the average number of subway rides a person takes each week.

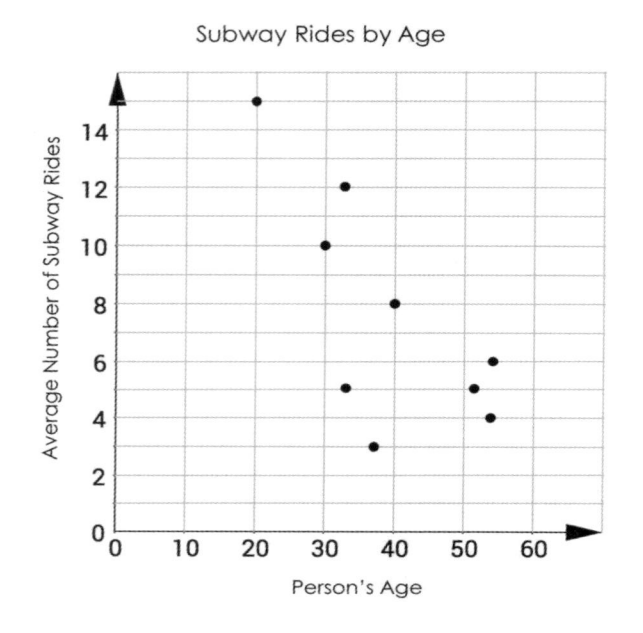

   Subway Rides by Age

   Which two data points would be used to determine the line of best fit?

   Ⓐ (31, 5) and (28, 8)
   Ⓑ (38, 3) and (50, 10)
   Ⓒ (20, 15) and (45, 12)
   Ⓓ (20, 15) and (55, 5)

   Algebra Wall: Want some help? You can always ask questions on the Algebra Wall and receive help from other students, teachers, and Study Experts. You can also help others on the Algebra Wall and earn Karma Points for doing so. Go to AlgebraNation.com to learn more and get started!

Section 10 – Topic 6
Residuals and Residual Plots – Part 1

Over a nine-month period, students in Mrs. Coleman's class at Satellite High School collected data on their total number of Instagram posts each month. The data is summarized below:

Instagram Posts

Month	1	2	3	4	5	6	7	8	9
# Posts	36	52	108	146	340	515	742	1,042	1,529

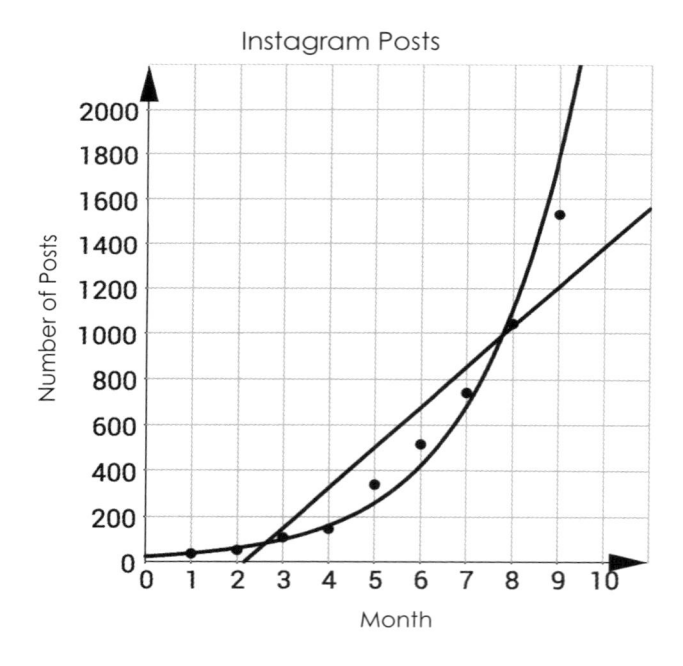

Instagram Posts

Let's consider which function should be used to fit the data: the linear function $f(x) = 176.32x - 380.47$ or the exponential function $g(x) = 23.30 \cdot 1.62^x$.

Section 10: Two-Variable Statistics

A **residual** is the difference between an actual data value and the predicted value.

> Residual = actual y – predicted y

Fill in the blanks to complete the following charts.

Linear Function: $f(x) = 176.32x - 380.47$

Month	# Posts	Predicted Value	Residual
1	36	−204.15	240.15
2	52	−27.83	79.83
3	108	148.49	
4	146	324.81	−178.81
5	340	501.13	−161.13
6	515	677.45	−162.45
7	742	853.77	−111.77
8	1,042	1,030.09	11.91
9	1,529		322.59

Exponential Function: $g(x) = 23.30 \times 1.62^x$

Month	# Posts	Predicted Value	Residual
1	36	37.75	−1.75
2	52	61.15	−9.15
3	108	99.06	8.94
4	146	160.48	−14.48
5	340		
6	515	421.16	93.84
7	742	682.28	59.72
8	1,042		
9	1,529	1,790.57	−261.57

What do you notice about the values of the residuals for the two models?

To determine whether or not a function is a good fit, look at a **residual plot** of the data.

> A residual plot is a graph of the residuals (y-axis) versus the x-values (x-axis).

The residual plot for the linear function $f(x) = 176.32x - 380.47$ is below.

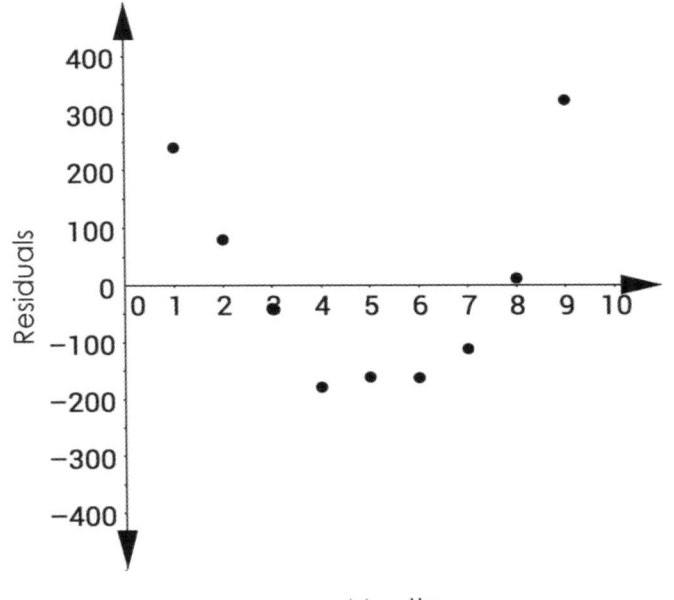

Section 10: Two-Variable Statistics

Let's Practice!

1. The residuals for the exponential function fitted to model the number of posts on Instagram are shown below. Use the table of residuals to construct a residual plot of the data.

Instagram Posts

x	1	2	3	4	5	6	7	8	9
Residual	−1.75	−9.15	8.94	−14.48	80.03	93.84	59.72	−63.29	−261.57

Try It!

2. Consider the residual plots for the linear and exponential models of the class's Instagram posts. Which function fits the data better: the linear or the exponential function? How do you know?

Algebra Wall

Want some help? You can always ask questions on the Algebra Wall and receive help from other students, teachers, and Study Experts. You can also help others on the Algebra Wall and earn Karma Points for doing so. Go to AlgebraNation.com to learn more and get started!

Section 10: Two-Variable Statistics

Section 10 – Topic 7
Residuals and Residual Plots – Part 2

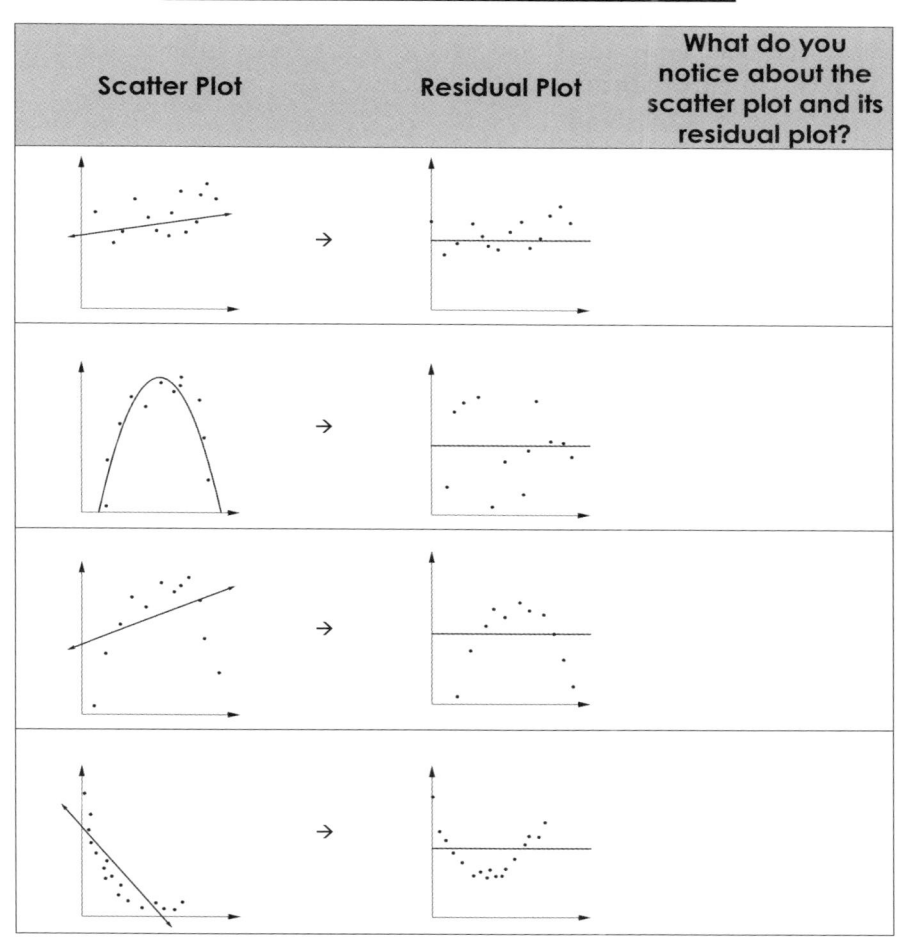

Scatter Plot	Residual Plot	What do you notice about the scatter plot and its residual plot?
	→	
	→	
	→	
	→	

Let's Practice!

1. If a data set has a quadratic trend and a quadratic function is fit to the data, what will the residual plot look like?

2. If a data set has a quadratic trend and a linear function is fit to the data, what will the residual plot look like?

Section 10: Two-Variable Statistics

Try It!

3. Suppose models were fitted for several data sets using linear regression. Residual plots for each data set are shown below. Circle the plot(s) that indicate that the original data set has a linear relationship.

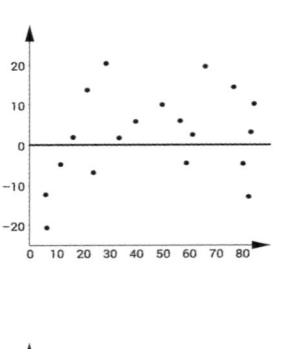

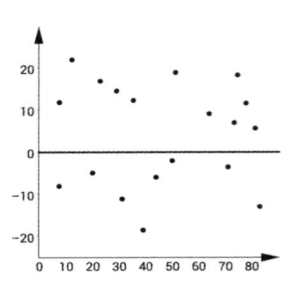

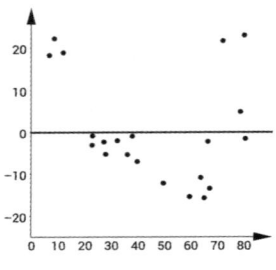

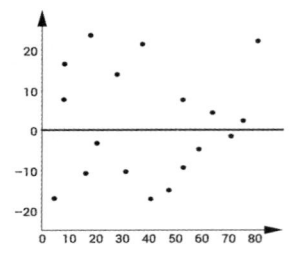

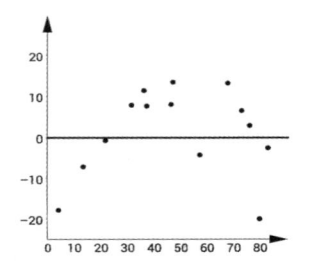

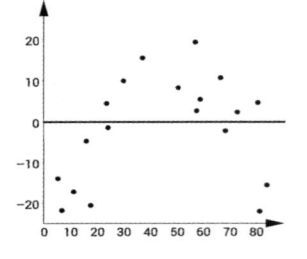

BEAT THE TEST!

1. Suppose a quadratic function is fit to a set of data. Which of the following residual plots indicates that this function was an appropriate fit for the data?

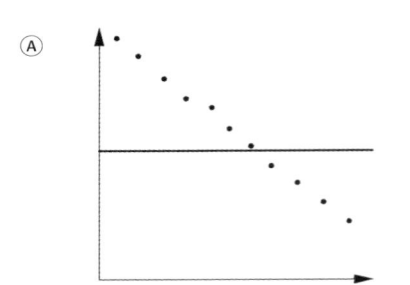

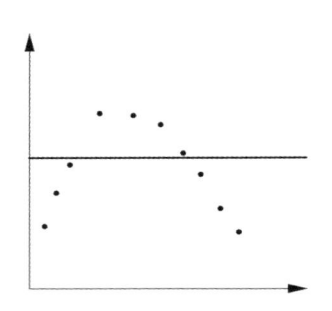

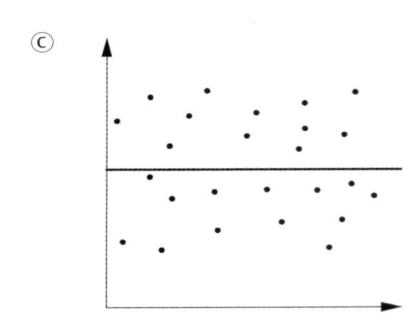

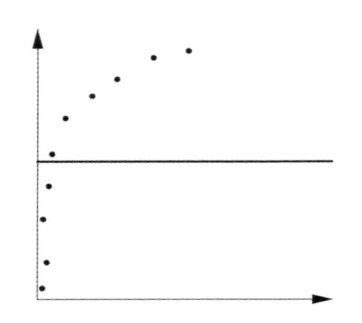

   Ⓐ   Ⓑ

   Ⓒ   Ⓓ

Algebra Wall

Want some help? You can always ask questions on the Algebra Wall and receive help from other students, teachers, and Study Experts. You can also help others on the Algebra Wall and earn Karma Points for doing so. Go to AlgebraNation.com to learn more and get started!

Section 10 – Topic 8
Examining Correlation

The scatter plot below shows the number of violent crimes in the United States from 1993 to 2012.

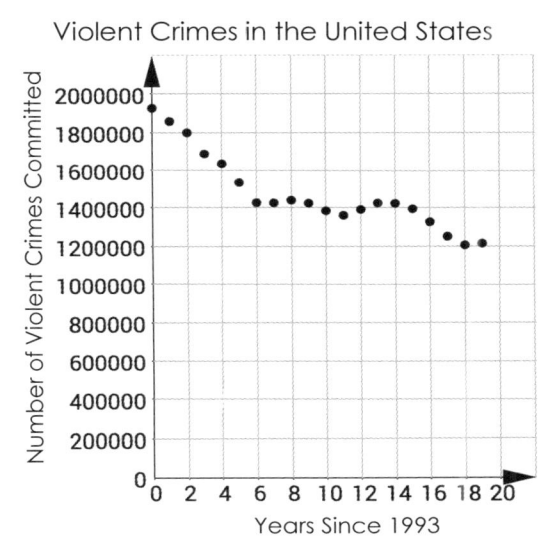

Violent Crimes in the United States

(scatter plot: Number of Violent Crimes Committed vs. Years Since 1993)

Source: United States Department of Justice, https://ucr.fbi.gov/

Describe the relationship between the years since 1993 and the number of violent crimes committed in the United States.

The **correlation coefficient**, r, measures the strength and direction of the linear association between two quantitative variables.

➢ $-1 \leq r \leq +1$

➢ r is unitless

Using the values in the boxes, indicate which of the following values of r best describes each of the scatter plots.

| $r = -0.001$ | $r = +0.790$ | $r = -0.991$ | $r = +0.990$ | $r = -0.547$ |

$r =$ _____ $r =$ _____ $r =$ _____ $r =$ _____ $r =$ _____

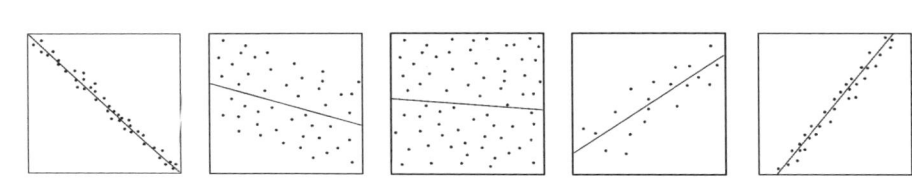

➢ The closer the points are to the line, the _____ the absolute value of r will be.

➢ The closer r is to 0, the _____ the relationship is between x and y.

➢ $r = +0.450$ and $r = -0.450$ both indicate the _____ strength of association between the variables.

Strength of a Linear Relationship

$r = -1.00$ $r = 0.00$ $r = +1.00$

Perfect Negative Linear Relationship   No Linear Relationship   Perfect Positive Linear Relationship

Section 10: Two-Variable Statistics

Let's Practice!

1. Albert, an ice cream vendor at Jones Beach, records the number of cones he sells each day as well as the daily high temperature. The table below shows his data for one week.

   Relationship between Temperature and Cones Sold

Temperature (°F)	81	72	88	85	89	90	87
Cones Sold	55	36	67	65	72	75	73

   Use a calculator to calculate the correlation coefficient.

   $r = $ _____

2. How do you think outliers affect the value of the correlation coefficient?

3. Recall the data for the number of violent crimes committed in the United States from 1993-2012. What does the value of the correlation coefficient, $r = -0.907$, mean in this context?

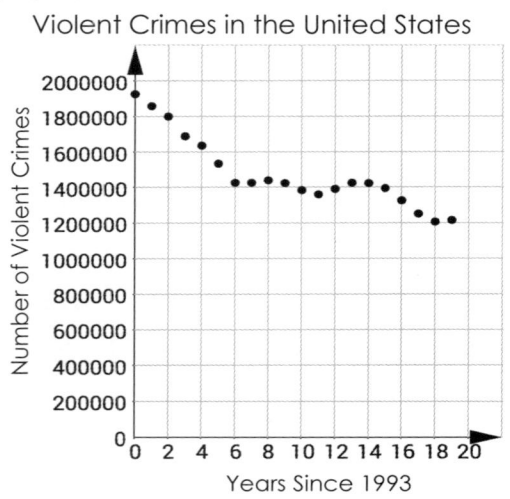

   Violent Crimes in the United States

   Source: United States Department of Justice,

Try It!

4. The table and scatter plot below show the relationship between the number of classes missed and final grade for a sample of 10 students.

   Relationship between Missed Classes and Final Grades

Missed Classes	0	7	3	2	3	9	5	3	5	5
Final Grade	98	86	95	85	81	69	72	93	64	88

   Use a calculator to find the correlation coefficient for the data above and explain what the value of the correlation coefficient means.

   Final Grade and Attendance

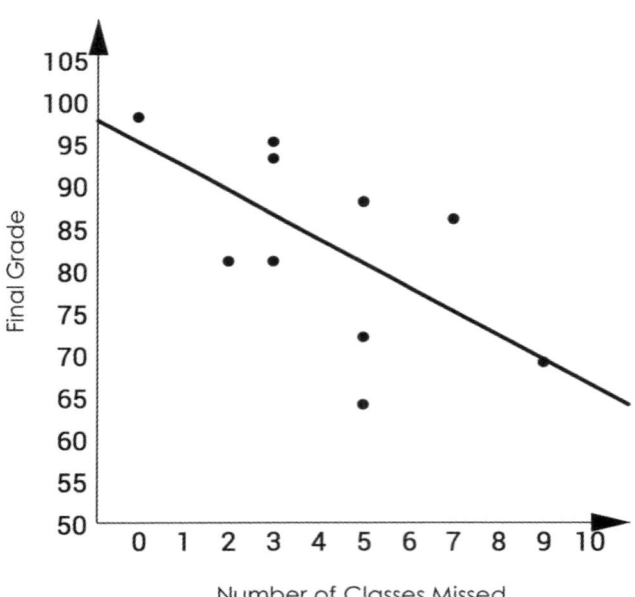

Section 10: Two-Variable Statistics

5. There is a strong positive association between the amount of fire damage (y) and the number of firefighters on the scene (x). Does having more firefighters on the scene cause greater fire damage? Justify your response.

STUDY EDGE TIP

Correlation does not imply causation!

➤ **Causation** is when one event causes another to happen.

➤ Two variables can be correlated without one causing the other.

BEAT THE TEST!

1. Which of the following represents the weakest correlation?

Ⓐ

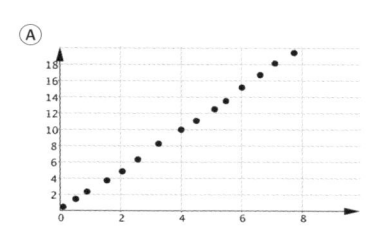

Ⓑ

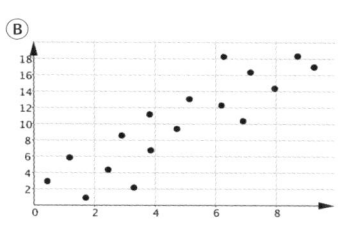

Ⓒ

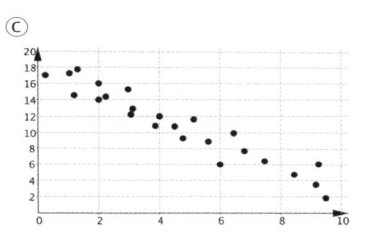

Ⓓ

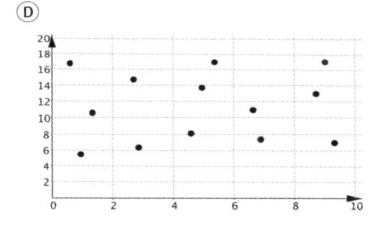

Great job! You have reached the end of this section. Now it's time to try the "Test Yourself! Practice Tool," where you can practice all the skills and concepts you learned in this section. Log in to Algebra Nation and try out the "Test Yourself! Practice Tool" so you can see how well you know these topics!

Section 10: Two-Variable Statistics

Index: Where Each Standard is Covered in Algebra Nation

A-APR.1:	Section 1 - Topics 1,7,8, and 9; Section 3 - Topics 3, 4, and 5
A-CED.1:	Section 2 - Topics 3, 5, 6, and 7; Section 5 – Topic 3
A-CED.2:	Section 2 - Topic 11; Section 4 - Topics 3 and 4; Section 8 – Topic 3
A-CED.3:	Section 4 - Topics 4, 6, 9, and 10
A-CED.4:	Section 2 - Topic 10
A-REI.1:	Section 2 - Topics 2, 3, and 11; Section 4 - Topics 4, 5, 6, 9 and 10; Section 6 - Topic 9; Section 8 - Topics 6, 7, and 8
A-REI.3:	Section 2 - Topics 1, 3, 5, 6, 7, 8, and 9
A-REI.4:	Section 5 - Topics 3, 4, 5, 6, 7, 8, 9, and 10; Section 6 - Topic 2
A-REI.5:	Section 4 - Topic 7
A-REI.6:	Section 4 - Topics 5, 6, 7, and 8
A-REI.10:	Section 2 - Topic 11; Section 4 - Topics 4 and 6; Section 8 - Topics 6, 7, and 8
A-REI.11:	Section 4 - Topics 5 and 6; Section 6 – Topic 9
A-REI.12:	Section 4 - Topics 9 and 10
A-SSE.1:	Section 1 - Topic 1; Section 6 - Topic 5
A-SSE.2:	Section 5 - Topics 2, 3 and 5
A-SSE.3:	Section 5 - Topics 2, 3, 4, 5, and 8; Section 7 - Topic 5
F-BF.1:	Section 4 - Topic 1; Section 7 - Topic 1; Section 8 - Topic 5
F-BF.2:	Section 4 - Topic 1; Section 8 - Topic 4
F-BF.3:	Section 3 - Topic 10; Section 6 - Topics 7 and 8
F-BF.4:	Section 3 - Topic 9
F-IF.1:	Section 3 - Topics 1, and 7
F-IF.2:	Section 3 - Topics 1 and 2
F-IF.3:	Section 4 - Topic 1; Section 7 - Topics 1 and 2
F-IF.4:	Section 3 - Topics 7 and 8; Section 5 - Topic 1; Section 6 - Topic 1; Section 8 - Topics 1 and 2
F-IF.5:	Section 3 - Topic 2; Section 8 - Topic 3
F-IF.6:	Section 4 - Topic 4; Section 8 - Topic 2
F-IF.7:	Section 3 - Topic 6; Section 6 - Topics 3, 4, 5, and 6; Section 7 - Topics 4 and 5, Section 8 - Topics 3, 4, 6, 7, and 8
F-IF.8:	Section 6 - Topics 3 and 4; Section 7 - Topics 5 and 6
F-IF.9:	Section 6 - Topic 6
F-LE.1:	Section 7 - Topic 2; Sections 8 – Topics 1 and 2
F-LE.2:	Section 7 - Topics 1, 2, and 3
F-LE.3:	Section 7 - Topic 2; Section 8 - Topic 1
F-LE.5:	Section 4 - Topics 2,3, 4 and 10; Section 7 - Topic 6
N-CN.1:	Section 1 - Topic 10
N-CN.7:	Section 6 - Topic 2
N-Q.1:	Section 1 - Topic 1; Section 4 - Topic 9
N-Q.2:	Covered throughout the workbook
N-Q.3:	Covered throughout the workbook
N-RN.1:	Section 1 - Topic 4
N-RN.2:	Section 1 - Topics 2, 4, 5, and 6
N-RN.3:	Section 1 - Topic 3
S-ID.1:	Section 9 - Topics 1, 2, 3, and 4
S-ID.2:	Section 9 - Topics 5, 6, and 7
S-ID.3:	Section 9 - Topic 8
S-ID.5:	Section 10 - Topics 1, 2, and 3
S-ID.6:	Section 10 - Topics 4, 5, 6, and 7
S-ID.7:	Section 4 - Topics 2, 3, and 4; Section 10 - Topic 5
S-ID.8:	Section 10 - Topic 8
S-ID.9:	Section 10 - Topic 8

Notes

Notes

Notes

Notes